THE FUTURE OF
AI AGENTS

Hayden Van Der Post

Reactive Publishing

CONTENTS

PREFACE

The story of AI agents is not just a chronicle of technological achievements; it is a narrative woven with the threads of human ingenuity, progress, and our enduring quest for betterment. From enhancing healthcare delivery to revolutionizing financial systems, from transforming education to creating new paradigms in entertainment, AI agents stand poised to be at the heart of our most significant advancements. This book acts as a lens through which you can observe these transformations, offering insights, predictions, and a balanced perspective on what lies ahead.

As we navigate through the chapters, you will uncover the foundational technologies—machine learning, neural networks, and natural language processing—that give AI agents their formidable capabilities. You will appreciate how these tools converge to create sophisticated systems capable of not only responding to stimuli but also anticipating needs, diagnosing problems, and crafting solutions in real-time. Our exploration is not limited to the technical but delves deep into the ethical fabric that binds this progress. The deployment of AI agents must be tempered with caution, responsibility, and unwavering commitment to ethical standards if we are to avoid the dystopian potential that has often been the subject of science fiction narratives.

The spectrum of AI agent applications is vast, touching upon every major sector from healthcare to agriculture, from autonomous transportation to personalized learning experiences. Each chapter stands as a testament to the transformative power of AI, illustrated through case studies, real-world applications, and future forecasts that highlight both the triumphs and the trials that lie ahead. These narratives reinforce the promise of AI agents while acknowledging the impediments—technical, ethical, and societal—that must be carefully navigated.

Data, the lifeblood of AI, warrants its dedicated exploration. The book delves into the intricacies of data management, privacy concerns, and the ethical considerations that accompany data-driven decision-making. Your understanding of AI agents will be incomplete without a nuanced perspective on how data is collected, processed, and utilized to enhance AI performance and user experiences.

Innovation is the cornerstone of AI agent evolution, and this book sheds light on the groundbreaking research and advancements that continue to propel the field forward. From quantum computing to swarm intelligence, the innovative horizons of AI are as promising as they are uncharted.

However, no exploration of AI would be complete without considering the broader implications on the global stage. Regional variances, governmental roles, and cultural impacts paint a diverse picture of AI agent adoption and integration worldwide. Challenges persist—technical limitations, security vulnerabilities, ethical dilemmas, and the potential misuse of these powerful tools. This book does not shy away from these realities, instead offering a balanced view to empower readers to participate in informed dialogues about the future we are collectively building.

As you turn these pages, may you be inspired not only by the technological feats of today but also by the visions for a future where AI agents contribute to a more equitable, efficient, and enlightened society. The final chapter invites you to envision the next decade of AI exploration, urging you to reflect on the profound impact these agents could have on global challenges, societal structures, and human creativity.

"The Future of AI Agents: Emerging Trends and Opportunities" is more than a book; it is a call to action. It implores you, the reader, to engage with the material deeply, to question, to envision, and ultimately to contribute to the unfolding story of AI agents. May this journey fill you with a sense of wonder, responsibility, and hope for the future we are about to co-create.

With heartfelt appreciation for your curiosity and critical thought,

Hayden Van Der Post

CHAPTER 1:
INTRODUCTION

Artificial intelligence agents have emerged as pivotal players in the wave of technological innovation characterizing our modern world. Unlike conventional software systems that rely on predefined instructions, these agents are uniquely designed to operate autonomously, learning and adapting to their environments in real time. They respond dynamically to stimuli, echoing the way living organisms interact with their surroundings.

The evolution of AI agents began with straightforward, rule-based systems, gradually maturing over the decades into sophisticated, self-learning entities. To appreciate their journey, we must explore their development alongside significant advancements in technology and shifts in computational paradigms.

In their early days, AI agents operated on a foundational concept known as the "sense-think-act" cycle. This basic framework involved perceiving the environment, analyzing the information to decide on an appropriate response, and executing that response. Such systems were commonplace in early robotics and game-playing applications, exemplified by IBM's Deep Blue, which famously triumphed over chess champion Garry Kasparov in 1997. While these initial agents had limited adaptability, they marked a critical milestone by demonstrating that machines could outperform humans in specific tasks.

As computational capabilities grew, so too did the complexity of AI agents. The advent of machine learning algorithms transformed these agents from rigid problem solvers into entities that could learn and evolve through experience. A striking example of this evolution is Google's AlphaGo, which not only mastered the strategic board game Go but also learned its strategies by imitating human players before developing its own unique tactics. This represented a paradigm shift from tailored solutions to a new breed of adaptable intelligence that could outthink human intuition and strategy.

A landmark advancement in AI agents' development was the incorporation of neural networks, which enable deep learning capabilities. Unlike their predecessors, AI agents equipped with deep learning can analyze vast datasets to identify patterns and make accurate predictions, crucial in fields such as medical diagnostics and autonomous driving. For instance, Tesla's self-driving cars continuously learn from extensive datasets that include human driving behaviors and data from external sensors, refining their navigation skills to adeptly handle real-world complexities over time.

Beyond the technical realm, the evolution of AI agents carries significant socio-economic implications, highlighting the importance of addressing ethical considerations as these agents gain autonomy. As AI agents begin to exhibit increasingly human-like capabilities, the distinction between machine and human intelligence becomes increasingly blurred, sparking fundamental questions about agency, accountability, and the ethical application of this technology.

Throughout their transformation, AI agents have evolved from basic tools into intricate systems that have redefined entire industries and profoundly influenced modern life. In the healthcare sector, for example, AI agents now play a crucial role in drug discovery, analyzing chemical databases at a speed and efficiency far beyond human researchers. Similarly, in the financial industry, these agents leverage predictive analytics to forecast market trends and optimize trading strategies, far exceeding traditional analytical methods.

The ongoing evolution of AI agents highlights their transformative potential across various sectors of society. This evolution exemplifies human ingenuity and the relentless quest for technological advancement, a journey that is both exciting and fraught with profound ethical considerations.

As we reflect on the past and look toward the future unfolding for AI agents, we must consider not only their technological capabilities but also their alignment with human values. It is at the intersection of technology, ethics, and human aspirations where the narrative of AI agents will be shaped, guiding their evolution in the years to come. This holistic approach is essential in ensuring that advancements in AI not only enhance functionality but also resonate with the ethical frameworks that govern our society.

Exploring the various types of AI agents—reactive, deliberative, and hybrid—reveals the rich tapestry of capabilities embedded in artificial intelligence systems. Each category represents a unique approach to how these agents perceive and respond to their environments, shaping the decisions they make based on the information at their disposal.

Reactive Agents: Instinctual Responders

Reactive agents are the most straightforward type of AI, operating on instinctual responses akin to reflexes in living organisms. These agents react to immediate stimuli, without retaining a historical context or wealth of knowledge about their surroundings. A prominent example of a reactive system can be found in the non-playable characters of classic video games, such as the ghosts in "Pac-Man." Here, the ghosts pursue the player guided solely by proximate rules; their movements dictated by immediate conditions rather than past experiences. While effective in scenarios that demand rapid, rule-based responses, reactive agents are typically confined to structured and predictable environments, where their lack of adaptive learning can be a limitation.

Deliberative Agents: Thoughtful Planners

In contrast, deliberative agents are designed with a more sophisticated framework, incorporating internal models of their environment to make informed decisions. These agents possess the ability to plan and reason about future actions based on their understanding of specific goals and situational contexts. Utilizing advanced data processing and optimization algorithms, deliberative agents meticulously analyze a myriad of possible actions to determine the optimal path forward. A striking example of a deliberative agent is the autonomous robots used in logistics, such as those deployed in Amazon's fulfillment centers. These robots continuously calculate the best routes to navigate through aisles and make decisions regarding the sequence of picking and sorting packages, all while factoring in variables like aisle congestion and delivery deadlines.

Hybrid Agents: The Best of Both Worlds

Real-world challenges often demand a blend of the reactive agility and the strategic foresight found in deliberative agents, giving rise to hybrid systems. Hybrid agents adeptly combine the strengths of both approaches, allowing them to handle unforeseen changes while also engaging in long-term planning and adaptation. A prime illustration of this is seen in autonomous vehicles developed by companies like Waymo and Tesla. These vehicles utilize reactive systems to respond to immediate stimuli, such as evading sudden obstacles or recognizing pedestrians. Concurrently, they employ deliberative planning to navigate effectively through intricate urban landscapes—taking into account traffic regulations and varying environmental conditions.

The evolution from simple reactive models to complex hybrid systems marks significant progress toward intelligent and adaptable technologies, capable of managing the dynamic intricacies of our world. As hybrid agents grow in sophistication and autonomy, it becomes increasingly critical to address the ethical implications that accompany their deployment across vital industries. This understanding equips us to design and implement AI systems that not only carry out tasks efficiently but also align with the ethical standards guiding contemporary technological advancements. From controlling the actions of basic game characters to orchestrating complex logistical operations, the foundational principles underlying these AI agent types are instrumental in shaping our digital landscape. Becoming well-versed in their diverse applications is paramount as we strive to leverage their capabilities for innovative solutions across various sectors.

Artificial intelligence (AI) agents are revolutionizing a diverse array of industries, seamlessly integrating into the core operations of businesses and services that shape our daily lives. Their influence ranges from boosting efficiency and productivity to enabling innovative new business models. In this exploration, we'll examine the multifaceted applications of AI across several key sectors, shedding light on their current implications and future possibilities.

Healthcare: Innovating Patient Care

In the healthcare sector, AI agents are fundamentally transforming the way patient care is delivered. One of the standout applications is predictive analytics in diagnostics. These insights empower healthcare providers to take proactive preventive measures, significantly enhancing patient outcomes. Additionally, AI-driven chatbots are reshaping patient interaction by providing virtual assistance for scheduling appointments and addressing routine health queries. This not only streamlines administration but also allows healthcare professionals to dedicate their time to more complex medical issues, thereby improving overall patient care.

Finance: Fortifying Security and Informed Decisions

The finance sector is increasingly harnessing the power of AI agents to enhance security measures and refine decision-making processes. One of the most notable innovations is in fraud detection systems, where machine learning models analyze transaction data in real-time to pinpoint suspicious activities. Furthermore, AI agents are pivotal in algorithmic trading, where they analyze market trends and execute trades based on historical data and predictive models. This capability maximizes investment returns while minimizing risks, illustrating AI's transformative impact on financial operations.

Retail: Elevating Customer Experiences

In the retail landscape, AI agents are redefining the shopping experience with a focus on personalization and operational efficiency. Recommendation engines, such as those utilized by Amazon, harness machine learning to tailor product suggestions to individual shoppers based on their preferences. Additionally, AI optimizes inventory management by accurately forecasting stock levels and demand fluctuations, ensuring that retailers maintain ideal inventory without the pitfalls of overstocking.

Transportation: Pioneering Autonomous Journeys

The transportation sector is undergoing significant evolution, particularly with the rise of autonomous vehicles, thanks to AI technology. Companies like Tesla are at the forefront, integrating sophisticated AI systems that process vast amounts of data from their surroundings to facilitate navigation and safe decision-making. These systems continually learn from different driving scenarios, improving their capability to handle various road conditions and traffic environments. Beyond personal transportation, AI is revolutionizing fleet management in logistics, optimizing delivery routes and minimizing fuel consumption. This not only results in substantial cost savings but also contributes to a smaller carbon footprint.

Manufacturing: Optimizing Production Processes

In manufacturing, AI agents are enhancing production pipelines and quality assurance processes. Advanced automated inspection systems, utilizing computer vision, can swiftly identify defects on the assembly line, ensuring that only products meeting rigorous quality standards reach consumers. Predictive maintenance solutions also play a critical role, monitoring machinery conditions to foresee potential failures and prevent unplanned downtimes.

Agriculture: Promoting Precision and Yield

The agricultural industry is witnessing a transformation towards precision farming driven by AI technology. Sophisticated AI systems analyze data from satellite and drone imagery to assess crop health and soil conditions, enabling farmers to make informed decisions on irrigation, fertilization, and pest control. This data-driven approach not only minimizes resource waste but also maximizes yields, paving the way for sustainable farming practices. Additionally, AI-powered robotic systems can autonomously harvest crops based on specific maturity criteria, enhancing both the speed and accuracy of the harvesting process.

Energy: Innovating for Sustainable Efficiency

In the energy sector, AI agents are essential in optimizing resource management and advancing sustainability initiatives. Smart grid technology employs AI to efficiently regulate electricity distribution, balancing supply and demand in real-time. This capability helps reduce energy consumption during peak periods, lowering both operational costs and environmental impact. AI also plays a crucial role in predictive maintenance for energy infrastructure, anticipating potential failures in power plants and wind turbines to ensure continuous operation and minimize costly outages.

The implementation of AI agents across these diverse industries exemplifies a significant paradigm shift toward smarter, data-driven operations that enhance efficiency, productivity, and innovation. Each application illustrates the remarkable potential of AI when aligned with specific industry needs, making a compelling case for the ongoing integration of these technologies into everyday practices. As AI continues to evolve, it promises even greater advancements, paving the way for unprecedented growth and improvements in how industries operate and create value.

Artificial intelligence agents are intricate systems built on a robust foundation of essential technologies, each serving a unique purpose in enabling these agents to execute complex tasks with autonomy and intelligence. Gaining insight into these underlying technologies is vital for appreciating the capabilities of AI agents as they adapt and thrive across various fields. The synergy of cutting-edge methods allows AI agents to excel in a wide array of tasks, from simple pattern recognition to sophisticated decision-making processes.

Machine Learning: The Heart of AI Intelligence

At the core of AI development lies machine learning (ML), a transformative technology that empowers AI agents to learn and progress through data-driven experiences. For example, in the realm of image recognition, models powered by convolutional neural networks have become indispensable in sectors like security and healthcare. These models, trained on extensive datasets, can identify intricate patterns and classify images with astounding accuracy, matching or even exceeding human expertise.

Natural Language Processing: Bridging Human

and Machine Communication

Natural Language Processing (NLP) plays a crucial role in enhancing interactions between AI agents and humans. This technology allows AI systems to comprehend, interpret, and generate human language in a contextually relevant manner. NLP underpins a variety of applications, including chatbots, virtual assistants, and language translation tools. For instance, advanced virtual assistants utilize NLP to analyze user inquiries and provide tailored responses that enrich the user experience. Notable models such as Google's BERT and OpenAI's GPT are at the forefront of this field, adept at navigating complex linguistic constructs to deliver coherent and contextually aware communications.

Computer Vision: Understanding the Visual World

The realm of computer vision is dedicated to enabling machines to interpret and understand visual data, radically transforming industries such as healthcare, automotive, and retail. For instance, in healthcare, computer vision is employed to analyze medical scans, rapidly identifying anomalies and thus expediting the diagnostic process while improving accuracy. In the automotive sector, self-driving vehicles rely on computer vision to perceive their surroundings and navigate safely in real-time, ensuring a seamless driving experience.

Robotics: Infusing Intelligence into Physical Entities

While many AI agents are software-oriented, robotics provides the dynamic intersection where artificial intelligence meets physical application. Through the integration of actuators, sensors, and control systems, robotics breathes life into intelligent systems, enabling machines to perform both simple and complex physical tasks. In manufacturing, AI-enabled robotic arms excel at assembling intricate components with unmatched precision and efficiency. Meanwhile, autonomous drones utilize AI algorithms for a plethora of applications, including aerial photography, disaster response, and logistics management. These examples highlight how robotics broadens the horizon for AI agents, delivering practical solutions that extend beyond the digital realm.

Cloud Computing: Enabling Scalability and Accessibility

Cloud computing serves as the backbone of AI deployment, providing the necessary infrastructure for scalability and accessibility. Leading cloud providers like Amazon Web Services (AWS) and Microsoft Azure offer specialized solutions that include pre-trained models and scalable computing power, facilitating swift AI development without the burden of extensive on-premises infrastructure. This democratization of technology accelerates the growth and spread of AI innovations across various sectors.

Internet of Things: Creating a Cohesive Ecosystem

The Internet of Things (IoT) plays an integral role in connecting an array of devices, sensors, and systems, fostering environments where AI agents can gather actionable data and influence their surroundings. In smart home settings, IoT devices continuously relay data to AI agents, enabling real-time adjustments to lighting, temperature, and security settings based on user habits and preferences. In industrial applications, IoT sensors monitor machinery and environmental conditions, providing critical data to AI systems that optimize processes and forecast maintenance needs. The interaction between IoT and AI exemplifies a powerful synergy that enhances data-driven decision-making capabilities.

Blockchain: Fortifying Trust in AI Systems

Although blockchain technology is not traditionally linked to AI, it offers a secure and transparent ledger system that significantly bolsters the integrity of data exchanges involving AI. Additionally, blockchain-enabled smart contracts can automate transactions between AI agents, streamlining workflows and minimizing human error. Each technology contributes distinct capabilities that collectively enhance the functionality and versatility of AI agents. As these technologies continue to evolve, they promise not only to improve existing applications but also to unveil new possibilities, ultimately reshaping the landscape in which AI agents operate.

Harnessing Machine Learning and Neural Networks: The Catalysts of AI Innovation

Machine learning and neural networks form the dynamic backbone of artificial intelligence (AI), propelling its capabilities and fostering its widespread adoption across diverse sectors. Their integral functions empower AI agents with the intelligence required to perceive, learn, and act autonomously, even in increasingly complex and unpredictable environments.

Machine Learning: The Bedrock of Evolving Intelligence

At its core, machine learning (ML) is the bedrock that enables machines to mimic human cognitive abilities by learning from experience. This trait renders ML indispensable for AI agents tasked with navigating intricate, data-heavy challenges.

Take predictive maintenance as a compelling illustration of ML in action. In industrial contexts, AI agents deploy machine learning algorithms to anticipate equipment failures, significantly reducing downtime and operational costs. This shift from reactive to proactive maintenance strategies not only enhances operational efficiency but also bolsters overall productivity.

Neural Networks: Emulating the Human Brain's Design

Neural networks, a specialized subset of machine learning, draw inspiration from the intricate neural architecture of the human brain. Comprising interconnected nodes or "neurons," these networks excel at processing high-dimensional data and are fundamental to tasks ranging from image recognition to natural language processing. Their ability to efficiently handle vast datasets and extract complex patterns is pivotal to the success of numerous AI applications.

Deep learning, an advanced variant of neural networks, marks a transformative leap in AI capabilities. Characterized by multiple layers of interconnected nodes, deep learning models have the depth required to unravel intricate data structures. A prime example is the use of convolutional neural networks (CNNs) in computer vision, where they meticulously analyze image data to identify objects with remarkable accuracy. In the healthcare sector, these models have proven adept at diagnosing diseases, such as cancer, from medical imaging, often achieving precision that surpasses that of human clinicians.

Revolutionizing Natural Language Processing with Neural Networks

Neural networks have also dramatically transformed the landscape of Natural Language Processing (NLP), enhancing how machines understand and generate human language. Recurrent neural networks (RNNs), along with their advanced successors like Long Short-Term Memory (LSTM) networks, are particularly effective in processing sequential data. These architectures are critical in applications such as language translation and text generation, where understanding context and maintaining coherence are vital.

Prominent advancements, such as OpenAI's GPT series, leverage transformer architectures—an innovative type of neural network adept at managing extensive datasets—to create text that closely resembles human writing. Applications range from customer support chatbots to sophisticated systems that generate coherent narratives, underscoring the versatility and power of neural networks in contemporary AI solutions.

Reinforcement Learning: Empowering AI
Agents through Experience

In contrast to supervised and unsupervised learning, reinforcement learning (RL) introduces a dynamic framework where AI agents learn by engaging with their environments to achieve designated objectives. Through a process of trial and error, these agents evaluate their actions based on feedback, fine-tuning their strategies to maximize cumulative rewards.

A classic instance of RL is seen in autonomous driving systems, where AI agents learn to navigate safely by simulating diverse driving conditions. The rapid assimilation of complex tasks by RL models mirrors human learning processes, albeit at an accelerated pace, demonstrating their profound potential.

Looking Ahead: The Synergy of Neural
Networks and Multi-Agent Systems

As we gaze towards the future, the synthesis of neural networks with multi-agent systems portends significant advancements. In such frameworks, multiple AI agents collaborate or compete, learning from both one another and their environments. This collaborative approach finds application in logistics optimization; for instance, a fleet of delivery drones can efficiently coordinate their routes and manage cargo distribution by leveraging collective insights derived from their neural frameworks.

As machine learning and neural networks continue to evolve, their roles as pivotal components in AI technology will only be reinforced.

Understanding the vital contributions of machine learning and neural networks is key to appreciating the breadth of their impact on AI. These technologies serve not only as enablers but also as defining elements that dictate the scope and scale of AI's influence, paving the way for ongoing exploration and transformation in this rapidly advancing field.

Ethical Considerations in the Deployment of AI
Agents: A Call for Responsible Innovation

As artificial intelligence (AI) agents become increasingly interwoven into the fabric of our daily lives, ethical considerations surrounding their deployment emerge as a complex and vital concern. The interplay between technology, governance, and human rights necessitates a nuanced approach to ensure that these innovations not only align with societal values but also mitigate potential adverse effects.

The Moral Imperative of Transparency and Accountability

At the heart of ethical AI deployment lies the principle of transparency. When AI systems function as "black boxes," their decision-making processes become nearly impossible to scrutinize. This opacity breeds skepticism among users and stakeholders alike. To cultivate trust, the development of explainable AI models is essential. For example, when AI aids in medical diagnoses, both patients and healthcare professionals should have access to comprehensible explanations of how conclusions are drawn. Providing straightforward justifications for AI-driven decisions not only builds trust but also enshrines accountability in operations.

Establishing a robust accountability framework is equally critical. When AI systems malfunction—as they inevitably will—clarity about responsibility must be firmly defined. Is accountability vested in the software developer, the deploying organization, or the AI itself? Clear guidelines are essential for managing repercussions in instances of error, fostering a culture of responsibility among AI developers.

Addressing Bias and Ensuring Fairness

AI systems often mirror the biases inherent in the data upon which they are trained, raising significant concerns about fairness and discrimination. A notable instance can be seen in recruitment AI agents, which may perpetuate gender or racial biases if trained on historically flawed hiring data. To counteract bias, it is essential to implement comprehensive testing and corrective measures. This might involve conducting extensive data audits, followed by adjustments to the algorithms that account for and rectify identified biases.

Moreover, fostering a diverse development team is crucial in combating homogeneous thinking that could overlook potential biases.

Privacy Concerns and Data Security

The advent of AI agents often entails the collection and analysis of vast quantities of personal data, intensifying concerns regarding user privacy. Robust data protection practices are imperative to prevent misuse of sensitive information, particularly in industries such as finance and healthcare.

Adopting strong encryption protocols, conducting regular data audits, and establishing clear consent processes are essential for upholding privacy. Additionally, applying 'privacy by design' principles throughout the development lifecycle ensures that data privacy considerations are embedded at every stage.

Autonomous Decision-making and Human Oversight

As AI systems increasingly gain autonomy, particularly in high-stakes environments such as autonomous vehicles or military applications, a critical question arises: How much independence should these entities possess? While greater autonomy can enhance operational efficiency, critical decisions impacting human life or societal norms should never be solely relegated to machines.

To navigate this challenge, frameworks that incorporate human-in-the-loop (HITL) oversight are essential. Such structures ensure that human judgment remains a key component in AI operations, especially when facing ethical dilemmas. For instance, even as autonomous vehicles make independent assessments in real-time, human operators should retain the ability to intervene in complex moral situations, such as those illustrated by the trolley problem.

Implementing Regulatory Standards

As the landscape of AI technology rapidly evolves, the establishment of comprehensive regulatory frameworks becomes crucial. These regulations should balance the promotion of innovation with the safeguarding of ethical practices to prevent potential misuse of AI technologies. Achieving global harmonization of AI regulations can mitigate the risk of regulatory arbitrage, where organizations might seek out jurisdictions with laxer ethical standards.

The European Union has initiated progress in this area through regulations like the General Data Protection Regulation (GDPR), which sets stringent benchmarks for data protection that AI technologies must adhere to. Such initiatives not only inspire international standards but also ensure ethical AI deployment on a global scale.

Encouraging Public Engagement and Dialogue

Facilitating a wide public discourse on the ethics of AI is vital for refining policies that resonate with societal values. Engaging diverse communities enables policymakers and researchers to incorporate varied perspectives, thereby fostering a more representative and inclusive approach to ethical AI considerations. Public forums, educational initiatives, and stakeholder collaborations are essential vehicles for democratizing the conversation surrounding AI's role in society.

Building an Ethical AI Future

The responsible deployment of AI agents demands ongoing vigilance and adaptive strategies to confront emerging ethical challenges.

Emphasizing ethical guidelines encapsulates a collective moral responsibility shared among developers, policymakers, and users alike. Together, these stakeholders play a pivotal role in shaping the ethical framework governing the deployment of AI, championing human dignity, equity, and rights in the face of technological advancement. Through this collaborative effort, we can pave the way toward a future where AI is not only advanced but also ethical and inclusive.

Distinguishing AI Agents from Traditional Software

Understanding the distinction between AI agents and traditional software is essential for grasping the transformative potential of AI-driven technologies. This differentiation extends beyond mere technical specifications; it encompasses the capabilities, adaptability, and roles these systems play in diverse environments. As we explore this comparison, the unique characteristics of AI agents emerge, highlighting their potential for intelligent behavior and decision-making.

Fundamental Structural Differences

At their core, traditional software operates according to a fixed, static set of instructions crafted by developers. This conventional method, often encapsulated in deterministic algorithms, guides the software through predetermined sequences of operations. For instance, a calculator exemplifies this paradigm, executing calculations from a rigid framework of rules with no capacity for deviation or contextual adaptation.

In stark contrast, AI agents are engineered with dynamic algorithms that facilitate learning and adaptability. Consider a chatbot powered by AI: it evolves its conversational strategies over time, improving its understanding and prediction of user intent as it interacts with a growing number of users. This capacity for adaptation represents a significant departure from traditional static programming.

Autonomy and Decision-Making Capacity

Traditional software is inherently reactive, performing tasks only when given explicit instructions by users or other systems. It lacks the autonomous decision-making ability and relies on human intervention for any deviation from its programmed path. For example, standard spreadsheet applications execute operations solely based on direct user inputs.

On the other hand, AI agents display a notable degree of autonomy, enabling them to make decisions based on environmental conditions, learned experiences, and strategic objectives. Take autonomous vehicles as an example: these AI agents analyze real-time sensor data to make split-second decisions regarding acceleration, braking, and navigation—often without any human input. This capability for autonomy empowers AI agents to function effectively in dynamic and unpredictable environments where traditional software would struggle.

Adaptability and Learning Capabilities

Adaptability is another pivotal characteristic that sets AI agents apart from traditional software. While conventional applications require manual updates to accommodate new features or respond to changing needs, AI agents continuously evolve through learning processes.

A prime illustration of this adaptability can be found in recommendation systems used by popular streaming services like Netflix. These AI-driven systems analyze user behavior over time, adjusting content suggestions based on changing viewing patterns. Through continuous refinement of their models via feedback loops, these recommendation engines remain relevant and effective over the long term—unlike static software, which risks obsolescence in a swiftly evolving digital landscape.

Context Awareness and Environmental Interaction

Traditional software lacks inherent context-awareness and primarily relies on predefined inputs and outputs. It processes data without grasping the broader environmental context. For instance, an email client handles messages as discrete items, adhering to predetermined sorting rules but lacking insight into the surrounding circumstances of email exchanges.

In contrast, AI agents are designed to understand and adapt to their environments. This might involve recognizing user emotions during customer service interactions or responding to physical changes detected by sensors in robotics. Smart home assistants, for instance, adjust operations based on contextual cues—like dimming lights when it senses the owner settling in for the evening. This level of contextual adaptability allows AI agents to deliver more nuanced and personalized interactions.

Role in Problem Solving and Innovation

AI agents excel beyond mere task automation—they actively participate in problem-solving and drive innovation by uncovering insights from complex data sets. Traditional software finds its strength in executing well-defined tasks and repeatable processes but struggles with the ambiguity of unstructured data or problems requiring cognitive rigor.

In industries such as finance, AI agents can analyze extensive arrays of market data, identify emerging trends, and propose investment strategies with a level of sophistication far beyond that of traditional software. This advanced problem-solving capability positions AI agents as invaluable tools for innovation, enabling businesses to leverage data in ways that were previously unattainable with conventional systems.

Case Study: AI Agents in Customer Service

A compelling illustration of the contrast between AI agents and traditional software can be found in the customer service industry. Historically, customer interactions were managed through rigid decision-tree scripts embedded in help desk software, which often struggled with complex and multifaceted inquiries.

In comparison, AI-driven customer service agents utilize natural language processing to comprehend and respond to a wide variety of customer queries. These agents continually evolve with each interaction, developing an understanding of user sentiment and context that allows them to deliver more accurate and empathetic responses than their non-AI counterparts.

Understanding the distinctions between AI agents and traditional software is crucial for appreciating the expansive scope and potential of AI technology. While both categories of systems have their respective advantages, AI agents herald a new paradigm of intelligent systems capable of learning, adapting, and autonomously navigating complex environments. As AI technologies advance further, they promise to redefine the software landscape, opening up unprecedented opportunities for innovation and societal transformation.

Major Milestones in AI Agent Development

The evolution of AI agents has been punctuated by a series of transformative milestones that have not only redefined technology but have also profoundly influenced societal dynamics. These landmarks in the journey of AI agents showcase the increasing sophistication and capabilities of artificial intelligence, reflecting significant technological advancements and breakthroughs that have shaped the design, deployment, and value of AI agents across various sectors.

Foundations of AI: From Symbolic Models to Early Heuristics

The origins of AI agents trace back to the mid-20th century when symbolic AI was at the forefront. Researchers during this era concentrated on rule-based systems and expert systems, striving to replicate human reasoning through logical frameworks. Notable examples of early AI agents include the General Problem Solver, developed in the late 1950s, and ELIZA, an early natural language processing program from the 1960s. These pioneering efforts laid the groundwork for more sophisticated and adaptable intelligent systems and paved the way for the vibrant field of AI we know today.

The Machine Learning Revolution

A pivotal moment in the advancement of AI agents occurred in the 1980s with the advent of machine learning. This shift marked a transition from rigid, static rule-based systems to more dynamic, data-driven methodologies.

The introduction of the backpropagation algorithm during this period illustrated the promise of neural networks in tackling complex, nonlinear problems. This advancement was foundational, opening doors for subsequent breakthroughs in deep learning, which would become critical for the evolution of intelligent agent technologies.

Landmark Achievements: Autonomy in Action

The visibility of AI's capabilities surged with landmark successes in complex gaming. IBM's Deep Blue made headlines in 1997 by defeating world chess champion Garry Kasparov, showcasing AI's ability to navigate intricate strategic scenarios. This was complemented by IBM Watson's sensational victory on the quiz show Jeopardy! in 2011, demonstrating the potential for AI agents to process natural language and draw upon an extensive knowledge base to craft nuanced responses.

These milestones illustrated that AI agents could not only perform complex tasks autonomously but could also compete with humans in specific domains, solidifying their status as valuable assets in various industries.

Deep Learning and the Rise of Intelligent Systems

The resurgence of deep learning algorithms marked another significant turning point in AI agent development. The early 2010s saw an explosion in computational power and the accessibility of large datasets, catalyzing breakthroughs in image and speech recognition. Technologies such as Convolutional Neural Networks (CNNs) and Recurrent Neural Networks (RNNs) became central to these innovations, enabling AI agents to achieve unprecedented accuracy in processing visual and auditory data.

A watershed moment occurred in 2012 when a deep learning system achieved a remarkable reduction in error rates during the ImageNet Challenge, heralding a new era of image classification capabilities. This success sparked immense interest and investment in deep learning, fueling rapid advancement in AI agent functionalities.

AI in Action: AlphaGo and Strategic Mastery

The integration of deep learning and reinforcement learning culminated in a historic achievement with AlphaGo's victory over renowned Go player Lee Sedol in 2016. Go, known for its tactical complexity, necessitates not just strategic thinking but also intuition. AlphaGo's remarkable win highlighted the potential of AI agents to not only analyze information but also engage in high-level decision-making and strategizing.

This achievement transformed perceptions of AI, showcasing it as a versatile tool capable of performing at a level that rivaled human expertise in sophisticated and creative domains.

AI Agents in Every Home: The Consumer Revolution

The launch and widespread adoption of AI-powered virtual assistants such as Apple's Siri, Amazon's Alexa, and Google Assistant marked a revolutionary moment in the integration of AI agents into daily life. These technologies leverage advances in natural language processing and machine learning to offer personalized assistance, enhancing productivity in ways that are now woven into our everyday routines.

This milestone signifies the transition of AI agents from niche research tools to indispensable components of consumer technology, utilized in a myriad of applications from smart home devices to healthcare, significantly enhancing convenience and accessibility.

Tackling Global Challenges: AI Agents in Healthcare

AI agents have also emerged as crucial players in addressing societal challenges, particularly in the healthcare sector. The COVID-19 pandemic showcased the impact of AI in predictive modeling, drug discovery, and vaccine development. AI systems played pivotal roles in diagnostics and patient care, particularly in telemedicine, thereby alleviating pressures on healthcare frameworks.

These contributions underscore the evolution of AI agents from mere analytical tools to proactive participants in solving critical global issues, demonstrating their transformative potential in various sectors.

Charting the Future: Ongoing Innovations and Possibilities

While these milestones highlight significant progress, the journey of AI agents is far from complete. Current innovations like Explainable AI (XAI) strive to enhance transparency in AI decision-making processes, addressing concerns related to bias and trust. Furthermore, the pursuit of generalized AI systems poses an exciting frontier—creating agents capable of tackling a wide array of tasks, ultimately approaching human-like cognition.

Understanding these pivotal developments in the history of AI agents is essential for stakeholders aiming to leverage AI responsibly and effectively. Each milestone represents not only a triumph in technology but also a reflection of our evolving relationship with intelligent systems. As AI agents continue to evolve, they promise to unlock unprecedented opportunities for advancement across a multitude of fields, setting the stage for future innovation and societal transformation.

AI Agents in Science Fiction Versus Reality

The depiction of AI agents in science fiction has long enthralled audiences, presenting narratives that oscillate between benevolent helpers and catastrophic adversaries. These imaginative portrayals have profoundly shaped societal perceptions of AI, igniting both hope and trepidation about this rapidly evolving technology. In stark contrast, the current landscape of AI agents is marked by pragmatic applications and significant benefits that diverge sharply from their fantastical representations.

The Captivating World of Fiction: From Asimov to Ex Machina

Science fiction has consistently cast AI as a double-edged sword, probing the intricacies of power, autonomy, and the essence of consciousness. Isaac Asimov's groundbreaking anthology, I, Robot, introduced robots governed by ethical laws instilled to safeguard humanity, striking a delicate balance between security and autonomy. Films like Blade Runner and Ex Machina delve into the philosophical ramifications surrounding identity and self-awareness, showcasing AI entities endowed with human-like characteristics and moral agency.

Television series such as Westworld and Black Mirror further examine the societal ramifications of advanced AI, resonating with contemporary concerns about control and surveillance in our increasingly digital lives. These narratives, while entertaining, prompt thoughtful reflection on the ethical dilemmas tied to the creation of intelligent systems that could potentially rival human intellect and moral judgement.

The Realities of AI: Practical Applications in the Present

Conversely, the current state of AI agents is primarily focused on enhancing efficiency in specific domains rather than embodying the autonomy and self-awareness portrayed in fiction. Today's AI excels in tasks such as data analysis, language processing, and customer service automation, which streamline operations and boost productivity, yet they do not possess the comprehensive cognitive abilities often attributed to their fictional counterparts.

Take, for example, modern AI-driven technologies like chatbots and virtual assistants—Siri, Google Assistant, and Alexa. These systems utilize natural language processing to perform tasks ranging from setting reminders to providing real-time weather updates. Despite their user-friendly interfaces, these AIs operate within tightly defined parameters, lacking the independent thought and ethical reasoning that fiction often ascribes to them.

Bridging the Gap: Advancements in Autonomous Systems

While today's AI agents may not mirror the self-aware beings found in science fiction, advancements in autonomous systems and the pursuit of artificial general intelligence (AGI) are pushing the boundaries of what is possible. Notable examples include AlphaGo's remarkable strategic capabilities and the development of autonomous vehicles, which demonstrate AI's potential to take on more complex responsibilities typically associated with human decision-making.

In the sphere of self-driving cars, companies such as Tesla and Waymo are pioneering AI agents that navigate intricate urban landscapes, highlighting the practical applications of AI in tasks that require both precision and adaptability—capabilities that can exceed human performance in terms of safety and efficiency.

Ethical Considerations: Lessons from
Fiction in AI Development

The imaginative portrayals of AI in fiction serve not only as a source of creativity but also as a cautionary lens for developers and policymakers. The ongoing discourse surrounding AI ethics has been fueled by these narratives, inspiring the establishment of comprehensive frameworks that prioritize safety and align technological advances with moral considerations. Asimov's Three Laws, though fictional, continue to resonate, informing modern guidelines that advocate for responsible AI usage.

Moreover, science fiction has been instrumental in sensitizing society to the implications of AI integration.

Looking Ahead: A Dual Vision of Coexistence

As we reflect on the relationship between AI agents in science fiction and their real-world counterparts, we find ourselves navigating a narrative woven from imagination and practicality. While science fiction inspires us to contemplate expansive possibilities and confront our deepest fears, the reality of AI development is centered on immediate solutions, efficiency, and ethical integrity.

As AI technology continues to evolve, the distinction between science fiction and reality is poised to blur even further. The advancement of AI agents holds the promise of unlocking extraordinary capabilities—yet it is imperative that ethical principles remain at the forefront of this evolution. In this ever-changing landscape, the story of AI stands as a testament to our journey toward harnessing technology for the greater good.

Purpose and Vision of the Book

"The Future of AI Agents: Emerging Trends and Opportunities" embarks on a captivating journey designed to illuminate the rapidly evolving realm of AI agents. This book serves as both a comprehensive guide and a source of inspiration for readers from diverse backgrounds. As artificial intelligence weaves itself deeper into the fabric of daily life and industry, it becomes essential that we expand our understanding of this intricate technology. Our aim is to demystify AI, making its concepts approachable for professionals, enthusiasts, and curious minds eager to explore its potential applications and impacts.

A Deep Dive into AI Agents

At the heart of this book is a thorough exploration of AI agents, highlighting both their current capabilities and future prospects. Throughout the chapters, readers will gain a foundational grasp of the various types of AI agents— reactive, deliberative, and hybrid models—empowering them to appreciate how these intelligent systems differ from traditional software. The adaptability and learning capacities of AI agents are key themes that will come to life through engaging examples.

Real-world applications are woven throughout the narrative, showcasing the transformative impact of AI across multiple sectors such as healthcare, finance, and transportation. Consider healthcare, where AI not only enhances predictive diagnostics but also facilitates the development of personalized treatment plans, steering the industry towards a more patient-centric paradigm.

Decoding the Technologies Behind AI

A vital component of our vision is to clarify the technologies that underpin AI agents. Delving into key concepts such as machine learning, neural networks, and advancements in natural language processing, readers will build a solid foundation of knowledge that reveals how these technologies converge to create sophisticated AI systems. The book will also explore groundbreaking innovations like quantum computing, which harbors the potential to redefine AI capabilities through extraordinary processing speeds.

Through detailed walkthroughs and engaging examples, we'll

guide readers on how leading machine learning frameworks such as TensorFlow and PyTorch can be harnessed to develop AI solutions. This ensures that we not only provide theoretical underpinnings but also practical insights, making the content actionable for those looking to implement AI technologies in their own endeavors.

Navigating Ethical Considerations

This book transcends mere technical exploration by placing a strong emphasis on the ethical and societal implications surrounding AI agents. Recognizing that technology functions within a broader context, we will highlight crucial ethical considerations such as data privacy, accountability, and bias mitigation. Compelling scenarios and problem-solving discussions will illustrate the importance of responsible AI deployment, reinforcing the notion that our technological advancements must be guided by moral integrity and social responsibility.

Fostering Innovation and Inclusive Progress

Inspiring readers to envision the future, the book encourages a forward-thinking mindset regarding the evolution of AI agents and their potential societal benefits. Through the integration of stories featuring innovators and change-makers in the field, we underscore the value of diverse perspectives in AI development. Readers are invited to consider how inclusivity can lead to more comprehensive and effective AI solutions, emphasizing collaboration across disciplines.

Workshops and mentorship initiatives exemplify actionable measures that promote diversity and inclusivity, demonstrating how communities can nurture a variety of talents for innovative problem-solving. This approach broadens the book's appeal to educators, policymakers, and community leaders who play a crucial role in establishing a collaborative and equitable AI landscape.

Bridging Science Fiction and Reality

Finally, this book aims to bridge the conceptual divide between the portrayal of AI agents in science fiction and their concrete counterparts in the real world. This dual approach enables readers to maintain a balanced view, empowering them to dream big while also being thoughtful about the future of AI.

In conclusion, "The Future of AI Agents" represents a harmonious blend of in-depth exploration, practical application, ethical discourse, and visionary insight. It is crafted not just to inform but also to invigorate readers in their journey towards shaping a future where AI agents are seamlessly integrated into society. Together, we can usher in a new era of innovation guided by ethical considerations and inclusive growth, ultimately fostering a brighter tomorrow for all.

CHAPTER 2: THE TECHNOLOGICAL LANDSCAPE

The remarkable capabilities of AI agents are rooted in a complex interplay of technologies that have undergone exponential growth in recent years. Central to these innovations is the ability to process vast quantities of data in real-time, empowering AI agents to make informed decisions with remarkable speed and precision. Driven by advanced algorithms, these technologies are reshaping interactions across both digital and physical landscapes, heralding a new era of intelligent engagement.

At the heart of AI's transformative power lies machine learning—a vital subset of artificial intelligence dedicated to creating systems that learn from and adapt to data. Through various methods, including supervised, unsupervised, and reinforcement learning, AI agents can discern patterns, forecast outcomes, and modify their behaviors in response to new information. A striking illustration of this capability is found in the healthcare sector, where machine learning algorithms sift through complex datasets to identify disease trends or recommend tailored treatment plans based on individual patient histories.

Deep learning, a more specialized branch of machine learning, further enhances the prowess of AI agents. For example, consider autonomous vehicles that rely on CNNs to analyze vast streams of sensor and camera data. This technology enables them to navigate safely in ever-changing environments, identifying obstacles and interpreting road signs with impressive accuracy.

Natural Language Processing (NLP) stands as another cornerstone in the advancement of AI agents, fostering more intuitive and effective human-computer interactions. NLP allows AI agents to comprehend and respond to human language with increasing sophistication, making it indispensable in applications like customer service chatbots and virtual assistants. Envision a banking chatbot capable of processing inquiries in multiple languages, offering personalized financial insights by accurately interpreting context and emotional tone.

The convergence of robotics and AI is another exciting frontier, empowering machines to execute tasks that demand both precision and flexibility. Take, for instance, the manufacturing industry, where AI-enhanced robots assemble products with meticulous accuracy, streamlining workflows and minimizing errors. This fusion of AI with robotics signals a significant transition to smart factories, where these autonomous systems partner with human workers to elevate productivity and innovation.

Moreover, the Internet of Things (IoT) plays a crucial role in expanding the capabilities of AI by incorporating sensors and connectivity into everyday objects. IoT devices create continuous data streams that AI agents can analyze to refine decision-making processes. In smart home settings, AI-powered IoT systems intelligently monitor energy consumption, learning from residents' habits to optimize resource management while enhancing comfort.

To address the substantial computational demands of these advanced AI agents, cloud computing emerges as a vital enabler. It provides scalable resources that facilitate intricate processing far beyond the limitations of standalone devices. Platforms such as Amazon Web Services and Microsoft Azure offer AI-as-a-Service solutions, giving developers access to powerful tools without the burden of heavy infrastructure investments. This democratization of AI resources allows even smaller enterprises to harness sophisticated AI agents within their operations.

As we navigate this evolving landscape, it is essential to recognize that the integration of these technologies also presents challenges. Issues such as data privacy and biases in machine learning models require our vigilant attention. Addressing these concerns is critical as we strive to maximize the potential of AI agents while adhering to ethical standards and societal values.

Artificial intelligence has made remarkable strides in its endeavor to replicate human thought processes, particularly within the domain of Natural Language Processing (NLP). This field plays a crucial role in bridging the communication divide between humans and machines, and recent enhancements have fundamentally transformed how AI interacts with us in our everyday lives. These innovations empower AI agents to understand, interpret, and generate human language with a sophistication that once seemed beyond reach.

Navigating the intricacies of human language requires advanced techniques grounded in machine learning and statistical modeling, which have witnessed impressive advancements in recent years. A key milestone in this evolution has been the emergence of Transformer models, with architectures like BERT (Bidirectional Encoder Representations from Transformers) and GPT (Generative Pre-trained Transformer) spearheading this change. These models revolutionize how context is understood, processing words in relation to all surrounding words rather than treating them in isolation. As a result, Transformer models achieve a level of insight that allows AI not just to grasp linguistic context but also to discern nuanced elements such as emotion and intention.

Consider the dynamic landscape of customer service as a practical illustration of NLP's impact. Advanced AI agents equipped with sophisticated NLP capabilities can accurately interpret a range of customer inquiries, distinguishing between a technical issue and a billing question. This enables them to generate swift and precise responses. Leveraging sentiment analysis, these agents can detect the emotional nuances within customer interactions, adjusting their tone to either empathize with or uplift the conversation based on the customer's mood. Such advancements have not only enhanced customer satisfaction but have also fostered loyalty, showcasing the real-world benefits stemming from progress in NLP.

Another compelling application of these advancements is the improved accuracy of real-time speech-to-text conversion. Virtual assistants like Amazon's Alexa and Apple's Siri harness NLP to comprehend spoken language, translating it into actionable tasks—be it setting reminders or relaying weather updates. These AI agents are finely tuned to accommodate various accents and dialects, promoting inclusivity within the vast spectrum of linguistic and cultural diversity.

Moreover, NLP has ushered in significant breakthroughs in machine translation, effectively dismantling language barriers that hinder multilingual communication. Services like Google Translate and DeepL leverage powerful neural networks to deliver translation quality that rivals human capabilities, capturing subtle meanings and idiomatic expressions with impressive precision. This not only facilitates global collaboration but also expands access to information across diverse linguistic backgrounds.

The training of these cutting-edge models hinges on vast datasets that feed the intricate algorithms underpinning

NLP's ongoing development. However, ensuring the quality and diversity of this data poses a significant challenge, as these elements critically influence model performance. Biases embedded within training data can lead to inaccurate interpretations or culturally insensitive outcomes. Addressing these concerns necessitates meticulous curation of datasets and the establishment of fairness criteria aimed at minimizing prejudice and enhancing inclusivity.

As we progress further into this realm, the computational demands placed upon modern NLP models call for robust infrastructural support. Organizations increasingly rely on cloud-based platforms to facilitate the immense processing power required by these applications. For instance, Google Cloud's machine learning capabilities provide scalable resources, enabling enterprises to implement sophisticated NLP solutions without incurring exorbitant costs associated with maintaining in-house infrastructure.

These technological advancements illuminate the importance of innovation within NLP while also emphasizing the ethical responsibilities of developers and stakeholders. As we strive to create trustworthy AI systems, it's vital to integrate transparency and accountability measures, ensuring that users are well-informed about the limitations and expected behaviors of these systems.

In our previous exploration of Natural Language Processing, we observed the remarkable strides AI agents have made in comprehending and generating human language, a feat largely attributed to advanced machine learning techniques. The backbone of this progress lies in the machine learning frameworks and tools that enable the development of these intelligent systems. These technologies not only accelerate the evolution of AI but also democratize access to sophisticated capabilities, empowering developers and organizations to create tailor-made solutions that address their specific challenges and aspirations.

At the forefront of this technological foundation is TensorFlow, an open-source framework pioneered by Google Brain. TensorFlow has emerged as a vital resource for training and deploying machine learning models, equipping developers with a comprehensive suite of tools designed for computational efficiency across diverse platforms—from mobile devices to vast data centers. Its flexible architecture allows practitioners to model complex challenges effectively, fostering an environment conducive to experimentation with various neural network designs, hyperparameter tuning, and performance optimization. As a result, developers are equipped to engineer highly effective AI agents capable of excelling in complex tasks.

Another major player in the AI landscape is PyTorch, a framework developed by Facebook's AI Research lab. PyTorch has garnered considerable attention, particularly within academic circles, thanks to its dynamic computation graph, which offers unparalleled flexibility. This adaptability makes PyTorch particularly attractive for iterative prototyping and experimentation. Researchers gravitate toward this approach because it mimics traditional programming paradigms, fostering innovation in both model architecture and training methodologies. Such flexibility is indispensable when refining AI agents for projects that require a nuanced understanding and agile adaptability.

For those venturing to integrate machine learning into enterprise applications, frameworks like Keras provide a high-level interface built on top of TensorFlow. Keras simplifies complex workflows, enabling developers to swiftly prototype and validate ideas without delving deep into the complexities of backend computations. Despite its user-friendly nature, Keras does not sacrifice functionality; it supports a wide array of machine learning models and techniques, making it a preferred choice for developers who desire both ease of use and computational prowess.

Consider a practical scenario in a retail environment where AI agents harness image recognition to revolutionize inventory management. Extensive training on labeled image datasets enables the AI to discern between various items, ensuring real-time updates to stock levels. With TensorFlow's optimization capabilities, developers can ensure that the system scales seamlessly, adeptly processing vast amounts of data with accuracy and reliability.

Moreover, the emergence of AutoML platforms, such as Google's AutoML and Microsoft's Azure ML, marks a significant shift in the landscape of AI development, making sophisticated model creation accessible even to those without deep expertise in AI. These platforms allow users to automate the end-to-end process of applying machine learning to practical problems, employing sophisticated algorithms to systematically explore various modeling options and optimize them for peak accuracy and performance. This democratization of AI helps bridge the skills gap, empowering businesses to leverage advanced technologies without needing an extensive in-house machine learning team.

Addressing concerns surrounding the limitations of data science resources, these frameworks and tools signify a transformative move towards enhanced accessibility and collaboration. This evolution is pivotal as organizations increasingly recognize the substantial advantages of AI integration across industries.

However, the allure of these tools and frameworks comes with a responsibility. Developers must remain acutely aware of the ethical implications tied to their usage. The potential for models to inherit biases from their training data underscores the importance of rigorous oversight throughout the model development and deployment process. Tools such as Fairlearn and AI Fairness 360 offer critical resources for assessing and mitigating bias, guiding developers to create equitable AI systems that align with societal values and ethical principles.

In conclusion, the evolution of machine learning frameworks and tools symbolizes the dynamic interplay between technological advancement and practical application. The true challenge—and opportunity—lies in responsibly wielding these tools, ensuring they enrich our society while upholding ethical integrity and social responsibility. The future of AI will be defined by this delicate balance, where cutting-edge technology meets thoughtful stewardship, creating a thriving and harmonious digital ecosystem.

Continuing from our investigation into the transformative impact of machine learning frameworks on intelligent systems, we now turn our attention to the exhilarating world of robotics and physical AI agents. This fascinating domain represents the confluence of software and the physical realm, infusing intelligence into the very fabric of our daily lives. The integration of artificial intelligence within robotics marks a significant evolution—moving beyond mere programmed machines to creating dynamic entities capable of adapting to complex and ever-changing environments.

Today, robots powered by AI are making their presence felt across a diverse range of industries, where they drive efficiency and spur innovation in unprecedented ways. In the manufacturing sector, for instance, robotic arms equipped with advanced AI vision systems are revolutionizing production lines. These machines not only assemble components but also meticulously inspect products for quality assurance, achieving a level of precision previously thought unattainable. This synergy between AI vision and robotic dexterity signifies more than just an upgrade in machinery; it heralds a paradigm shift towards fully automated and intelligent manufacturing processes.

A prominent illustration of AI-driven robotics can be found in warehouse logistics. Companies like Boston Dynamics have pioneered autonomous machines capable of navigating intricate storage environments with remarkable efficiency. Endowed with sophisticated AI algorithms, these robots can make real-time decisions, maneuver around obstacles, and optimize transport routes, all while ensuring the swift and safe transfer of goods. This capability enhances operational efficiency, significantly reducing the need for human labor in repetitive tasks, thereby allowing personnel to concentrate on more strategic and fulfilling responsibilities.

In the healthcare arena, the marriage of robotics and AI is making impressive strides. Robotic systems such as the Da Vinci Surgical System utilize AI to guide instruments with exceptional precision during complex surgeries. This technology not only improves surgical outcomes but also reduces recovery times, marking a revolutionary step forward in patient care. Here, the predictive and analytical prowess of AI complements the finesse and dexterity of robotics, improving the quality of healthcare services.

Nonetheless, the deployment of AI in robotics is not without its challenges. As these systems gain autonomy and make independent decisions, the importance of creating robust decision-making frameworks cannot be overstated. Take, for example, self-driving cars that must navigate unforeseen obstacles; they require ethically sound programming to determine the best course of action. This underscores the critical need for responsible ethical considerations that must accompany technological advancements.

The task facing developers is multifaceted—juggling the intricacies of risk management, safety protocols, and adherence to regulatory standards to ensure safe and ethical operation of robotic systems. Comprehensive testing and validation methodologies are essential to create agents that align with societal norms, mitigating potential risks and ensuring reliability even in unpredictable scenarios.

The convergence of AI and robotics also opens doors to creating highly interactive environments, crucial for AI agents operating in social contexts. Humanoid robots powered by AI are increasingly deployed in public domains, such as customer service and eldercare. Utilizing natural language processing and sentiment analysis, these robots engage in human-like interactions, offering valuable assistance and fostering meaningful connections.

Consider Pepper, a humanoid robot designed specifically to interact with customers. Pepper's AI capabilities enable it to perceive human emotions and respond accordingly, making interactions feel more empathetic and relatable. This goes beyond merely assisting customers; Pepper's AI-driven analysis also empowers it to provide personalized product recommendations, enriching the overall user experience.

However, as we celebrate these technological advances, it is imperative we reflect on the profound implications of human-robot interactions, raising questions about ethical boundaries and cultural sensitivities. Guidelines and perceptions surrounding AI vary significantly across nations, presenting unique challenges in ensuring that AI agents are harmoniously integrated into everyday life.

The rapid advancement of robotics, underpinned by AI, signals the dawn of an era that intertwines machine learning's predictive capabilities with tangible actions, fundamentally reshaping how industries function and interact with the world. As developers and innovators progress in their quests to refine these physical agents, the challenge transcends technical achievement; it encompasses a commitment to ethical stewardship of technological breakthroughs. This endeavor aims to cultivate a future where robotic intelligence enhances human experience, all while aligning with moral foundations and cultural values.

As we explore the realms of robotics and AI, we unveil the

extraordinary potential for machines not only to emulate but also to elevate human capabilities. This journey is one marked by both excitement and caution, prompting an inquiry into not just what these technologies can achieve, but, more importantly, what they ought to accomplish. This sets the stage for an ongoing evolution of the digital landscape, one that balances innovation with ethical responsibility.

The convergence of AI agents with the Internet of Things (IoT) heralds a groundbreaking evolution in the way interconnected devices communicate, interact, and learn from one another, ultimately forging a seamlessly intelligent network. This powerful integration—commonly referred to as AIoT—amplifies the capabilities of individual devices while significantly enhancing the collective potential of smart environments. Building upon our previous exploration of AI-driven robotics, this discussion ventures into the realm of ubiquitous connectivity, revealing possibilities that extend far beyond conventional applications.

At its core, IoT encompasses a network of physical devices equipped with sensors, software, and other technologies that permit the exchange of data with other devices and systems via the internet. The infusion of AI transforms these devices from passive participants into proactive agents capable of processing, analyzing, and learning from the vast amounts of data they generate. This dynamic ability empowers AI agents to make informed decisions autonomously, fostering environments that are not only responsive but also intuitively adaptable to user needs.

One of the most compelling illustrations of AIoT in practice is the emergence of smart cities. These urban ecosystems harness data collected from a multitude of IoT devices to enhance infrastructure, refine public services, and elevate residents' quality of life. Picture a city where AI agents adeptly manage traffic signals in real-time by tapping into data streams from cameras, sensors, and vehicle communication systems.

AIoT also holds transformative potential in smart homes, where AI-driven IoT devices automatically regulate lighting, climate, and security settings to enhance comfort and safety. Imagine a home that learns from your daily patterns: the AI adjusts the thermostat just before you arrive, dims the lights as you unwind, and secures the premises as you settle in for the night. Such devices harness machine learning algorithms to anticipate and fulfill individual preferences, delivering a personalized experience that merges convenience with energy efficiency.

In industrial contexts, the collaboration between AI and IoT creates robust predictive maintenance systems. Intelligent sensors embedded within machinery continuously monitor performance and detect anomalies, sending real-time data to AI algorithms that forecast potential failures before they manifest. For instance, in a manufacturing facility outfitted with IoT sensors, an AI system can analyze operational status and forecast when machinery might require servicing.

Nonetheless, the deployment of AI agents alongside IoT comes with challenges that must be addressed to ensure success. The sheer volume of data generated by interconnected devices demands sophisticated data management and analytical capabilities. Here, cloud computing plays a pivotal role, providing scalable infrastructure to process and store this data influx. Leveraging cloud-based AIoT platforms allows organizations to harmonize data from diverse sources, ensuring seamless integration and real-time responsiveness.

Security concerns also pose significant obstacles in the realm of AIoT. As devices become increasingly interconnected, the potential for cyberattacks grows. Safeguarding against these risks calls for robust cybersecurity measures specifically tailored for IoT environments. AI algorithms can enhance these defensive strategies by identifying unusual network behaviors and responding to threats instantaneously, thus protecting sensitive information and maintaining system integrity.

Interoperability stands as another essential consideration in the integration of IoT and AI. For AI agents to operate effectively across various IoT devices, common standards and protocols must be established to enable seamless communication among disparate systems. This endeavor requires collaborative efforts from technology developers, industry groups, and regulatory bodies to create frameworks that foster interoperability and align with evolving industry standards.

Despite these hurdles, the landscape of AIoT applications continues to evolve, driving innovation across multiple sectors. In healthcare, for instance, wearable IoT devices equipped with AI can monitor patient vitals and deliver real-time diagnostics, facilitating proactive healthcare management through continuous observation and early intervention. In agriculture, AIoT systems analyze soil moisture data and weather patterns to optimize resource utilization, directing precision irrigation efforts and ultimately boosting crop yields.

The marriage of AI agents with IoT represents a significant leap toward the creation of intelligent ecosystems designed to simplify tasks, enrich user experiences, and optimize resource management. These advancements not only elevate personal convenience and operational efficiency but also empower organizations and societies to confront complex challenges on a larger scale. As the domain of AIoT continues to advance, it promises to reshape our living and working environments through enhanced connectivity and actionable insights, paving the way for a future where interconnected intelligence drives innovation and fosters sustainable growth.

Cloud computing has emerged as a cornerstone for the

scalability of artificial intelligence (AI), providing the vital infrastructure and resources needed to handle the vast data processing and storage demands that accompany AI-driven initiatives. As AI agents increasingly permeate various industries, harnessing the capabilities of cloud computing becomes not just beneficial but also essential for optimizing and enhancing AI performance.

Central to the cloud computing model is its ability to deliver on-demand computing resources over the internet, offering organizations unparalleled flexibility and efficiency in deploying AI solutions. One of the most remarkable features of cloud services is their capacity for dynamic scaling of computational resources, which allows organizations to adjust their infrastructure to meet shifting demands from AI tasks. This scalability ensures that AI systems can perform at their peak even during high-traffic periods, all while avoiding the exorbitant costs associated with maintaining dedicated physical hardware.

Take, for instance, a retail organization that employs AI agents to anticipate consumer behavior and manage inventory efficiently. During bustling shopping seasons like Black Friday, the surge in consumer engagement necessitates a significant uptick in computational power. Cloud computing enables the retailer to scale their AI infrastructure quickly, facilitating real-time data processing for accurate trend forecasting and responsive inventory adjustments. Once the shopping frenzy subsides, the organization can seamlessly reduce its cloud resources, effectively managing costs without compromising on performance.

Moreover, cloud platforms offer a wealth of AI-specific services that simplify the development and implementation process for businesses. With offerings like machine learning models as a service (MLaaS), artificial intelligence as a service (AIaaS), and databases as a service (DBaaS), organizations gain access to pre-built tools and frameworks. This allows developers to concentrate on refining and training AI models without getting mired in technical complexities. From natural language processing APIs to advanced computer vision algorithms, these services empower businesses to incorporate sophisticated AI capabilities swiftly and efficiently.

The collaborative nature of cloud environments further enhances the scalability of AI by enabling distributed computing and teamwork among dispersed development teams. Multiple developers can engage on a single AI project simultaneously, irrespective of their geographic locations, fostering an innovative ecosystem that accelerates development cycles. For example, a team dedicated to creating an AI-driven smart city application can utilize cloud-based development tools to synchronize their efforts, test interactions in real time, and iterate on their designs with agility—ultimately driving faster, more effective innovation.

Data management, an integral component of any AI initiative, is significantly improved through cloud computing. The ability to store, access, and analyze large datasets in cloud environments allows AI projects to work with the most recent data, ensuring the accuracy and relevance of AI models. As AI systems adapt to process increasingly diverse data from multiple sources, the extensive storage options and sophisticated data management tools provided by cloud services are critical for powering efficient AI workflows.

However, the integration of cloud computing with AI presents certain challenges that organizations must address. Foremost among these is data security; given the sensitive nature of information involved in AI training, it is crucial to implement robust encryption and access controls to mitigate risks of unauthorized access and data breaches. Leading cloud service providers offer an array of security measures and compliance certifications to safeguard data integrity, yet organizations bear the responsibility of managing these resources to align them with their unique security policies.

Latency is another important consideration, particularly when real-time processing is a necessity. To counteract potential delays associated with cloud infrastructure, edge computing emerges as a complementary solution. Organizations can adopt a hybrid model that utilizes both cloud and edge computing, thus extending AI capabilities into areas where immediate data processing is critical.

The landscape of cloud computing is continually evolving, paving the way for emerging technologies that will further enhance the scalability of AI agents. Innovations such as Kubernetes for orchestrating containerized applications and serverless computing for automatically scaling resources in response to real-time demands are revolutionizing the development and deployment of AI applications. These advancements are instrumental in shaping smart, responsive systems capable of effectively managing complex, data-intensive tasks across a variety of domains.

In conclusion, cloud computing not only provides the scalable infrastructure essential for the flourishing of AI agents but also equips organizations with the tools needed to innovate and respond swiftly to a rapidly changing technological environment.

Data management and real-time processing are critical pillars in the architecture of AI agents, serving as the foundation for advanced data-driven insights and decisions. As AI agents increasingly permeate diverse industries—from autonomous vehicles and healthcare to financial services—the capacity to adeptly manage and process data in real time is no longer just advantageous; it is essential for successful implementation and enduring performance.

At the core of real-time processing is the ability to make swift decisions informed by the continuous influx of data. This capability directly influences the responsiveness and efficiency of AI agents. Take autonomous vehicles, for instance; these agents must accurately interpret an array of sensor inputs—including signals from cameras, LIDAR, and radar—allowing them to adapt their driving behavior dynamically while prioritizing passenger safety. Through real-time data processing, AI systems can effectively analyze their surroundings, anticipate potential dangers, and execute rapid maneuvers that not only avert hazards but also enhance overall traffic efficiency.

Efficient management of data flows is paramount in enabling this real-time responsiveness, particularly concerning data ingestion, storage, and retrieval. Today's data management platforms are built to handle the immense volume, speed, and variety of data produced by advancing technologies. Stream processing frameworks like Apache Kafka and Apache Flink empower organizations to ingest and analyze large-scale, real-time data streams, converting raw data into actionable intelligence on the fly. These platforms support event-driven architectures, allowing AI systems to engage with fresh data as it arrives and react dynamically—rather than relying on slower, batch-processing methods.

For example, consider a financial institution employing AI agents for fraud detection. This capability necessitates seamless integration of stream processing technologies with the institution's existing systems, ensuring that each transaction undergoes automatic analysis and scoring for potential fraud as it is processed. When coupled with machine learning models trained on historical transaction data, the AI agent can pinpoint subtle patterns indicative of fraudulent behavior, thereby preventing financial losses.

Beyond real-time data streams, robust data management also involves the systematic and efficient storage of historical data, which is vital for training AI models and enhancing their performance over time. Databases optimized for rapid read-write operations, such as NoSQL databases (e.g., MongoDB, Cassandra), offer scalable solutions for managing vast quantities of structured and unstructured data. When paired with advanced analytical tools, these databases facilitate the swift retrieval and assessment of historical data, enabling developers to continuously refine AI models and strategies.

However, tackling the intricacies of data management and real-time processing is not without its challenges. One significant obstacle is ensuring data quality and integrity. Data inaccuracies or inconsistencies can lead to flawed model predictions and misguided decisions. Therefore, it is crucial to implement stringent data validation protocols. This includes employing data cleansing techniques, establishing comprehensive data governance policies, and regularly auditing data pipelines to identify and correct potential discrepancies before they ripple through downstream AI processes.

Latency management represents another vital consideration that can greatly influence the performance of real-time systems. While cloud computing offers scalability for handling enormous datasets, latency issues may arise from delays in data transmission between on-premises systems and cloud data centers. Employing edge computing and localized data processing solutions can significantly mitigate latency, bringing computational resources closer to data sources and minimizing the need for back-and-forth data transmission between cloud and edge devices.

Additionally, security and privacy concerns are vital aspects in the realm of data management and real-time processing, particularly in sensitive fields such as healthcare and finance. Protecting sensitive data necessitates rigorous access controls, robust encryption methods, and adherence to regulations like GDPR and CCPA. Establishing transparency in how data is collected, processed, and utilized by AI agents is essential in building user trust and ensuring compliance with global data protection laws.

In conclusion, effective data management and real-time processing are integral to AI agent functionality, paving the way for revolutionary applications across various sectors by facilitating timely insights and actions. Organizations that skillfully integrate these critical elements can leverage the full potential of AI to reform their operational frameworks, drive innovation, and sustain competitive advantages in an ever-evolving landscape. Achieving this requires not just the adoption of advanced technologies but also a strategic approach emphasizing agility, security, and ethical stewardship in managing the vast reservoir of data that powers AI today.

As artificial intelligence (AI) agents become increasingly integrated across diverse sectors, they bring with them a host of cybersecurity challenges that demand immediate and comprehensive attention. The inherent capabilities and vast interconnectivity of AI systems make them appealing targets for malicious actors eager to exploit potential vulnerabilities for harmful purposes. Consequently, addressing the complexities of AI cybersecurity is imperative, necessitating robust strategies that consider both technological weaknesses and the human dynamics inherent in AI deployment.

One of the most pressing threats in the AI landscape is the phenomenon of adversarial attacks. These attacks occur when cybercriminals intentionally manipulate input data to mislead AI models, resulting in incorrect outputs with potentially dire consequences. A striking example can be seen in the realm of autonomous vehicles where an adversarial attack might involve subtly altering images of stop signs. Such manipulations can deceive an AI system into misclassifying the sign, posing serious risks not only to the vehicle's operation but also to public safety. To counter these threats, developers are increasingly encouraged to implement adversarial training during the AI development lifecycle. This proactive approach involves exposing AI models to various perturbations during their training phase, thereby enhancing their robustness and better preparing them to withstand deceptive inputs.

Another significant cybersecurity concern is data poisoning, a tactic where attackers compromise the datasets used for training AI models. For instance, tampering with financial records in algorithmic trading systems could distort market predictions, leading to catastrophic financial decisions. Mitigating this risk requires the implementation of rigorous data validation processes and regular audits to ensure the integrity and reliability of datasets utilized in AI training.

Moreover, the rapid advancement of AI technologies raises substantial concerns about data privacy breaches. Given that AI systems often rely on extensive volumes of personal information, unauthorized access or unauthorized data exposure can lead to severe privacy violations. In the healthcare sector, where AI is increasingly applied for optimizing patient care, it is vital to implement stringent protective measures to safeguard sensitive health records. Employing advanced encryption methods, such as homomorphic encryption, can allow data to be processed in an encrypted state, maintaining privacy while still enabling the essential functionalities of AI.

Additionally, the implementation of AI systems brings its own set of challenges related to insider threats and human error. Employees with access to sensitive AI systems may misuse their privileges—whether intentionally or unwittingly —leading to significant security breaches. To mitigate these risks, organizations must establish comprehensive access control measures that restrict data access based on clearly defined roles and responsibilities. Integrating techniques like multi-factor authentication and real-time monitoring of user activities can further enhance security by promptly identifying and addressing suspicious behavior.

Addressing AI cybersecurity challenges also involves identifying and addressing potential vulnerabilities within AI algorithms themselves. Researchers have highlighted the existence of backdoor vulnerabilities, which are specific patterns in input data that can trigger unauthorized actions within AI systems. Regular security reviews and thorough vulnerability testing of AI algorithms should become a standard practice. Here, the use of AI-enhanced automated security tools can facilitate the detection and remediation of vulnerabilities within the system architecture more effectively.

To bolster cybersecurity for AI systems, collaboration among various stakeholders is essential. Partnerships across industry, academia, and government can pave the way for developing standardized cybersecurity frameworks and best practices tailored specifically to AI agents. These frameworks should encompass all stages of the AI lifecycle—ranging from design and data management to deployment and ongoing maintenance—ensuring that security is seamlessly integrated into the AI development process rather than treated as an afterthought.

Furthermore, it is worth noting that AI agents can themselves play a critical role in the enhancement of cybersecurity defenses. Machine learning algorithms are adept at analyzing network traffic patterns, allowing them to identify anomalies indicative of cyber threats in real-time. AI-driven security measures not only improve the speed and accuracy of threat detection but also provide organizations with a proactive line of defense against emerging cyber threats.

In conclusion, the cybersecurity challenges associated with AI agents necessitate a multifaceted approach that blends technical solutions, strategic planning, and collaborative efforts. Adopting proactive cybersecurity strategies not only safeguards the integrity of AI systems but also fosters consumer and stakeholder trust, reinforcing the transformative potential of AI innovations when embraced responsibly.

Choosing between open-source and proprietary AI agent platforms is a decision that carries significant consequences for organizations, influencing not only budget allocations but also development flexibility and security measures. A deep understanding of the subtle distinctions between these two types of platforms can provide valuable insights into strategic deployment choices, reflecting broader themes in AI agent development and integration.

Open-source AI platforms shine in their transparency and collaborative spirit. They empower developers worldwide to access, modify, and enhance the source code, creating a dynamic ecosystem where knowledge and innovation are shared freely. This open collaboration often leads to accelerated advancements and inventive solutions. Notable projects such as TensorFlow and PyTorch exemplify this trend, having found extensive applications in various industries, including healthcare and finance. For instance, TensorFlow's adaptable architecture allows for exceptional scalability and easy integration with diverse data sources, making it a prime choice for crafting intricate, bespoke AI models that cater to specific business requirements.

Nonetheless, embracing open-source platforms does come with its own set of challenges. The absence of commercial support can be a significant hurdle for organizations lacking substantial technical expertise. Additionally, the constant stream of updates and contributions from a distributed global community can complicate version control and compatibility management. This situation often necessitates a dedicated development team to oversee and maintain the platform, which may diminish the cost-saving advantages for smaller enterprises.

On the other hand, proprietary AI platforms deliver tailored solutions typically backed by committed customer support, alleviating some of the pressures associated with managing and troubleshooting complex AI systems. Established corporations like IBM (with Watson) and Microsoft (with Azure AI) develop these platforms, providing advanced features rigorously tested for reliability and performance. Proprietary solutions are particularly attractive to enterprises that prioritize stability and robust security, as they come equipped with comprehensive cybersecurity measures and compliance assurances. These elements are vital in sectors such as finance or healthcare, where data sensitivity and regulatory adherence are paramount.

However, the appeal of proprietary platforms is tempered by certain restrictions. They can often constrain organizations to vendor-specific protocols, which limits customization options. Furthermore, the cost of licensing and the long-term commitment to proprietary systems can have a substantial impact on operational budgets. Companies must carefully weigh the benefits of vendor support against the potential limitations on innovation and flexibility that these platforms may impose.

Consider the practical example of a startup in the autonomous vehicle sector. An open-source platform like OpenAI Gym could facilitate early-stage research and development, allowing for experimentation and adaptation without incurring hefty upfront costs. As the startup grows, transitioning to a proprietary platform may offer the essential infrastructure and security assurances needed to fulfill industry standards and establish commercial relationships with automotive partners.

Ultimately, the choice between open-source and proprietary AI platforms should be informed by the organization's specific objectives, available resources, and technical capabilities. A hybrid approach that combines the advantages of both platforms can provide a balanced strategy. For instance, leveraging an open-source platform for initial development, followed by transitioning to a proprietary solution for deployment, can harness the strengths of both methodologies.

In conclusion, this decision is not merely technical; it significantly influences an organization's cultural and strategic trajectory.

Exploring the Future of AI Agents: Innovation, Integration, and Ethics

As we look ahead to the future of AI agents, it becomes essential to navigate through the rapid technological advancements and evolving trends that are redefining artificial intelligence. This journey isn't merely about technological evolution; it's about understanding how groundbreaking innovations can alter industries and reshape societal norms. Building upon the foundational concepts of AI integration and ethical considerations, we can envision a landscape where AI becomes an integral part of our lives.

The Convergence of Technologies: Unlocking New Potentials

At the forefront of this transformation is the convergence of AI with other cutting-edge technologies. Take, for instance, the burgeoning field of quantum computing. While still in its formative stages, quantum computing holds tremendous potential to revolutionize AI capabilities by significantly enhancing processing power. Imagine AI agents equipped with quantum computing abilities, tackling complex problems that once seemed insurmountable. Tasks such as drug discovery and climate modeling could be accelerated to new heights, with AI simulating molecular interactions with extraordinary precision. This could pave the way for developing groundbreaking pharmaceuticals or sustainable energy solutions, transforming vital sectors for the better.

Alongside quantum advancements, the integration of AI with

the Internet of Things (IoT) is creating a multi-faceted environment for real-time data interaction. Envision smart cities where AI agents harness data from millions of sensors to optimize traffic systems. These agents will not just manage traffic flow; they will reduce congestion and enhance public transportation efficiency, making urban living increasingly sustainable. In the realm of agriculture, AI-powered IoT systems can provide farmers with precise insights into soil health and crop requirements, encouraging sustainable practices that improve yield while preserving the ecosystem.

The Ethical Landscape of AI Development

As we forge ahead, the conversation around AI ethics must also advance. The development of ethical AI technologies is vital to ensure responsible deployment. Imagine AI agents that can autonomously audit their algorithms for biases or potential harmful behaviors. Integrating established ethical frameworks directly into AI systems will not only build public trust but also ensure compliance in sensitive applications like law enforcement and human resources, where the stakes are particularly high.

Enhancing Human-AI Interactions

A significant aspect of future technological strides lies in advancements in natural language processing (NLP). As these algorithms evolve, AI agents will gain an unprecedented ability to understand and interpret the nuances of human communication. This enhancement will allow virtual assistants to engage more meaningfully across various sectors—think healthcare or education—by fostering natural and effective interactions. For instance, in mental health care, AI agents could provide empathetic support, accurately recognizing emotional cues through text and voice analysis to offer timely interventions and personalized recommendations.

Collective Intelligence: The Swarm Approach

Another captivating development on the horizon is the concept of swarm intelligence, inspired by the cooperative behaviors found in nature. Through decentralized decision-making, these systems can rapidly adapt to changes in their environment, unlocking innovative solutions through teamwork.

Redefining Human-Computer Interaction

As AI continues to evolve, so will the interfaces that connect us with these intelligent agents. Innovations in augmented reality (AR) and virtual reality (VR) will redefine our engagement with AI, providing immersive experiences that go beyond traditional interfaces. Picture an architect using an AR headset to design a building in real time, leveraging AI insights into structural integrity and aesthetics. This fusion of technology and creativity will redefine industries and elevate user experiences to unprecedented levels.

Embracing the Future: Challenges and Responsibilities

The future of AI agents paints a vibrant picture of integration into our daily lives and societal frameworks. However, the path forward is not without its challenges. Issues such as data privacy, algorithmic bias, and ethical AI use must be prioritized as we evolve.

In conclusion, the future of AI agents is a rich tapestry woven from technological innovation and ethical responsibility. As organizations seek to harness the power of AI, staying attuned to these developments is essential—not only for profitability but also for enhancing the well-being of humanity. The journey is just beginning, and it promises to reshape our world in remarkable ways.

CHAPTER 3: KEY INDUSTRIES AND APPLICATIONS

The healthcare landscape is undergoing a remarkable transformation thanks to the emergence of AI agents. These intelligent systems are not merely supplemental tools; they are reshaping patient care, streamlining operational workflows, and providing critical support to healthcare professionals in unprecedented ways. Let's explore how AI is revolutionizing healthcare, illustrated through concrete examples and their significant implications.

In the realm of healthcare administration, AI agents act as virtual assistants, expertly managing a variety of tasks, from scheduling appointments to monitoring vital signs. Imagine a busy hospital equipped with an AI-driven system designed for optimizing patient flow. This sophisticated technology utilizes data analytics to dynamically allocate resources, forecast peak times, and adjust staffing levels in real-time. The result? Reduced wait times and a more effective utilization of hospital resources, which significantly enhances overall patient satisfaction.

When it comes to diagnostics, AI agents demonstrate extraordinary capabilities. They can process medical images with a speed and accuracy that far exceed human potential. For instance, an AI solution using deep learning algorithms can analyze millions of radiology images, swiftly recognizing patterns linked to diseases such as cancer or pneumonia. This rapid analysis enables earlier interventions, which are crucial for improving patient outcomes and can potentially save lives.

Telemedicine, too, has been transformed by the integration of AI agents, especially in underserved rural areas where access to healthcare providers remains limited. Virtual health assistants can perform initial assessments by interpreting patient symptoms communicated through text or voice. In these remote locations, patients can engage with AI-driven bots that draw from extensive medical knowledge databases, offering preliminary consultations. This not only minimizes the need for costly travel but also ensures that patients receive timely medical advice.

Moreover, the administrative side of healthcare benefits tremendously from AI automation. Tasks like billing, data entry, and processing insurance claims are streamlined by intelligent systems. For example, an AI application can automatically verify insurance claims against current policies, swiftly identifying discrepancies or potential fraud. This automation enhances cash flow for healthcare providers while also reducing the manual errors that often lead to delays in patient care.

Personalized medicine represents another significant area where AI agents are making waves. A compelling example lies in pharmacogenomics, where AI algorithms predict how patients will respond to different medications. This capability allows for tailored prescriptions that maximize therapeutic effectiveness while minimizing adverse side effects, ushering in a new era of precision medicine that aligns treatments with an individual's unique genetic profile.

However, the integration of AI in healthcare does not come without its challenges, particularly concerning ethical considerations. Data privacy remains a paramount concern, as safeguarding patient information within AI systems requires implementing stringent cybersecurity measures. Healthcare organizations must prioritize encryption, access controls, and continuous monitoring to protect sensitive data and ensure compliance with regulations like HIPAA.

The evolution of AI agents has also sparked vital discussions about the irreplaceable role of human empathy in healthcare —something technology cannot replicate. While AI excels in managing data-driven tasks, it lacks the compassionate understanding that defines effective patient-provider relationships. Thus, rather than replacing the human touch, AI serves to complement healthcare professionals, allowing them to concentrate more on complex and empathetic dimensions of patient care.

Looking ahead, as the healthcare sector increasingly embraces AI technologies, the collaborative synergy between human expertise and machine intelligence will shape its future. AI agents will not substitute for doctors or nurses; instead, they will empower these medical professionals by providing insights and efficiencies that were previously unattainable. The ongoing challenge lies in responsibly harnessing this technological potential, ensuring that advancements align seamlessly with ethical standards and prioritize patient-centric values.

This journey toward integrating AI agents into healthcare is one of innovation, accountability, and collaboration. The aim extends beyond merely improving medical outcomes; it involves fostering an environment that is as compassionate as it is advanced. As we move forward, the integration of AI must ultimately enhance the human experience, creating a healthcare ecosystem that prioritizes not only efficiency but also empathy and compassion.

One area where AI agents are making a particularly profound impact is in fraud detection and prevention. With the integration of sophisticated machine learning algorithms, financial institutions can analyze vast amounts of data at remarkable speed, enabling them to identify unusual patterns indicative of fraudulent activity. For instance, some banks now utilize AI solutions that offer real-time transaction monitoring, leveraging historical data to detect inconsistencies or anomalies swiftly. This proactive strategy not only reduces potential financial losses but also cultivates a high level of trust among customers, who can feel secure knowing their assets are vigilantly protected.

The landscape of risk assessment and management has also undergone significant enhancement through the implementation of AI technologies. Resources like AI agents excel at evaluating risks by dissecting complex, multi-layered data sets, empowering financial entities to make more informed decisions. Consider an insurance company that harnesses AI to analyze past claims, socio-economic indicators, and even environmental data such as weather patterns.

Customer service is evolving rapidly, thanks to the rise of AI-powered virtual assistants. These intelligent agents can seamlessly handle customer inquiries, dispense financial advice, and facilitate transactions. A notable example includes AI chatbots that banks employ to engage with customers across digital platforms. These bots are capable of managing a wide array of functions—from simple balance inquiries to complex fund transfers and offering insights based on a customer's spending habits. This not only enhances customer satisfaction through 24/7 availability but also allows human representatives to concentrate on more intricate issues requiring personalized engagement.

Investment management is also experiencing a transformation, as AI agents deliver real-time insights and portfolio management solutions to investors. Algorithm-based trading platforms leverage AI to perform sophisticated quantitative analyses that surpass human capabilities, optimizing trading strategies to drive better returns. A prime example is the rise of AI-driven robo-advisors, which assist clients in managing their investment portfolios. These advisors utilize advanced algorithms to craft tailored portfolios reflective of individual risk profiles and prevailing market conditions, providing personalized investment recommendations without the hefty fees commonly associated with traditional advisory services.

Additionally, the role of AI in personal finance management is becoming increasingly significant. Financial applications powered by AI track individual spending patterns, generate budget recommendations, and forecast future financial health. Envision an application that consolidates transaction data from various bank accounts, analyzes spending behaviors, and alerts users to potential savings opportunities or undesirable spending habits. This customized financial management empowers individuals to make informed choices that align with their long-term financial objectives.

However, while the potential of implementing AI agents in the financial sector is vast, it is essential to recognize the challenges that accompany this shift. Data privacy and security remain paramount concerns, as financial institutions are custodians of highly sensitive client information. The demand for robust encryption methods, fortified cybersecurity protocols, and rigorous compliance with regulatory frameworks is critical in safeguarding data integrity and upholding client confidentiality.

Moreover, the ethical considerations surrounding AI implementation in finance are not to be overlooked. Issues such as algorithmic transparency, accountability, and bias require urgent attention to ensure fair treatment for all customers. Financial institutions must prioritize the development of unbiased algorithms, ensuring equitable service delivery that fosters a culture of trust and loyalty among clients.

As financial companies continue to integrate AI agents into both operational processes and customer-facing strategies, the industry stands on the cusp of an era rich with opportunities and responsibilities. For AI to truly excel in finance, it must work harmoniously alongside human expertise, allowing professionals to focus on high-level strategic decision-making and value creation. The future of finance, augmented by AI, promises enhanced precision, efficiency, and customer satisfaction—ultimately paving the way for a more resilient and responsive industry that meets the evolving needs of its clientele. This commitment to transformation not only highlights the potential for AI technology to reshape financial services but also emphasizes the importance of upholding the highest standards of security, ethics, and customer care.

The retail industry is on the cusp of a transformative era, propelled by the advancements of artificial intelligence (AI). These innovations are reshaping how businesses interact with consumers and operate internally, leading to enhanced customer experiences, improved inventory management, and more meaningful engagement with patrons through personalized offerings.

One of the most compelling applications of AI in retail is the personalization of the shopping experience. Retailers harness the power of machine learning algorithms to delve into customer data, revealing insights into preferences and buying behaviors. For instance, a fashion retailer may analyze a customer's purchase history and online browsing habits to craft tailored recommendations. Imagine a shopper visiting an online store and being greeted with curated outfit suggestions that resonate with their unique style. This level of individualized attention not only increases the probability of a purchase but also fosters a deeper sense of brand loyalty, making the shopping experience more relevant and enjoyable for consumers.

Inventory management is another critical area where AI is making a significant impact. Advanced AI systems facilitate real-time tracking and management of stock levels, mitigating issues related to stockouts and excess inventory. Consider a grocery store chain that employs AI-driven demand forecasting models, utilizing historical sales data and external factors like weather patterns to accurately predict product demand. This approach allows the chain to optimize inventory, ensuring that items such as fresh produce are stocked in adequate quantities while minimizing waste. Such efficiency not only boosts profitability but also aligns with sustainability efforts—an increasingly important consideration for modern consumers.

The rise of self-service checkout experiences powered by AI is further revolutionizing the retail landscape. Leveraging cutting-edge computer vision and sensor technologies, these systems automatically identify and charge for items as customers exit the store, bypassing traditional checkout procedures. Amazon Go is a prime example, where shoppers enjoy the seamless experience of walking in, selecting products, and leaving without engaging with a cashier. This innovation not only accelerates the shopping process but also caters to the demand for convenience prevalent in today's fast-paced society.

In addition to logistical enhancements, AI agents are transforming customer service interactions. Retail websites routinely feature virtual assistants and chatbots that provide instant responses to queries, assist with product selection, and clarify store policies. For instance, an electronics retailer might deploy a chatbot capable of guiding customers through tech troubleshooting or suggesting compatible accessories for their newly purchased devices. Such automation elevates customer support efficiency while enriching the overall shopping experience with immediate assistance available around the clock.

Moreover, AI-driven sentiment analysis tools empower retailers to gather insights from customer feedback and social media discussions, unraveling consumer sentiments and brand perceptions. For example, an AI tool might monitor social media for reactions to a newly launched product, equipping retailers to respond proactively to customer concerns or celebrate positive feedback, thus fostering a more agile and responsive business model.

However, the incorporation of AI in retail does not come without its challenges. As retailers collect and analyze vast amounts of consumer data, privacy concerns inevitably arise. It is essential for businesses to implement robust data protection measures, ensuring compliance with regulations and maintaining consumer trust. Transparency in how data is collected, stored, and utilized is crucial, as is a commitment to safeguarding customer information.

Additionally, the issue of biased AI algorithms presents a significant challenge. Retailers must prioritize the development of unbiased AI systems, ensuring that algorithms reflect fairness and do not inadvertently perpetuate societal biases. This dedication to ethical practices not only reinforces consumer confidence but also enhances engagement with AI-enhanced retail experiences.

As the retail sector embraces AI, it stands to gain unprecedented opportunities for improving efficiency and enriching customer relationships. The future of retail lies in a landscape where AI seamlessly integrates into every facet of the consumer journey, promising a dynamic and responsive industry that not only meets but exceeds the evolving expectations of shoppers. This progression illustrates a proactive response to the demands of contemporary consumers, highlighting AI's potential to revolutionize retail in ways that are both innovative and profoundly human-centered.

The integration of artificial intelligence (AI) into transportation is fundamentally transforming the landscape of autonomous vehicles (AVs), heralding a future characterized by unprecedented efficiency, heightened safety, and innovative mobility solutions. As one of the most remarkable strides in modern transportation technology, AVs are the product of a powerful synergy between AI advancements, data analytics, and machine learning algorithms.

At the heart of autonomous vehicle development lies the intricate use of computer vision and sensor technologies. These sophisticated systems allow vehicles to interpret their surroundings by processing vast streams of visual data in real-time. Utilizing advanced sensors—such as LIDAR (Light Detection and Ranging), radar, ultrasonic sensors, and high-definition cameras—AVs create intricate, constantly refreshed maps that guide their navigation systems. A prime example is Tesla's Autopilot, which employs eight cameras paired with a dozen ultrasonic sensors and an onboard computer to provide a comprehensive 360-degree view of the vehicle's environment. This technology facilitates sophisticated functions such as adaptive cruise control, lane centering, and obstacle avoidance.

Machine learning algorithms play a crucial role in the decision-making capabilities of AVs, enabling them to adeptly react to ever-changing road conditions. Consider Waymo's advanced self-driving system, which is powered by a vast neural network trained on billions of simulated miles to ensure precise predictions and safe navigation, especially in intricate urban settings.

The influence of autonomous vehicles extends well beyond personal transportation. It is reshaping the economic and societal landscapes as well, particularly within the freight and logistics sectors. Companies like TuSimple and Daimler are pioneering autonomous trucks designed to enhance long-haul efficiency by mitigating the limitations posed by human driver fatigue. This paradigm shift has the potential to dramatically reduce delivery times and costs, contributing to a more robust and agile supply chain.

Public transportation is yet another arena where the impact of AI-enhanced vehicles is evident. Trials of autonomous buses and shuttles are currently underway in multiple cities around the globe, aimed at providing flexible and seamless mobility solutions. For instance, Las Vegas has piloted electric self-driving shuttles as a complementary option to its public transit system, offering residents an eco-forward and accessible alternative to conventional buses. Such initiatives exemplify the capacity of AVs to mitigate traffic congestion, diminish emissions, and enhance urban mobility, making transportation more accessible for all.

However, as with any transformative technology, the rise of autonomous vehicles brings forth significant ethical and regulatory challenges. The paramount concern is ensuring safety, which demands exhaustive testing and validation of AV systems under diverse and unpredictable conditions. Furthermore, the legal frameworks governing these vehicles must evolve to address complexities around liability and accountability in the event of accidents involving AVs. Creating these regulations necessitates collaboration among policymakers, technology innovators, and insurance providers to cultivate public trust and acceptance of this emerging technology.

Privacy issues also loom large in the discussion around autonomous vehicles, given their continuous data collection and analysis from both passengers and their surroundings. Companies must prioritize transparent data practices, ensuring users' privacy is protected. This commitment involves not only adopting anonymization techniques but also implementing robust cybersecurity measures to safeguard against unauthorized access.

As AVs become increasingly embedded into transportation networks, their potential to promote sustainable urban development grows. However, realizing this potential requires strategies that emphasize shared mobility solutions over traditional ownership models.

The future of autonomous vehicles is rife with opportunities that could revolutionize our understanding of transportation. The intersection of cutting-edge AI technologies with practical transportation solutions is creating a new paradigm in which autonomy and human oversight harmoniously blend. This evolution promises to deliver a safer, more efficient, and environmentally responsible mobility landscape. Achieving these advancements necessitates thoughtful navigation of ethical considerations and a commitment to innovation that aligns with societal aspirations, ultimately guiding the future of AVs towards the goal of fostering a globally connected and sustainable world.

In the ever-evolving landscape of agriculture and food production, artificial intelligence (AI) is paving the way for transformative advancements that redefine age-old farming practices and optimize the food supply chain. As the global population continues to rise, so too does the demand for efficient and sustainable food production. In this context, AI-driven innovations are emerging as essential allies in promoting sustainable agricultural practices and enhancing food security.

One of the most significant applications of AI in agriculture is precision farming. This innovative approach leverages advanced data analytics and automation to maximize crop yields and streamline resource management. A prime example of this technology in action is demonstrated by John Deere, where AI-powered systems utilize sophisticated machine learning algorithms to deliver actionable insights to farmers.

These insights facilitate informed decision-making regarding planting, irrigation, and harvesting, ultimately leading to more efficient agricultural operations.

The integration of drones and satellite imagery into farming practices represents another noteworthy advancement. These AI-equipped drones are capable of surveying vast areas of farmland, capturing high-resolution images that reveal discrepancies in crop health. This technology identifies regions impacted by diseases or pest infestations, enabling farmers to respond proactively. For instance, the Dutch startup Connecterra employs AI to analyze drone footage, providing farmers with detailed diagnostics that inform targeted interventions. This not only reduces the reliance on broad-spectrum pesticides but also optimizes resource allocation.

AI agents are also revolutionizing livestock management. Through AI-driven facial recognition technologies, farmers can monitor the health, behavior, and dietary needs of individual animals within their herds. This approach prioritizes animal welfare while enhancing production efficiency. A noteworthy company, CattleEye, utilizes AI to scrutinize video footage of dairy herds, identifying early signs of health issues such as lameness.

In the larger context of the food supply chain, AI is instrumental in optimizing logistics and minimizing waste. Machine learning algorithms can dissect patterns within supply chain operations to better forecast demand, streamline inventory practices, and predict disruptions. One leading example in this sphere is IBM, which provides AI-driven blockchain solutions that deliver end-to-end traceability for food products. Such systems ensure that every product adheres to quality standards throughout the supply chain, from farm to table, ultimately mitigating food spoilage and enhancing supply chain transparency.

Moreover, AI is playing a crucial role in the development

of innovative food products. NotCo, for instance, harnesses AI technology to formulate plant-based products that mirror the flavors and textures of animal-derived foods. These AI-generated insights serve as a foundation for crafting products that align with sustainable dietary choices.

However, embracing AI in agriculture presents formidable challenges. The technical complexity inherent in deploying advanced AI systems necessitates significant investments in technological infrastructure and the upskilling of local farming communities. Ensuring equitable access to AI technologies across varied geographic regions is pivotal in mitigating a potential digital divide, which could exacerbate existing disparities in agricultural productivity. Additionally, it is imperative to navigate ethical considerations around data privacy and ownership to safeguard farmers' proprietary information and facilitate fair use of agronomic data.

As AI continues to evolve, it holds immense potential to reshape the future of agriculture, striking a harmonious balance between productivity and ecological responsibility. Realizing this transformative potential calls for a united effort involving policymakers, technology developers, and the agricultural community, creating an ecosystem where innovation aligns with sustainability goals and societal needs.

The successful integration of AI in agriculture and food production symbolizes technology's profound capacity to foster positive change. Such innovations are essential in building a resilient food system agile enough to confront future challenges. Through these advancements, we can envision a future where technology and tradition coexist harmoniously, ultimately enhancing our quest for global food security and environmental stewardship.

The integration of AI agents in education is revolutionizing how learning experiences are designed and delivered, ushering in a personalized approach that responds to the unique needs of each student. This transformation not only enhances student engagement but also optimizes learning pathways, making education more inclusive and effective for all learners.

At the core of AI's role in education is its ability to analyze extensive datasets that capture student performance. For instance, platforms like Kidaptive utilize AI to monitor student interactions and adapt content delivery in real-time, thereby enhancing understanding and retention of material. These intelligent systems continually evolve based on student performance, fine-tuning teaching strategies to better support each individual educational journey.

Moreover, AI is transforming the landscape of assessment in education. Traditional testing methods often overlook the multifaceted nature of student learning. In contrast, AI-driven assessments can evaluate a variety of skills, from critical thinking to problem-solving abilities. Imagine an AI system that assesses a student's engagement with complex mathematical concepts through interactive simulations.

AI's impact is also felt in the classroom through the emergence of AI-powered teaching assistants. These virtual aids streamline administrative tasks, enabling educators to dedicate more time to meaningful student interactions. A prominent example is IBM's Watson, which has been successfully incorporated into educational settings to assist with lesson planning, grading, and responding to student inquiries.

In the realm of higher education, AI's influence is growing even more pronounced. Universities are harnessing AI to create smart learning environments that provide adaptive and immersive experiences. This includes virtual laboratories, where students can conduct scientific experiments safely before progressing to practical applications. AI algorithms facilitate simulations of real-world scenarios, allowing students to visualize theoretical concepts in action. Arizona State University's SmartCampus initiative exemplifies this, with AI-supported tools designed to enhance and personalize the on-campus experience.

AI's contributions extend to language learning as well. Applications like Duolingo harness AI to tailor exercises based on individual proficiency levels, ensuring that lessons remain engaging and appropriately challenging. This targeted approach not only increases retention but also accelerates language fluency, accommodating varying learning abilities.

However, the integration of AI in education presents several challenges that must be addressed. Concerns regarding data privacy and user profiling are paramount, necessitating robust measures to protect sensitive student information. Additionally, the digital divide remains a pressing issue, as access to the technology that supports AI-driven education varies widely across different regions and socioeconomic backgrounds. To unlock the full potential of AI in education, it is vital to address these disparities and ensure that AI solutions are developed with pedagogical and ethical considerations in mind.

Equipping educators with the necessary training and resources to incorporate AI effectively into their teaching practices is also crucial. Successful integration requires a thorough understanding of AI tools and their capabilities, supported by ongoing professional development. Schools and universities should prioritize creating collaborative frameworks that promote a harmonious relationship between educators and AI, leveraging technology as a complement to human insight and interaction.

The emergence of AI in education heralds a new era in how we approach learning. Its potential to customize educational experiences, support diverse learning needs, and provide innovative teaching tools makes AI an invaluable partner in the modernization of education.

This intricate fusion of technology and personalized education lays the groundwork for a future in which learning is a dynamic and individualized experience. As AI continues to advance, it promises to further enhance educational systems, driving them towards greater inclusivity, adaptability, and effectiveness. Through these developments, we envision a future where every student has the opportunity to realize their full potential, supported by AI-powered learning experiences that are responsive to their individual journeys.

The fusion of artificial intelligence (AI) agents with smart home technology is fundamentally transforming our domestic environments, establishing unprecedented standards for comfort and efficiency. This powerful integration is evolving homes into intelligent ecosystems, interconnected systems capable of streamlining everyday tasks and significantly enhancing our quality of life.

At the heart of this transformation is the AI agent, functioning as a master controller for an array of systems—including lighting, security, entertainment, and climate control—via a cohesive interface. These agents employ advanced machine learning algorithms that adapt to the daily habits and preferences of occupants, optimizing energy consumption while maximizing comfort. For instance, the Google Nest thermostat intelligently learns the rhythms of its residents, automatically adjusting the temperature to maintain an ideal climate. This not only promotes energy efficiency but also ensures a comfortable living environment tailored to the family's needs.

Voice-activated AI ecosystems, exemplified by Amazon Alexa, empower users to command their surroundings with effortless ease. From adjusting the ambiance by dimming lights to setting reminders or curating music playlists, these technologies make home management intuitive and enjoyable. As AI agents evolve, they are increasingly proficient at understanding and anticipating user needs, leveraging natural language processing to effortlessly execute complex commands and improve interaction.

Security, a paramount concern for homeowners, is another domain where AI agents shine in smart home applications. Sophisticated surveillance systems equipped with AI capabilities can process real-time video feeds, discerning normal activity from unusual behavior and differentiating between residents, visitors, and potential intruders. Take, for example, the Arlo security camera system; it intelligently alerts homeowners to suspicious events while minimizing false alarms by recognizing familiar faces. This proactive approach not only enhances home security but also bolsters residents' peace of mind.

Beyond efficiency and security, AI agents enrich our lives through personalization. Whether creating a morning routine or providing tailored entertainment experiences, these agents seamlessly integrate with consumer electronics. AI-driven devices, such as Sonos speakers, optimize sound settings based on room acoustics and individual preferences, delivering an audio experience that feels uniquely designed for each user.

However, as the integration of AI into smart homes expands, it brings privacy issues to the forefront. The constant data collection necessary to enhance services necessitates a robust approach to safeguarding personal information. While employing data encryption and strict access controls can offer a layer of protection, manufacturers must prioritize transparent privacy policies that clearly outline data collection practices to reassure users.

The accessibility of smart home technology remains uneven, underscoring a digital divide that must be addressed to ensure everyone can benefit equitably. Initiatives that promote wider internet connectivity and make smart technology affordable can facilitate inclusive adoption, allowing diverse populations to partake in the advantages of connected living.

User-centric design is paramount for maximizing the effectiveness and widespread acceptance of AI technologies in smart homes. Developers bear the responsibility of ensuring these systems are intuitive and accessible to people with varying technological expertise. This involves creating straightforward interfaces and establishing comprehensive support systems that engage users and enhance their overall experience.

Consumer education regarding the capabilities and constraints of AI-powered smart homes is equally critical. Workshops, online tutorials, and community forums can serve as valuable resources, informing users about the potential benefits and best practices for integrating AI into their daily lives. This knowledge empowers homeowners to make informed decisions as they embark on their digital transformation journey.

The integration of AI agents into smart homes represents not just a passing technological trend but a profound evolution towards more responsive living environments. As AI continues to drive advancements in smart home systems, we can expect even greater levels of automation and personalization that fundamentally redefine modern living.

Industry 4.0, often hailed as the fourth industrial revolution, is reshaping the manufacturing realm through the integration of Artificial Intelligence (AI) with cutting-edge technologies. This transformation reaches unprecedented heights of automation, data exchange, and real-time monitoring, establishing an era of smart factories characterized by interconnected machines, systems, and products. The result is a manufacturing landscape that embraces remarkable efficiencies and unparalleled agility.

At the heart of Industry 4.0 lies the Internet of Things

(IoT). This innovative framework weaves together sensors and devices, enabling real-time data capture throughout the manufacturing process. This data is not just information; it serves as the vital essence that fuels AI agents, empowering them to analyze and optimize manufacturing workflows with a level of precision previously deemed impossible. A notable example of this is predictive maintenance. Companies like Siemens are at the forefront of this innovation, developing solutions that utilize AI algorithms to analyze historical and real-time data, predict machine malfunctions, and recommend proactive maintenance schedules.

Furthermore, AI agents play a pivotal role in enabling mass customization within manufacturing. This capability allows factories to produce highly personalized products efficiently, all while maintaining economies of scale. Advanced manufacturing techniques, such as additive manufacturing and 3D printing, empower AI agents to optimize design configurations, minimizing material waste and expediting production speed. For instance, Adidas has embraced this approach in their production of custom footwear, swiftly tailoring products to meet individual consumer preferences.

Quality control has also witnessed a significant boost thanks to AI-driven vision systems, which meticulously ensure that every item produced aligns with the highest quality standards. These sophisticated systems inspect products at every stage of the manufacturing process, detecting defects and inconsistencies with accuracy far surpassing that of traditional human inspection. In a marketplace where consumer expectations grow ever higher, this capability is indispensable for guaranteeing that products meet rigorous quality benchmarks prior to their market release.

Complementing these advancements are collaborative robots, or cobots, that epitomize the harmonious relationship between humans and machines in the context of Industry 4.0. Designed to assist human workers, cobots handle routine and physically demanding tasks, thereby enhancing productivity while freeing up human employees to focus on more complex problem-solving roles. Universal Robots has made strides in this area, creating cobots that can adapt to various tasks and environments, showcasing the flexibility and ingenuity that AI agents contribute to modern manufacturing.

Nevertheless, the transition to Industry 4.0 is fraught with challenges. One of the most pressing concerns is data security, as the interconnectedness of systems exposes manufacturers to increased cyber threats. It is imperative for organizations to adopt robust cybersecurity measures to safeguard sensitive information and maintain operational integrity. Strategies such as encryption and continuous network monitoring are critical in protecting smart factory environments, mitigating the risk of data breaches and ensuring the safety of essential infrastructure.

Moreover, the workforce must evolve in tandem with these technological advancements. As automation becomes more prevalent, upskilling and reskilling initiatives are vital to equip employees with the capabilities necessary to operate and manage these sophisticated technologies. Participating in training programs and forming partnerships with educational institutions can empower workers with the skills needed to thrive in AI-enhanced workplaces.

The ethical dimensions of increased automation also warrant significant attention. While AI agents can dramatically enhance efficiency, they also raise valid concerns about potential job displacement. Employers have a responsibility to navigate this landscape thoughtfully, considering strategies that balance technological progress with social accountability. This may include fostering work environments that augment human capabilities rather than replace them entirely.

The transition toward a more automated and interconnected manufacturing sector holds deep implications for global competitiveness. Entities that adeptly harness AI technologies within their manufacturing frameworks position themselves to lead in innovation and productivity, effectively redefining production standards on a global scale.

In summary, Industry 4.0, characterized by the integration of AI agents, represents a seismic shift in manufacturing, placing a premium on efficiency, customization, and quality. This evolution signifies not just an advancement in manufacturing capabilities but a broader commitment to market responsiveness and ethical standards, setting a new benchmark for success in the industrial landscape.

The entertainment industry is experiencing a transformative renaissance, largely fueled by advancements in artificial intelligence. This intersection of creativity and technology is reshaping how content is crafted, personalized, and enjoyed, unlocking a myriad of possibilities for both creators and audiences.

One of the most striking examples of AI's impact can be found in music production. Today's AI algorithms have become remarkably proficient in composing original music, creating melodies and harmonies that are often indistinguishable from those written by human composers. Tools like Amper Music are empowering musicians and content creators to effortlessly develop soundtracks that reflect specific moods or themes, spanning a diverse range of genres from orchestral to electronic. This democratization of music creation enables artists to experiment boldly, crafting high-quality compositions even without extensive formal training.

In the realm of storytelling and scriptwriting, AI technologies, particularly models like OpenAI's GPT, have made significant strides. These advanced neural networks can analyze existing literature, screenplays, and various narrative forms to generate coherent and engaging plots. Filmmakers are increasingly leveraging these capabilities to brainstorm storylines or refine dialogue, often using AI-generated suggestions as a springboard for their own creativity. Rather than replacing human writers, these tools serve as collaborators, enhancing their ability to explore new creative landscapes.

The influence of AI extends powerfully into visual media as well, particularly in animation and special effects. Machine learning tools are revolutionizing the animation process by automating labor-intensive tasks such as rigging and motion capture. Pioneering studios like Pixar harness AI to elevate animation quality, ensuring seamless transitions and heightened realism. Although deepfake technology raises ethical questions, it also highlights AI's remarkable ability to alter and generate video content with astonishing precision. As the industry navigates these ethical waters, it remains committed to exploring the expansive potential of these innovative tools responsibly.

Furthermore, AI is redefining audience engagement in film and television. This level of personalization not only enhances viewer engagement but also ensures that the content delivered aligns closely with audience desires. Streaming giants like Netflix utilize sophisticated recommendation algorithms to cater to an increasingly diverse global viewer base, optimizing content delivery through data-driven insights.

The gaming sector stands at the cutting edge of AI utilization, demonstrating immersive experiences like never before. AI algorithms govern non-player characters (NPCs) with increasingly complex behaviors, enriching realism and interactivity within expansive virtual worlds. Additionally, procedural content generation powered by AI allows game environments to tailor themselves uniquely for each player, creating personalized narratives that adapt based on player choices. This level of engagement fosters replayability, making each interaction within the game universe compelling and deeply rewarding.

AI's role in entertainment does not stop at creation; it significantly enhances distribution strategies as well. Algorithms manage content scheduling, determine optimal release windows, and optimize marketing efforts tailored to specific demographics. With the help of AI-driven analytics, marketers can track trending topics across social media, ensuring that campaigns resonate with contemporary audience interests and behaviors while maximizing exposure and profitability.

Despite the remarkable opportunities presented by AI, the integration of technology into entertainment raises important ethical considerations. Issues surrounding intellectual property, privacy, and the authenticity of AI-generated content require careful navigation. It is essential for creators to address these challenges with sensitivity, respecting original artistic intentions while contemplating the broader cultural implications of AI-fueled media.

Ultimately, AI agents are fundamentally reshaping the entertainment landscape, creating novel avenues for artistic expression and personalization. As the industry continues to blend human creativity with machine intelligence, it is poised to deliver richer, more immersive experiences that cater to the ever-evolving tastes of audiences worldwide. Embracing these advancements while upholding an ethical framework will be crucial as we forge a inclusive and vibrant future in content creation. The harmonious convergence of human ingenuity and AI capabilities heralds a new era of artistic innovation, offering an exciting trajectory for the evolution of the entertainment industry.

Artificial intelligence is poised to play a pivotal role in advancing social good initiatives and driving sustainability efforts across a multitude of sectors. As the climate crisis escalates, AI's remarkable ability to analyze vast datasets and generate predictive insights emerges as a beacon of hope for innovative solutions. This intersection of technology and ethical responsibility is central to our narrative, highlighting AI's potential to create positive societal and environmental outcomes.

One of the most compelling applications of AI in promoting social good is its role in climate change mitigation and adaptation strategies. For example, IBM's Watson has been effectively integrated into flood prediction systems, enhancing communities' preparedness and response capabilities.

Energy management is another vital area where AI's influence is making significant strides. Through the application of sophisticated machine learning algorithms, AI optimizes energy grids, enabling more efficient distribution and minimizing waste. Google's DeepMind has made headlines for dramatically reducing power consumption at its data centers, showcasing how technology can contribute to cutting carbon footprints, promoting energy conservation, and fostering the development of sustainable infrastructure in our increasingly digital world.

In the realm of agriculture, AI is transforming traditional practices to boost food production while minimizing environmental impact. Precision farming, augmented by machine learning, empowers farmers to analyze soil conditions, crop health, and weather forecasts with remarkable precision. Take Blue River Technology, for instance; their AI-driven smart sprayers can distinguish between crops and weeds, allowing for targeted pesticide application.

Moreover, AI is proving invaluable in biodiversity conservation efforts. Conservationists utilize AI to monitor wildlife populations, enabling real-time cataloging and tracking of endangered species. Innovative technologies, such as drones equipped with computer vision algorithms, facilitate the observation of animal migration patterns and the assessment of ecosystem health with minimal human interference. This data-driven methodology not only enhances our understanding of biodiversity but also informs policy decisions and conservation strategies aimed at preserving endangered species and protecting ecosystems across the globe.

Despite the enormous potential of AI in driving social good and sustainability, challenges remain. Concerns related to data privacy, equitable access, and the inherent biases in AI systems require careful consideration. The responsible deployment of AI technologies calls for a collaborative approach that blends technological expertise with insights from local communities, stakeholders, and policymakers.

Additionally, the environmental impact of AI itself is a growing concern. Training large AI models necessitates substantial computational power, often resulting in heightened energy consumption. This paradox underscores the urgent need to focus on developing energy-efficient algorithms and advocating for renewable energy sources in AI infrastructure.

Fostering transparency and accountability in AI systems is essential for building trust and ensuring responsible usage. OpenAI serves as a commendable example with its dedication to sharing research and collaborating with organizations to ensure that the benefits of AI are distributed equitably.

Ultimately, the application of AI for social good and sustainability encapsulates a broader vision of harmonizing technological progress with ecological responsibility and social equity. The success of these initiatives relies on a steadfast commitment to ethical principles, innovative partnerships, and a united goal of cultivating a resilient future for our planet. As AI technology continues to evolve, its capacity to drive positive change shines brightly, leading us toward a world where technology serves as the cornerstone for achieving our global social and environmental objectives.

CHAPTER 4: THE ROLE OF DATA IN AI AGENTS

The relationship between big data and artificial intelligence (AI) agents is a dynamic partnership characterized by mutual enhancement, where vast datasets provide the essential fuel that enables intelligent systems to learn, adapt, and grow. As we delve into this complex interplay, it becomes increasingly clear that the effectiveness and reach of AI agents hinge on their capacity to process, analyze, and extract valuable insights from extensive information troves. The significance of big data extends beyond its sheer volume; it empowers AI agents to execute sophisticated tasks with remarkable accuracy and responsiveness.

To appreciate this transformative relationship, let's consider an AI-driven healthcare system designed for predictive diagnostics. Such a system relies on an extensive array of data, including patient records, medical histories, diagnostic images, and treatment outcomes. This wealth of information, amassed over years from diverse populations, equips AI with the tools to uncover patterns that human practitioners might overlook. The greater the volume of data processed, the more precise and tailored the AI's predictions become, ultimately elevating the quality of personalized care that patients receive.

A parallel scenario unfolds in the retail sector, where AI agents leverage big data to decode consumer behaviors. For example, an AI-driven recommendation engine on an e-commerce platform may not only propose products based on previous purchases but can also foresee future demands by detecting market trends from aggregated user data.

Nonetheless, harnessing the power of big data depends not just on its acquisition but significantly on astute data processing and management capabilities. Real-time analytics are crucial, particularly in sectors like autonomous vehicles, where AI agents must immediately interpret sensor data to make split-second decisions that could prevent accidents. This ability to analyze and react to big data instantaneously showcases the potential for AI agents to revolutionize industries by delivering responsive and adaptive solutions.

Conversely, big data continuously broadens the capabilities of AI agents across various fields. In agriculture, for instance, AI systems can analyze satellite imagery and soil moisture levels, providing farmers with precise guidance on crop rotation and irrigation strategies. This integration of data leads to enhanced yields and more efficient resource management. In the realm of finance, AI agents harness big data analytics to monitor and predict market fluctuations, facilitating informed investment decisions and effective risk management.

However, the advantages of big data come with a set of challenges that merit careful attention. The enormous volume of data necessitates robust infrastructure and sophisticated storage solutions. Additionally, as AI agents evolve, establishing an effective data governance framework becomes critical to ensure data security, integrity, and quality—factors that are vital for the reliability of AI operations.

One practical approach to overcoming these challenges is the deployment of scalable cloud-based systems that offer the computational power needed to handle large datasets. Platforms such as Apache Hadoop and Apache Spark play a pivotal role, enabling the parallel processing and analysis of big data across extensive clusters of computers. This infrastructure provides the agility and efficiency essential for high-performance AI applications.

The dynamic interplay between structured and unstructured data lies at the core of the vast landscape of big data, fundamentally shaping the capabilities of artificial intelligence (AI) agents. To harness the full potential of AI systems, it's crucial to understand these distinct data categories and their unique characteristics.

Structured Data: The Building Blocks of Analysis Structured data is characterized by its organized nature, existing within predefined fields and columns. Typically stored in relational databases like SQL servers, this type of data includes numerical values, dates, and categorical labels, making it amenable to straightforward manipulation and analysis with traditional programming languages such as SQL. For instance, consider a retail customer database: each record may contain structured fields such as customer ID, purchase history, and transaction dates. This structured format enables AI agents to effortlessly extract trends, optimizing processes such as inventory management and targeted marketing efforts.

Unstructured Data: A Vast Ocean of Insights On the other hand, unstructured data—comprising a significant portion of the global data landscape—presents a challenge due to its lack of a predetermined format. This data type includes diverse assets like images, audio, video, social media interactions, emails, and free-text documents, all of which require advanced AI techniques for meaningful processing. Within this expansive repository lies a wealth of latent insights waiting to be uncovered through powerful AI technologies, such as natural language processing (NLP) and image recognition systems. For instance, social media data, rich with consumer sentiments, can be effectively analyzed using sentiment analysis algorithms to discern emerging trends and public opinions.

Unlocking Value from Unstructured Data To derive value from unstructured data, AI systems often leverage machine learning models and deep learning frameworks that can identify patterns and context within these complex datasets. A prominent example is the application of convolutional neural networks (CNNs) for image classification. In the realm of autonomous vehicles, AI agents utilize CNNs to interpret visual data, enabling them to detect obstacles, traffic signals, and pedestrians in real-time, thereby enhancing safety and navigation.

The Power of Data Integration The fusion of structured and unstructured data further amplifies the efficacy and versatility of AI. In the healthcare sector, for instance, patient information systems typically merge structured data, such as demographics and medical histories, with unstructured data like radiological images and physician notes. AI models processing this rich dataset can significantly improve diagnostic accuracy, leading to more personalized treatment plans. Similarly, in financial services, structured transaction records can be enriched with unstructured data from customer interactions, allowing for the creation of predictive models that evaluate creditworthiness and detect potential fraud.

Navigating the Challenges However, the heterogeneity present between structured and unstructured data presents significant challenges. It's essential to establish robust data integration frameworks that can accommodate various data formats and promote seamless interoperability. Achieving this often involves the creation of hybrid databases and data lakes that unify diverse data structures for comprehensive processing. Platforms like Apache Hadoop's HDFS and Amazon S3's object storage play pivotal roles in supporting such hybrid data environments, ensuring efficient and scalable data handling.

The Role of Advanced AI Tools The continuous evolution of AI-driven data transformation tools, such as TensorFlow and PyTorch, has been essential in refining the management of unstructured data. These tools empower developers to build neural networks capable of executing complex tasks, including language translation and autonomous navigation, making them invaluable for industries seeking to expand AI application across various domains.

The Evolution of Data Collection Techniques

Data collection has undergone a remarkable transformation over the years. It has shifted from simplistic manual entries and survey methods to complex automated processes capable of real-time data acquisition. Central to this evolution is the dynamic interplay between data collection practices and technological innovations, which together form the backbone of effective AI models.

In the Internet of Things (IoT) landscape, sensor networks serve a pivotal role in acquiring environmental data. Consider smart agriculture; IoT devices continuously monitor soil moisture, temperature, and sunlight exposure, supplying AI models with crucial information that optimizes irrigation systems. As a result, farmers can enhance crop yields while conserving valuable resources.

2. Surveys and Questionnaires

Even in an era dominated by automation, traditional tools like surveys and questionnaires remain vital. These methods excel in gathering subjective data directly from individuals, providing insights that automated processes might overlook. In the healthcare sector, for instance, patient-reported outcomes surveys are essential for gauging treatment efficacy from the patient's viewpoint—an aspect often neglected by automated data analysis.

3. Social Media Monitoring

Social media has emerged as a treasure trove for real-time data collection, offering deep insights into public sentiment and behavioral trends. Unstructured data from these platforms is crucial for sentiment analysis and trend forecasting, utilized by marketers and policymakers alike.

4. Crowdsourcing

Crowdsourcing harnesses the collective power of a large group of individuals, often through online platforms, to gather diverse data and opinions. This approach allows organizations to amass a wide array of data points quickly and cost-effectively. A typical application is in image labeling tasks; services like Amazon's Mechanical Turk leverage crowdsourcing to create extensive datasets for training computer vision algorithms.

5. Online Tracking and Analytics

With the surge of digital services, online tracking via cookies and analytics software has become a common data collection strategy. These tools monitor user interactions, page visits, click-through rates, and other metrics, yielding granular insights into user behavior. However, while these methods are powerful, they raise significant ethical concerns regarding privacy. As such, they necessitate a commitment to transparency and informed consent from users.

Challenges in Data Collection

Despite its transformative capabilities, data collection is riddled with challenges, including privacy concerns and data quality issues. The backlash against intrusive data practices emphasizes the urgent need for robust data privacy regulations, such as the General Data Protection Regulation (GDPR) in the European Union, which enforces explicit consent and mandates safeguards for personal data.

Ensuring data quality is equally crucial, given that biased or inaccurate data can lead to flawed AI outcomes. Techniques such as data cleaning, validation checks, and representative sampling are vital for mitigating these risks, ensuring the integrity and reliability of the collected data.

The Technological Influence on Data Collection

Ongoing technological advancements continuously reshape data collection methodologies, enabling the capture of increasingly varied and nuanced data sets. Wearable technology, for instance, gathers health-related information like heart rates and activity levels, providing a constant stream of data for predictive health models.

Looking Ahead: The Future of Data Collection

As AI technologies continue to advance, the demand for sophisticated data collection methods will only grow. Effectively navigating the ethical and technical challenges associated with these methodologies is paramount for the responsible and effective use of AI.

The future of data collection will undoubtedly influence the evolution of AI development, ensuring these intelligent systems remain finely attuned to the complexities of human experience and the intricacies of the natural world.

Data privacy and security are at the forefront of discussions surrounding artificial intelligence (AI) development, particularly as these technologies increasingly integrate into sensitive areas of personal and organizational life. Navigating these concerns is essential for building trust, ensuring regulatory compliance, and protecting against the potential misuse of the vast quantities of data that AI systems require.

The Importance of Data Privacy and Security

As AI systems continue to evolve in complexity and capability, they depend on large datasets that frequently contain personal and sensitive information. This dependence gives rise to significant privacy challenges related to how data is collected, stored, processed, and shared. AI technology must strike a delicate balance between leveraging this data and respecting user privacy—a challenge all the more pressing in an era marked by rapid technological advancements.

Key Privacy Challenges

1. Data Collection and Usage AI applications often necessitate access to a plethora of personal information, ranging from consumer preferences to health information. The pressing challenge lies in ensuring that data is collected with explicit informed consent and that it is only used for legitimate purposes. In the healthcare domain, for instance, AI diagnoses must maintain the utmost confidentiality regarding patient records; unauthorized access could not only violate privacy but also undermine trust in AI healthcare solutions.

2. Transparency and Consent Upholding principles of transparency and informed consent is vital across all AI implementations. However, the intricate nature of AI processes can obscure how data is handled, leading to confusion among users. Enhancing transparency entails more than just clear communication; it requires intuitive privacy settings that allow users to exert control over their data. Take mobile applications utilizing location data as an example—these apps should provide explicit choices regarding data collection and the specific contexts in which it will be utilized.

3. Data Retention Policies Establishing effective data management protocols includes the development of clear data retention policies. Keeping data longer than necessary not only increases the risk of privacy breaches but also complicates the processes involved in managing and securing that data. Companies like Google have addressed this through periodic data

retention strategies that enable automatic deletion after a specified duration, achieving a balance between utility and privacy.

Security Challenges in AI Systems

The reliance of AI agents on significant and sensitive datasets also makes them prime targets for cyberattacks, including data breaches and adversarial manipulation. To safeguard data integrity and prevent unauthorized access, robust security measures are essential.

1. Encryption and Access Controls Implementing strong encryption protocols is crucial for ensuring the protection of data both in transit and at rest. Complementing this are access controls that restrict sensitive information to authorized personnel only. In the financial sector, for example, stringent encryption standards are vital to protect transaction data from unauthorized access, thereby preserving both user trust and institutional integrity.

2. Anonymization Techniques Employing data anonymization is a powerful strategy for minimizing privacy risks by concealing identifiable information within datasets. Techniques such as data masking and differential privacy allow data to be utilized for machine learning while safeguarding individual identities. For example, location-based services might rely on aggregated data models that prevent exact tracing back to individuals, enhancing user privacy.

3. Regular Security Audits and Penetration Testing To proactively identify vulnerabilities, organizations should prioritize regular security audits and penetration testing. These practices reveal potential weaknesses that could be exploited by malicious entities, enabling organizations to implement

preventative measures. The infamous Equifax data breach, which affected millions of individuals, underscores the urgent need for such proactive strategies to safeguard sensitive information.

Ethical and Legal Considerations

In addition to technological solutions, ethical and legal frameworks play a significant role in shaping conversations about data privacy and security. Regulations like the General Data Protection Regulation (GDPR) in the EU impose stringent standards for data protection, mandating careful attention to consent, data rights, and lawful processing of personal information. Adhering to these regulations represents not only a legal obligation but also an ethical imperative, reinforcing the accountability of AI developers and organizations to protect user information.

Future Directions

As AI technologies become increasingly embedded in our daily lives, the quest to address privacy and security concerns will remain a vital and evolving challenge. It is crucial to develop adaptive security measures designed to preempt emerging threats while embedding privacy-by-design principles into the AI development lifecycle.

In summary, addressing data privacy and security issues is fundamental for the sustainable advancement of AI technologies. This balance will lead to the creation of more trustworthy and autonomous AI solutions, ultimately benefiting society as a whole.

Data ethics and the responsible use of artificial intelligence (AI) are not just buzzwords; they are foundational elements shaping the current discourse around AI development. As technological capabilities continue to evolve and become more embedded in our daily lives, the call for moral responsibility has never been more pressing. Developing ethical frameworks for AI not only ensures compliance with legal standards but also aligns with societal values, minimizing potential harm and fostering a climate of trust.

Understanding Data Ethics

At its core, data ethics encompasses the principles and guidelines that govern the responsible use of data within AI systems. This includes paramount considerations such as data privacy, fairness, accountability, and transparency. As AI increasingly influences decisions that impact individuals and communities, steadfast adherence to these principles becomes essential. Upholding data ethics is crucial for building public confidence and maximizing the positive contributions that AI technologies can offer.

Fundamental Ethical Principles

1. Fairness and Bias Mitigation Achieving fairness in AI systems is critical to preventing the perpetuation of existing biases. Often, bias is an inherent problem stemming from skewed training data, which can produce unfair outcomes that discriminate against certain demographics. A notable case highlighted by researchers Joy Buolamwini and Timnit Gebru involves certain facial recognition technologies that exhibit significant errors, particularly with dark-skinned individuals and women. To combat this, AI systems must be designed with algorithms that are not only transparent but regularly audited to ensure equitable performance across diverse populations.

2. Transparency and Explainability For AI to truly be effective and trustworthy, it must operate in a transparent manner. Users and stakeholders should have access to clear explanations regarding how AI systems make decisions. This transparency is vital; for example, when financial institutions use AI to evaluate loan applications, applicants

deserve to understand what factors influence their creditworthiness.

3. Consent and Autonomy Respecting individual autonomy is fundamental in the context of AI. It is essential that AI systems seek explicit consent for data collection and usage, allowing users to make informed choices about the data they share and how it is utilized. A prime example can be seen in Apple's implementation of App Tracking Transparency, which grants users greater control over their personal data and enhances their privacy rights.

Committing to Responsible AI Development

Embracing responsible AI practices entails weaving ethical considerations throughout the entire AI lifecycle—from the initial design phase to deployment and beyond.

1. Ethical Design and Development Practices An ethically responsible approach to AI development invites the participation of a diverse array of voices —ethicists, sociologists, and various stakeholders alongside developers and engineers. For instance, forming multidisciplinary teams to review AI outputs can help identify potential biases and rectify them prior to public release.

2. Continuous Monitoring and Evaluation Ethical compliance is not a one-time checkbox but an ongoing commitment. Continuous monitoring of AI systems is necessary to adapt to the dynamic nature of real-world environments. Implementing real-time data tracking mechanisms can alert developers to any deviations that might pose ethical concerns, allowing for prompt corrective measures.

3. Stakeholder Engagement and Feedback Cultivating

a feedback loop involving a wide range of stakeholders—including users, community advocates, and regulatory agencies—enhances the ethical evaluation of AI systems. This collaborative approach helps refine AI technologies to ensure they meet ethical standards. For example, Microsoft's AI Ethics Committee serves as a vital platform for gathering external input, thereby promoting ethical stewardship across AI initiatives.

Navigating Legal and Regulatory Frameworks

While ethical considerations stand on their own, they often intersect with legal frameworks designed to protect individuals and communities. Regulations such as the General Data Protection Regulation (GDPR) mandate principles of data protection that align closely with ethical standards, requiring organizations to ensure lawful processing, informed consent, and respect for data subject rights. Adhering to these legal obligations not only fulfills compliance requirements but also fortifies the ethical use of AI, embedding core values within formal governance structures.

Envisioning Future Trajectories

As we look ahead, the realm of data ethics in AI is poised to grow in both complexity and significance. Emerging innovations, such as AI-driven autonomous systems, call for heightened ethical scrutiny, as these technologies often operate with diminished human oversight yet wield considerable influence. The future of AI ethics may involve evolving standards and metrics designed to address the unique challenges posed by these cutting-edge technologies. Establishing and consistently adhering to comprehensive ethical standards will enable the AI community to ensure that advancements positively impact society, upholding individual rights and promoting fair treatment for all influenced by AI. This commitment to ethics is not merely an option; it is essential for fostering a sustainable digital ecosystem and unlocking the full potential of AI as a transformative force for good in our world.

The Vital Role of Data Quality in Artificial Intelligence

In the multifaceted landscape of artificial intelligence, data acts as both the bedrock and the driving force behind the performance of AI systems. High-quality data is essential for developing robust AI models that yield accurate, reliable, and actionable results. In stark contrast, poor data quality can severely compromise AI performance, resulting in flawed predictions, biased insights, and a detrimental erosion of trust among users and stakeholders. A thorough understanding of data quality issues, along with effective strategies to address them, is crucial for the successful deployment and ongoing operation of AI technologies.

The Detrimental Effects of Poor Data Quality

Data quality challenges can arise from various sources, including inaccuracies, incompleteness, inconsistency, and redundancy. If these issues remain unaddressed, they can permeate the entirety of the machine learning lifecycle, skewing outputs and undermining the overall effectiveness of AI systems.

1. Inaccuracy and Its Consequences When data is inaccurately collected or labeled, the consequences can be profound. For example, if a healthcare AI system relies on mislabeled patient data, its ability to predict diagnoses or recommend appropriate treatments can be fundamentally compromised. Such inaccuracies pose serious risks not only to patient safety but also to the overall credibility of AI in healthcare. Implementing rigorous data validation processes during data ingestion can dramatically reduce the likelihood of errors entering the system.

2. Incompleteness and the Risk of Unreliable Predictions Incomplete datasets present a substantial challenge, as they limit the AI model's ability to generalize effectively across scenarios. Consider a sales forecasting system that receives partial transactional records; without a complete dataset, predictions can become increasingly unreliable. This illustrates the necessity for comprehensive data collection strategies that ensure all pertinent data is captured, providing a solid foundation for model training.

3. Inconsistency and Its Impact on Reliability Inconsistencies arise when conflicting information exists across various datasets. Take, for instance, an AI used in financial services for fraud detection. If data from different sources do not align, legitimate transactions may be incorrectly flagged as fraudulent, while illicit activities could go undetected. To combat this, implementing data harmonization processes is essential for reconciling disparate sources into a cohesive, reliable dataset.

4. Redundancy and Degradation of Model Efficiency Redundant data can lead to significant inefficiencies during model training, as the system wastes computational resources processing duplicate information. In natural language processing, an abundance of redundant text samples can lead to overfitting, reducing the model's ability to generalize and respond effectively to new inputs.

Addressing Data Quality Challenges: Strategies and Techniques

To mitigate the adverse effects of poor data quality, organizations must adopt systematic and proactive approaches to enhance data integrity throughout the AI development lifecycle.

1. Data Preprocessing and Cleaning Effective data preprocessing is crucial prior to model training. Techniques such as data cleansing, normalization, and transformation help eliminate errors, standardize formats, and prepare datasets for precise analysis. For instance, data practitioners can utilize tools like Python's Pandas library to automate data cleaning tasks, ensuring that datasets are free from discrepancies.

``` python import pandas as pd

\#\# Load the dataset
data = pd.read_csv('dataset.csv')

\#\# Replace missing values with the median
data.fillna(data.median(), inplace=True)

\#\# Remove duplicates
data.drop_duplicates(inplace=True)

\#\# Normalize numerical columns
normalized_data = (data - data.mean()) / data.std()
```

1. Implementing Data Governance Frameworks Establishing robust data governance frameworks enables organizations to uphold high data quality standards consistently. These frameworks elucidate protocols for data stewardship, ensuring data consistency and accuracy across various departments. Leveraging frameworks like DAMA-DMBOK (Data Management Body of Knowledge) can streamline data management processes and foster a culture of quality maintenance.

2. Continuous Quality Monitoring Real-time data monitoring systems can track various data quality metrics, providing timely alerts when anomalies or

errors are detected. Automated monitoring tools, such as Apache Airflow and Kibana, empower organizations to swiftly address data issues, minimizing manual intervention and maintaining the stability and performance of AI models.

3. Integrating User Feedback Loops Establishing feedback loops that incorporate insights from end-users, domain experts, and machine learning engineers is vital for identifying and rectifying data quality challenges. Soliciting continuous user feedback on AI model performance can uncover hidden data flaws and prompt necessary adjustments. Collaborative efforts ensure that corrective measures are aligned with user needs, ultimately enhancing the quality of AI solutions.

The Road Ahead: Evolving Quality Standards

As AI systems grow increasingly sophisticated and their applications expand, the need for high-quality data will only intensify. Organizations must remain vigilant, continually refining data quality standards to align with shifts in technological advancements.

In this dynamic, data-centric environment, prioritizing data quality transcends operational necessity; it becomes a strategic imperative. Embracing this ethos paves the way for meaningful, trustworthy AI practices that stand the test of time.

Techniques for Data Augmentation and Manipulation

In the world of artificial intelligence, the quality and variety of data are paramount. AI models thrive on diverse datasets, which enhance their ability to learn and make accurate predictions. However, challenges often arise in acquiring the extensive datasets needed for optimal model performance, whether due to data scarcity or the high costs of extensive data collection. Herein lies the transformative power of data augmentation and manipulation techniques—essential strategies that expand and enrich datasets, allowing AI models to perform better without the need for additional data collection efforts.

Data Augmentation: Expanding the Dataset

Data augmentation is a vital strategy for increasing both the size and diversity of datasets by applying various transformations to existing data. This approach is particularly prevalent in fields such as computer vision and natural language processing, where it helps models generalize more effectively to new and unseen data.

In computer vision, data augmentation involves applying transformations like rotation, translation, flipping, and adjustments to brightness and contrast. These techniques yield a rich array of training images that enable models to adapt to variations in their input, reducing the risk of overfitting.

For example, imagine a dataset of images used to train a model to identify specific animal species. Implementing simple augmentations can exponentially increase the dataset's size and complexity, thus enhancing the model's ability to recognize animals in diverse environments.

```python
from keras.preprocessing.image import ImageDataGenerator

datagen = ImageDataGenerator(rotation_range=40,
width_shift_range=0.2,
height_shift_range=0.2,
shear_range=0.2,
zoom_range=0.2,
horizontal_flip=True,
fill_mode='nearest')

\#\# Assuming 'images' is the array of training images
```

```
augmented_images = datagen.flow(images, batch_size=32)
```
` ` `

2. Text Augmentation: Diversifying Linguistic Input

In the realm of natural language processing, augmentation techniques can include word replacements, synonym substitutions, and the introduction of noise.

` ` `python from textblob import TextBlob import random

```
def add_noise(text):
blob = TextBlob(text)
words = blob.words
words_with_noise = []

for word in words:
if random.uniform(0, 1) > 0.8: \# 20% chance to replace the
word
synonym    =    word.synsets[0].lemmas()[0].name()    if
len(word.synsets) > 0 else word
words_with_noise.append(synonym)
else:
words_with_noise.append(word)
return ''.join(words_with_noise)

augmented_text = add_noise("Data augmentation enhances
the dataset's diversity.")
```
` ` `

Data Manipulation: Optimizing Model Training

Data manipulation refers to techniques that adjust datasets to make them more conducive to effective model training. Below, we explore key manipulation strategies that significantly enhance AI outcomes:

Normalization rescales data to a specific range—typically between 0 and 1—while standardization adjusts data so that it possesses a mean of zero and a standard deviation of one. These techniques are especially crucial in fields such as financial modeling, where differences in scale among input variables can skew results.

``` `python   from   sklearn.preprocessing   import
StandardScaler

scaler = StandardScaler()
standardized_data = scaler.fit_transform(original_data)
``` `
```

## 2. Feature Scaling and Selection

Scaling ensures that all features of a dataset exert equivalent influence during model training, thus preventing any one feature from overpowering others. Simultaneously, feature selection techniques help identify the most relevant attributes, ultimately improving the efficiency and performance of the model.

## 3. Synthetic Data Generation

In cases where real data is scarce or sensitive, synthetic data generation offers a compelling alternative. Techniques such as Generative Adversarial Networks (GANs) and variational autoencoders can create realistic datasets that mimic the properties of real-world data, providing valuable inputs for model training.

```python
``` `python from keras.models import Sequential from
keras.layers import Dense, LeakyReLU

\#\# Example: A simple GAN architecture
def build_generator():
model = Sequential()
model.add(Dense(256, input_dim=100)) \# 100-dimensional
latent space
model.add(LeakyReLU(alpha=0.2))
model.add(Dense(mnist_images_shape, activation='tanh'))
return model
```

```
generator = build_generator()
generated_data = generator.predict(noise_vector)
```
` ` `

4. Balancing Class Distribution

Imbalanced datasets—where certain classes dominate—can bias AI models and lead to skewed predictions. Techniques such as resampling, which includes oversampling minority classes and undersampling majority classes, help to create a more balanced dataset, ensuring fair learning across categories.

` ` `python from imblearn.over_sampling import SMOTE

```
smote = SMOTE()
oversampled_data,        oversampled_labels        =
smote.fit_resample(original_data, original_labels)
```
` ` `

Fostering Innovation Through Creative Data Handling

The strategic application of data augmentation and manipulation not only enhances model effectiveness but also inspires innovative solutions in data-constrained environments.

Engaging in progressive data handling practices requires a commitment to exploring cutting-edge methodologies and seamlessly integrating them into existing workflows. This approach underscores the broader narrative of responsible, informed AI development, wherein data transformation plays a critical role in delivering intelligent and equitable technologies.

Real-Time Data Processing and Responsiveness

Real-time data processing stands as a crucial pillar in the architecture of modern artificial intelligence systems. As AI becomes increasingly integral to essential applications—

ranging from autonomous driving to stock market analysis —the capability to swiftly ingest, analyze, and act on incoming data is not just advantageous; it is vital. This agility enhances immediate decision-making while enabling AI agents to respond adeptly to fluctuating scenarios and dynamic environments.

The Crucial Role of Real-Time Processing

Real-time data processing embodies the continuous ingestion and analysis of data, allowing AI systems to react almost instantaneously. In fields where timing is paramount, such as healthcare or transportation, the ability to swiftly incorporate new information can be the decisive factor between triumph and failure. For instance, AI-driven patient monitoring systems rely on rapid data analysis to alert healthcare professionals to critical changes in patient conditions, enabling timely interventions that could save lives.

Consider a smart traffic management system designed to optimize traffic light sequences based on real-time congestion data captured through sensors. Its efficacy hinges on the capability to analyze this data in real time, significantly reducing wait times and enhancing urban mobility.

Technologies Empowering Real-Time Processing

The essence of real-time data processing lies in the advanced technologies and infrastructures capable of handling vast streams of data with remarkable speed. Prominent among these technologies are:

1. Stream Processing Frameworks

Platforms such as Apache Kafka, Apache Flink, and Apache Storm offer robust solutions for managing real-time data streams. These frameworks are engineered to distribute and process extensive quantities of data with minimal latency, ensuring that decision-making can occur rapidly after data arrival.

```python
from pyspark.streaming import StreamingContext from pyspark import SparkContext

sc = SparkContext(appName="RealTimeProcessing")
ssc = StreamingContext(sc, 1) \# Set the micro-batch interval to 1 second

\#\# Example: Process data from a stream every second
data_stream = ssc.textFileStream("path/to/data")
processed_data = data_stream.map(lambda x: x.split(",")).filter(lambda x: x[2] > threshold)
```

1. Event-Driven Architecture

Leveraging an event-driven architecture is fundamental for real-time processing. Systems are crafted to react to individual events as they transpire, a model particularly relevant in the realm of the Internet of Things (IoT).

A practical illustration of this is a smart power grid that dynamically adjusts electricity distribution by continuously analyzing real-time consumption data, optimizing energy use while minimizing waste.

1. In-Memory Computing

By storing data in RAM rather than slower disk storage, in-memory computing drastically accelerates processing times. Solutions such as Redis or Apache Ignite employ in-memory data grids, enabling instantaneous access to frequently utilized data.

```java
import org.apache.ignite.Ignition; import org.apache.ignite.Ignite; import org.apache.ignite.IgniteCache;

try (Ignite ignite = Ignition.start("examples/config/example-ignite.xml")) IgniteCache cache = ignite.getOrCreateCache("myCache"); cache.put(1, "Real-time
```

Data"); System.out.println("Saved: " + cache.get(1));

` ` `

Designing for Optimal Responsiveness

Beyond technology, successfully developing real-time systems hinges on thoughtful design principles aimed at enhancing responsiveness. Key considerations include efficient algorithm design, intelligent load balancing, and the prioritization of critical tasks. Resilience, scalability, and the ability to adapt to varying data input volumes without compromising performance are non-negotiable attributes.

In high-frequency trading, for example, algorithms must be fine-tuned to maintain peak responsiveness amidst extreme data traffic. Rapid execution of trades within milliseconds of receiving new market data is essential for capitalizing on fleeting price changes.

Diverse Real-Time Applications

Real-time data processing has found extensive applications across diverse industries, capitalizing on its ability to facilitate immediate reactions and adaptability:

- Autonomous Vehicles: The processing of real-time sensor data is fundamental for navigating complex environments—detecting obstacles and making split-second driving decisions autonomously.

- Smart Manufacturing: Factories equipped with IoT technology utilize real-time data from production lines to anticipate machinery failures, enhance safety protocols, and improve overall efficiency through just-in-time decision-making.

- Digital Advertising: Algorithms leveraging real-time consumer interaction data enable advertising platforms to dynamically adjust campaigns, optimizing effectiveness based on evolving user preferences.

Achieving Seamless Real-Time Integration

To effectively implement real-time processing, organizations must strategically integrate technology with skilled personnel and innovative methodologies that support rapid adaptation. Continuous refinement of algorithms and adoption of scalable infrastructure are essential to sustaining real-time capabilities as data volumes continue to rise. Moreover, accountability in decision-making processes—especially in critical fields such as healthcare and finance—is indispensable, given the profound impact of AI-driven actions on human lives and financial well-being.

As organizations increasingly deploy AI agents reliant on real-time data, fostering a culture of agility and responsiveness becomes paramount.

The Vital Role of User Feedback in Enhancing AI Agents

User feedback serves as an indispensable catalyst in the ongoing evolution of artificial intelligence agents, significantly shaping their development to meet the diverse needs and expectations of end-users. While cutting-edge algorithms and powerful computing capabilities lay the groundwork for the technology, the rich insights provided by users ensure that these agents are not just technically proficient but also genuinely valuable in real-world applications.

Embracing Diverse Feedback Loops

Effectively integrating user feedback into AI systems relies on understanding a wide array of user experiences. This diversity enriches the functionality of AI agents, enabling them to adapt to various contexts and scenarios. Collecting feedback involves creating multiple feedback loops that capture an extensive range of user interactions—from direct comments to subtle patterns in usage behavior. For instance, AI-driven customer service chatbots thrive on data derived from real user conversations. Feedback regarding clarity, relevance, and overall satisfaction becomes crucial metrics guiding their continuous refinement.

Consider the impact of user feedback on voice-activated virtual assistants. Insights concerning voice recognition accuracy, response relevance, and overall usability inform developers about critical areas for improvement. As a result, updates are made not just to enhance algorithms but also to ensure that interactions feel more natural and intuitive.

Strategies for Efficient Feedback Collection

To systematically gather and analyze user feedback, various methodologies can be employed to ensure comprehensive insights:

1. Surveys and Questionnaires

Targeted surveys are powerful tools to elicit specific feedback on performance and user satisfaction. These should encourage subjective reflections and include open-ended questions, providing deeper insights into user expectations and areas for improvement.

1. User Analytics and Behavior Tracking

Analyzing user interaction patterns—such as click behavior, frequency of use, and task completion rates—offers valuable insights into how effectively an AI agent fulfills its intended purpose. This form of implicit feedback is often more objective, shedding light on real-world user experiences.

```python
``` python ## Example code snippet for analyzing user behavior patterns import pandas as pd

df = pd.read_csv('user_interaction_log.csv')
engagement_metrics          =          df.groupby('user_id')
['interaction_type'].count()
```
```

```
` ` `
```

1. A/B Testing

Implementing A/B tests provides a controlled environment in which different iterations of an AI system can be compared. This allows developers to assess user preferences based on direct interaction with varying versions.

1. Direct User Engagement

Facilitating user-group discussions or workshops invites qualitative feedback that can delve into user challenges and suggestions, offering richer insights than quantitative measures alone.

Analyzing and Integrating Feedback

The incorporation of user feedback into AI development necessitates a structured approach to ensure insights lead to meaningful enhancements:

- Prioritizing Feedback

Not all feedback can be acted upon at once. An effective strategy involves classifying feedback based on its impact, feasibility, and frequency. This hierarchical approach enables teams to focus on the most crucial enhancements that will yield significant improvements in user experience.

- Collaborative Development

Engaging regularly with developers, UX designers, and end-users fosters a deeper understanding of user needs, ensuring that solutions are aligned with practical complexities. This collaboration, integral in both feedback collection and implementation, drives continuous evolution of AI agents.

- Automating Feedback Integration

Utilizing AI tools to process large volumes of user feedback can streamline the improvement cycle. Techniques like sentiment analysis and natural language processing automate the extraction of insights, facilitating swift adaptations in response to user sentiments.

```python
## Example of sentiment analysis on user feedback
from textblob import TextBlob

feedback = TextBlob("The new feature improved my work efficiency significantly.")
sentiment = feedback.sentiment
```

Real-World Applications and Persistent Challenges

As AI systems become increasingly woven into the fabric of both professional and personal spheres, their reliance on user feedback intensifies. This feedback-driven evolution is particularly pronounced in sectors like healthcare, where AI support tools benefit significantly from clinician insights, enhancing diagnostic accuracy and reliability.

In the realm of e-commerce, user feedback related to product recommendations refines personalization algorithms, boosting customer satisfaction and elevating sales. However, the journey of integrating feedback is not without challenges, such as overcoming biased responses, managing large volumes of input, and distinguishing actionable insights from noise.

Ultimately, the integration of user feedback into AI development is a multifaceted endeavor. It requires an unwavering commitment to listening, interpreting, and responding to the diverse voices of users. This approach not only fosters technological innovation but also cultivates true user satisfaction and trust, ensuring that AI agents remain agile and responsive to the changing landscape of user demands and expectations. In this way, they contribute meaningfully to sustained utility and success in a rapidly evolving digital world.

Future Trends in Data Utilization for AI

The rapid evolution of artificial intelligence is intricately tied to the strategies we employ in managing, processing, and utilizing data. As AI technologies advance, so too do the methodologies surrounding data use, fundamentally transforming how these systems are constructed and how effectively they generate insightful and relevant outcomes.

The Rise of Real-Time Data Processing

A significant trend reshaping the AI landscape is the increasing demand for real-time data processing. Industries are seeking swift insights and agile decision-making capabilities, necessitating AI systems that can seamlessly manage streaming data. This shift is of particular importance in critical sectors like finance and healthcare, where timely data can determine vital outcomes. Emerging technologies, such as edge computing, are being adopted to enable AI to process information closer to its source, thereby minimizing latency and reducing bandwidth consumption.

An illuminating example can be found in autonomous vehicles. These sophisticated systems rely on real-time data from a network of sensors to make instant navigation and safety-related decisions.

Embracing Data Diversity and Complex Integration

As data becomes increasingly multifaceted, incorporating everything from unstructured text to sophisticated multimedia, AI systems are challenged to blend these diverse data types into cohesive analytical frameworks. This complexity calls for significant advancements in data fusion techniques, which integrate disparate sources into a unified, actionable narrative. AI agents, especially those focused on natural language processing and computer vision, will need to simultaneously interpret and synthesize varied information from texts, images, and videos.

Take smart city initiatives, for instance. Here, the integration of traffic data, environmental metrics, and social media insights forms a holistic city management platform. Such comprehensive data amalgamation empowers urban planners to make informed decisions, enhancing infrastructure and optimizing resource allocation.

The Evolution of Data Governance and Ethical Practices

Given the rising focus on data privacy and security, the demand for robust data governance frameworks will only intensify. Organizations must ensure compliance with ever-evolving regulations while establishing transparent data usage policies. AI systems will be instrumental in automating compliance checks, helping maintain ethical standards in data management.

For example, in financial institutions, AI-driven compliance monitoring can facilitate adherence to anti-money laundering regulations by continuously scrutinizing transaction data patterns and flagging any anomalies that may arise.

The Emergence of Synthetic Data for AI Training

In response to the growing need for large, high-quality datasets, the generation of synthetic data has surfaced as a viable solution. This approach involves creating artificial datasets that mirror real-world data properties, allowing AI models to train effectively even when genuine data is scarce.

Within the healthcare sector, synthetic data is increasingly used to develop predictive models for rare diseases, thereby addressing the lack of available patient data while maintaining privacy. These models can predict disease progression and treatment outcomes, enabling advanced insights without compromising sensitive information.

Advancements in Data Augmentation Techniques

To bolster the generalization capabilities of AI models, data augmentation techniques are evolving, providing a wider array of data variations for training purposes. These methods involve altering existing data through techniques such as rotation, cropping, or changing colors, significantly expanding the dataset's diversity and robustness.

In the realm of computer vision, augmented data is extensively employed to enhance the performance of image classification models.

```python
## Example of data augmentation for image classification
from keras.preprocessing.image import ImageDataGenerator

datagen = ImageDataGenerator(
rotation_range=20,
width_shift_range=0.2,
height_shift_range=0.2,
horizontal_flip=True)

\#\# Assuming 'images' is a numpy array of image data
augmented_images = datagen.flow(images, batch_size=32)
```

Harnessing User Feedback for Continuous Improvement

The integration of user feedback into data cycles creates opportunities for the ongoing refinement and enhancement of AI systems.

E-commerce platforms are a prime example, leveraging user feedback to fine-tune recommendation systems.

Implications for Future AI Development

As AI technologies increasingly intertwine with societal frameworks, these trends in data utilization will significantly inform their evolution. Developers and organizations must remain agile, adopting state-of-the-art data management strategies while prioritizing transparency and accountability. This dual focus will not only enhance AI systems' accuracy and efficiency but also align them with ethical standards, paving the way for a future where data-driven insights enrich every facet of life. This strategic approach will further entrench AI as an indispensable partner in addressing the complexities of contemporary existence and tackling the challenges that lie ahead.

CHAPTER 5:
DESIGNING AND
DEVELOPING
AI AGENTS

A fundamental element of designing successful AI agents lies in understanding the distinct needs and goals of end-users. The design journey should commence with a clear identification of the target audience and the specific challenges the AI agent aims to address. Engaging in contextual inquiries, conducting user interviews, and administering surveys can yield invaluable insights into user behaviors, preferences, and pain points. For example, when developing a virtual assistant for the healthcare sector, it's imperative to grasp both patients' needs and healthcare providers' workflows. This holistic understanding ensures the agent enhances operational efficiency and improves patient care outcomes.

Equally important is the principle of clarity and simplicity in interface design. AI agents must convey information in an intuitive and accessible manner, thus reducing the cognitive load on users. Take, for instance, a chatbot integrated into a customer service framework: a conversational flow that is both coherent and user-friendly enables customers to resolve their issues quickly, minimizing frustration and boosting overall satisfaction. To achieve optimal usability, designers often utilize wireframing and prototyping tools, allowing for iterative testing and refinement of the user interface. This process ensures that interactions feel seamless and natural.

In addition to clarity, personalization has become a cornerstone of AI agent design. Agents that adapt to individual user preferences and behaviors can offer a more engaging experience. Leveraging machine learning algorithms is crucial in this context, as they empower agents to learn from user interactions and customize responses dynamically. For instance, an embedded recommendation engine within an e-commerce platform can analyze past purchasing behavior to suggest products that align with user interests, thereby enhancing satisfaction and driving sales.

Ethical considerations must also be at the forefront of AI agent design. Developers should establish robust ethical guidelines that address data usage, privacy concerns, and bias mitigation. Integrating fairness principles into the development process is vital to preventing discrimination and fostering inclusivity. This commitment is particularly significant in systems like automated hiring tools, where impartial decision-making is essential to support organizational diversity and equity.

Robustness and reliability are additional critical facets of effective AI agent design. These agents must be equipped to handle a variety of input scenarios with grace, including unexpected or ambiguous user requests. Thorough testing against diverse datasets is essential to ensure high performance across different contexts. For example, a financial advisory tool's ability to provide accurate and responsible responses to complex financial inquiries can significantly influence user trust and decision-making.

Finally, the principle of continuous improvement through user feedback is fundamental to the sustained success of AI agents. Designers should implement mechanisms for collecting and analyzing user input, which can then inform iterative design enhancements. For instance, deploying periodic surveys or incorporating feedback options within the application allows users to share their thoughts, facilitating ongoing optimization and responsiveness to user needs.

In conclusion, the journey of designing AI agents intricately weaves together technical expertise, empathetic understanding of user requirements, ethical considerations, and adaptability. This thoughtful approach paves the way for the meaningful and responsible deployment of technology within increasingly diverse and complex environments.

In the rapidly evolving field of AI agent design, a steadfast commitment to user-centric principles is paramount for crafting systems that genuinely resonate with users' needs while simultaneously fostering trust and satisfaction. Unlike traditional software applications that operate within predictable parameters, AI agents engage users in dynamic and often unpredictable environments. This necessitates a design approach that prioritizes the user experience as not merely beneficial, but essential.

At the heart of user-centric design lies an in-depth understanding of the user's environment and the specific context in which they operate. This understanding is achieved through immersive research techniques such as contextual inquiries, where designers and developers observe and interact with users in their natural settings. For example, when creating an AI-powered virtual assistant for remote learning, it becomes vital to explore varied user scenarios —encompassing different learning styles, environments, and technical expertise. Such comprehensive insights provide a strong foundation for crafting tailored solutions that significantly improve educational experiences.

Incorporating tools like storyboarding and personas into the design process helps ensure that user perspectives remain at the forefront. Personas—fictional characters that embody the diverse user types—serve as valuable tools for visualizing needs, experiences, and goals of different user segments. When developing a navigation system for visually impaired individuals, for instance, creating detailed personas allows the design team to dive deeply into specific user requirements, facilitating the iteration of design features such as audio feedback and tactile interfaces that align with user expectations and adhere to accessibility standards.

Engaging users directly in the design journey through collaborative sessions or co-creation workshops is another powerful strategy. In the realm of healthcare applications, involving patients and healthcare professionals can shine a light on critical features—like secure data management and intuitive appointment scheduling—that developers might unintentionally overlook.

Iterative prototyping is a cornerstone of user-centric design within AI development, allowing designers to explore, refine, and enhance products based on user feedback. The journey often begins with low-fidelity prototypes—such as wireframes or simple sketches—that enable validation of basic concepts without significant investment. These initial ideas evolve into high-fidelity prototypes equipped with interactive features, ready for user testing in realistic environments. Gaming companies, for example, frequently employ this iterative approach to fine-tune AI behavior and improve user interactions, resulting in a more immersive and rewarding experience.

Another critical element is incorporating usability testing into each design iteration, ensuring that the product interface is intuitive and aligns with user expectations. This process involves closely observing users as they engage with prototypes, identifying pain points and areas ripe for enhancement. In the case of an AI-driven grammar checking tool, usability testing can reveal whether users find the interface helpful and easy to navigate, complete with clear explanations that enhance their writing without imposing unnecessary complexity.

Moreover, maintaining transparency within the AI system is vital. Users should have a clear understanding of how an AI agent functions, especially regarding the decisions it makes autonomously. This is where Explainable AI (XAI) techniques come into play, offering users insights into the decision-making processes of the AI, thus boosting trust and confidence. For instance, an AI responsible for credit scoring that clearly explains its decision-making criteria can foster user trust and demystify the rationale behind individual scores, rather than leaving users guessing.

Finally, accessibility must be a primary consideration in AI agent design. This commitment entails ensuring that AI systems are usable by individuals with varying abilities, incorporating features that adapt to diverse needs. Functionalities such as voice recognition for hands-free operation, compatibility with screen readers, and customization options for different sensory preferences can greatly enhance the accessibility of AI technologies, making them usable for a broader audience.

In conclusion, anchoring AI agent design within user-centric principles ensures that these technologies are not only innovative and effective but also deeply attuned to the needs and contexts of users. Such thoughtful design not only amplifies user capabilities but also enriches interactions with technology, ultimately enhancing the overall user experience.

The successful development of AI agents is fundamentally anchored in the strategic choice of robust frameworks and methodologies. These elements play a critical role in enhancing both the efficiency of the development process and the quality of the final product. The frameworks and methodologies selected significantly impact the flexibility, scalability, and maintainability of AI agents, ultimately affecting their performance and sustainability in a rapidly evolving field.

Exploring Development Frameworks

To begin with, familiarizing oneself with the landscape of available frameworks is essential. TensorFlow and PyTorch stand out as two of the most widely adopted tools for building machine learning models within AI agents. TensorFlow boasts a flexible architecture that supports deployment across various platforms, making it a versatile option for diverse applications. In contrast, PyTorch is celebrated for its dynamic computational graph, which allows developers to modify their models on-the-fly during runtime.

The decision between these frameworks often depends on the specific needs of the AI project. For example, when tasked with predicting customer behavior in an e-commerce environment, TensorFlow's scalability and rich suite of features for deep learning can be invaluable. Its high-level APIs enable developers to train and deploy intricate models efficiently, addressing complexities inherent in large datasets. On the other hand, if a project requires rapid prototyping and iterative experimentation—key to advancing in a competitive market— PyTorch's intuitive interface can provide the necessary agility, allowing teams to explore various scenarios without being hindered by cumbersome configurations.

The Importance of Structured Methodologies

In addition to selecting appropriate frameworks, embracing structured methodologies can significantly enhance the development process. Agile methodologies, known for their emphasis on flexibility and incremental progress, prove particularly advantageous in the realm of AI agent development. The iterative nature of Agile aligns seamlessly with the experimental and adaptive mindset essential to successful machine learning projects.

Scrum and Kanban represent two distinct yet complementary

Agile practices frequently utilized in AI development. Scrum employs a structured framework with clearly defined roles, regular meetings, and established artifacts that foster collaboration and communication. Within Scrum, projects are divided into time-boxed iterations known as sprints— typically lasting two to four weeks. During these sprints, cross-functional teams work together to address prioritized tasks from a product backlog, resulting in a deliverable increment at the end of each cycle. For instance, when developing a language translation AI, the structured feedback mechanism inherent in Scrum's sprint reviews and retrospectives becomes crucial, facilitating continuous refinement and responsiveness to linguistic nuances over time.

Conversely, Kanban focuses on visualization of the workflow and limitation of work-in-progress, promoting a continuous delivery model instead of fixed iterations. This approach enhances overall process efficiency, making it easier to pinpoint bottlenecks and optimize resource allocation. In the context of creating an AI-driven diagnostics tool in healthcare, Kanban's visual task management can provide clarity regarding progress and priorities, ensuring that urgent features receive prompt attention without delay.

Adopting a Hybrid Approach

Integrating these methodologies often involves a hybrid approach tailored to the unique dynamics and demands of each project. For example, a development team might initiate the process with Scrum to establish an organized framework and regular assessment cycles. As the project progresses and stabilizes, elements of Kanban may be incorporated, allowing for greater flexibility and responsiveness to changing requirements.

The Role of CI/CD in Agility

Furthermore, the principles of Continuous Integration and Continuous Deployment (CI/CD) are pivotal in reinforcing agility throughout the AI development lifecycle. For instance, in the realm of real-time fraud detection within the financial sector, a CI/CD pipeline enables rapid updates to model algorithms in response to new fraud patterns, thereby enhancing the system's overall resilience and effectiveness.

In summary, the careful selection and implementation of development frameworks and methodologies are crucial in determining the success of AI agent projects. Utilizing frameworks like TensorFlow and PyTorch alongside methodologies such as Agile, Scrum, Kanban, and CI/CD practices allows development teams to optimize their workflows, adapt to emerging challenges, and create robust AI solutions. These foundational elements serve as the backbone of successful AI initiatives, ensuring they not only meet user expectations but also retain the flexibility to evolve in line with technological advancements and shifting market needs.

In the rapidly evolving landscape of AI agent development, incorporating stakeholder feedback is both an art and a science. It serves as a vital mechanism for ensuring that technological innovations resonate with user needs and expectations. The capacity to gather, interpret, and implement insights from a diverse range of stakeholders can dramatically elevate the relevance, usability, and acceptance of AI solutions.

Understanding Stakeholder Feedback

In the context of AI projects, stakeholders refer to a wide array of individuals and organizations that have a vested interest in the outcomes of the system. This group includes end-users, project sponsors, executive leaders, regulatory bodies, and developers. Each of these stakeholders brings a distinct perspective that, when effectively integrated, can significantly inform design decisions and prioritize features, ultimately ensuring that the AI agent achieves its intended goals.

Effective Channels for Collecting Feedback

Establishing robust channels for feedback collection is crucial to integrating insights into the development process. While traditional methods like surveys and structured interviews remain fundamental, contemporary AI development has embraced more dynamic approaches:

1. Beta Testing Programs: These programs allow a carefully selected group of users to interact with a pre-release version of the AI product, providing real-time insights into its functionality and usability. For instance, in launching a customer service chatbot, beta testers can pinpoint weaknesses in understanding natural language queries, prompting targeted improvements before the public rollout.

2. Focus Groups and Workshops: Facilitating in-depth discussions with stakeholders can yield deeper insights into user experiences and expectations. For example, in developing a patient monitoring system in healthcare, focus groups comprising healthcare professionals and patients can identify critical usability issues, leading to enhancements that promote user satisfaction and adherence to medical protocols.

3. Feedback Loop Systems: Continuous feedback collection can be achieved post-deployment through in-app feedback features or automated survey prompts. This strategy ensures that stakeholder perspectives are consistently captured over time, allowing for ongoing improvements based on real-world usage.

Analyzing and Prioritizing Feedback

The power of stakeholder feedback is realized in its careful analysis and prioritization. Not all feedback can or should be addressed at once, necessitating the establishment of evaluation criteria. Key considerations include:

- Relevance and Feasibility: Each suggestion should be assessed for its relevance to the project's objectives and technical feasibility.
- Impact on User Experience: Feedback that leads to significant enhancements in user experience or addresses critical pain points should take precedence.
- Alignment with Strategic Goals: Recommendations that align with broader organizational or project objectives should be prioritized, ensuring that development efforts are directed where they will have the most significant impact.

For example, in the creation of a financial advisory AI tool, feedback highlighting the need for improved data visualization might be prioritized over specialized feature requests, as clear visual representation can enhance overall decision-making.

Strategies for Integration

Once feedback is analyzed, it is crucial to effectively incorporate it into the development cycle. Agile methodologies are particularly suited to this process due to their iterative nature and focus on continuous improvement. Integrating feedback can be achieved through several strategies:

1. Iteration and Prototyping: By incorporating feedback into successive iterations, developers can test new features or modifications in a controlled setting before full rollout. This approach mitigates risks and ensures that changes deliver value to the final product.

2. Cross-Disciplinary Collaboration: Stakeholder feedback often raises issues that require insights from various expertise areas, such as design, engineering, and psychology. Facilitating

collaboration among these disciplines ensures that comprehensive solutions are developed and effectively implemented.

3. Transparent Communication: Maintaining open communication channels with stakeholders throughout the development process builds trust and keeps them informed about how their input is being utilized. For instance, regularly updating stakeholders on how their feedback has influenced the product development process can strengthen their commitment to the project's success.

Real-World Implementation Examples

A notable example of effective stakeholder feedback integration can be seen in the development of a personalized learning AI for educational settings. Early feedback from stakeholders highlighted a disconnect between the AI's recommendations and the realities of classroom dynamics. Through iterative development and regular feedback sessions, the resulting AI was tailored to offer adaptive learning pathways, significantly enhancing educational outcomes for a wide range of students.

The integration of stakeholder feedback is an essential element in the successful development of AI agents, championing a user-centric approach that resonates with a variety of needs and expectations. This approach not only enhances technical performance but also ensures that AI innovations fulfill their promise of facilitating meaningful advancements across diverse industries and sectors. In this way, the voices of stakeholders become a vital compass guiding the evolution of AI technologies.

In the dynamic world of artificial intelligence (AI) development, prototyping and iterative development stand out as essential strategies for creating innovative and user-focused solutions. These methodologies empower teams to explore intricate design landscapes and systematically enhance AI functionalities through ongoing refinement and adjustment.

The Art and Science of Prototyping

Prototyping is more than just a preliminary step; it is a crucial means of transforming abstract ideas into tangible, interactive models that embody the fundamental features of a prospective AI system. Unlike fully realized products, prototypes are often simplified versions that allow developers and stakeholders to assess whether the initial design aligns with user expectations. This phase encourages experimentation and embraces imperfection, prioritizing rapid feedback and insights over polished final products.

In the realm of AI, the prototyping process can take various forms based on specific project needs. For instance, in the development of a natural language processing agent, an early prototype may emphasize basic conversational capabilities, honing in on language comprehension rather than diving deep into complex dialogue structures. This targeted approach enables early testing and helps identify and correct misunderstandings in how users interpret AI responses.

Iterative Development: A Cycle of Continuous Improvement

Building on insights garnered from prototyping, iterative development represents a methodical approach where systems undergo successive refinements through multiple cycles. Each iteration comprises planning, development, testing, and evaluation phases. The feedback collected during each cycle is indispensable, shaping the next iteration and ensuring the project's evolution is grounded in both technological viability and users' expectations.

This methodology is particularly advantageous for AI projects, given the complexities and unpredictabilities inherent in machine learning models. For example, the development of a predictive analytics AI might begin with a straightforward algorithm-based prototype, which is gradually expanded to include diverse parameters and datasets. As understanding deepens, so too do the insights the system can provide.

Maximizing Impact through Collaborative Prototyping

The potency of effective prototyping lies in collaborative engagement. Success is contingent upon the active participation of a diverse group of contributors, including developers, designers, and end users. This diversity fosters the identification of potential blind spots, ensuring the prototype is not only functional but also user-friendly and widely accepted.

Imagine creating a healthcare application designed to aid hospital staff with scheduling tasks. Involving doctors, nurses, and administrative employees in the prototyping process allows the development team to highlight critical features such as shift preferences, break timings, and overtime allocation. The feedback gained during these sessions plays a vital role in guiding subsequent design iterations.

Harnessing the Right Tools and Techniques

A variety of tools are available to support the prototyping journey, from rudimentary paper sketches, which allow for quick adjustments, to sophisticated software platforms like Adobe XD or Figma, which facilitate the creation of interactive and visually engaging models. The choice of tool should reflect the project's complexity and the level of clarity required to communicate ideas effectively.

For instance, when creating a customer relationship management AI, initial wireframes can outline user interfaces effectively, while more advanced interactive prototypes can simulate user actions, accurately depicting intricate workflows for managing customer data.

Adapting to Change through Iteration

Change is an inherent aspect of the iterative development

process. Each cycle presents an opportunity to implement learnings from prior phases, refining the AI's capabilities and bringing them in line with stakeholder needs. A proactive and structured approach to change ensures that systems evolve in tandem with technological advancements and shifting user expectations.

A noteworthy example can be found in a retail AI-driven platform that begins with a basic recommendation engine suggesting similar products. As iterations progress, the platform can integrate more complex models that analyze user behavior and manage inventory effectively, ultimately offering personalized shopping experiences that enhance user satisfaction and engagement.

A Real-World Example of Iterative Development Success

The progression of autonomous vehicle AI systems exemplifies the power of iterative development. Initial prototypes focused on fundamental self-driving functionalities within controlled environments. Subsequent iterations introduced more sophisticated elements, such as real-time sensor data processing and adaptive traffic navigation. Thorough testing across varied driving conditions allowed developers to continuously refine algorithms, resulting in systems capable of handling the nuanced challenges of real-world driving.

Balancing Benefits and Challenges

The iterative prototyping approach provides a host of benefits, including risk reduction, enhanced communication with stakeholders, and products finely tuned to meet genuine user needs. However, challenges remain, particularly in striking the right balance between rapid iteration and maintaining thorough documentation, as well as avoiding feature creep—the addition of excessive features that do not enhance the user experience.

To navigate these challenges effectively, it is essential to establish clear project goals that guide each iteration cycle. This discipline ensures a focused progression on key areas, while accountability and clear communication within teams help to guarantee that every development phase leads to actionable results aligned with strategic objectives.

Prototyping and iterative development offer a robust framework for achieving innovative, user-centered AI solutions. As AI continues to evolve, embracing these methodologies ensures that new applications are both groundbreaking and responsible, harnessing their potential to transform industries and enrich lives.

Testing and Performance Evaluation of AI Agents

In the realm of artificial intelligence (AI) development, the stages of testing and performance evaluation are not merely procedural; they are foundational to ensuring that AI agents are both reliable and effective. These critical processes help ascertain that the agents function as intended while also meeting user needs and expectations.

Comprehensive Testing Strategies

Given the intricate nature of AI agents, a multifaceted approach to testing is essential to guarantee the optimal performance of all components in a variety of conditions. The testing process can be categorized into several key strategies:

1. Unit Testing: At the core of effective testing is unit testing, which involves verifying the functionality of individual components. Each unit is tested independently to confirm its correctness before being integrated into the overall system. For instance, in a chatbot application, unit tests would target specific modules, like message parsing functions, ensuring they provide accurate responses.

2. Integration Testing: Following unit validation, integration testing scrutinizes the interactions

among combined components. This step is critical to ensure that data flows seamlessly between modules. For example, when assessing a recommendation engine, the integration of the data processing module with the predictive algorithms is essential for ensuring robust and accurate functionality.

3. System Testing: Moving beyond component interactions, system testing evaluates the entire AI framework as a cohesive unit. This comprehensive assessment confirms that the system meets all specified requirements and works harmoniously. For instance, in an e-commerce AI system, simulating user interactions allows for validation of features, including recommendation accuracy and billing processes.

4. User Acceptance Testing (UAT): This stage is paramount for gauging end-user satisfaction. UAT involves real users engaging with the system in realistic scenarios, providing critical feedback on usability and efficacy. For example, testing an AI-based language tutor with a group of students can uncover insights regarding its practicality and educational value.

5. Performance Testing: Performance testing assesses how an AI agent performs under various conditions, focusing on metrics such as latency, response time, and overall efficiency. For instance, in AI-driven analytics platforms, subjecting the system to simulated heavy data queries evaluates its speed and accuracy, which is crucial for user satisfaction.

Key Performance Metrics

Evaluating AI agents' performance requires a clear understanding of specific metrics that indicate both success and areas for improvement. Some essential metrics include:

- Accuracy: This metric measures the correctness of the AI's outcomes, whether in predictive accuracy or search result relevance.
- Precision and Recall: Particularly vital for classification tasks, these metrics evaluate the AI's ability to correctly identify relevant versus irrelevant data points, which is essential in applications like spam detection.
- F1 Score: This metric represents a harmonic mean of precision and recall, providing a balanced evaluation for classification models.
- Latency: Critical for applications that rely on speed, latency measures the response times of AI systems, such as in real-time language translation services.
- Scalability: The ability of an AI system to maintain performance while managing increased data loads or user demand is crucial, particularly for systems predicted to expand.

Real-World Case Studies

Examining the journey of a machine learning model developed for fraud detection in a financial institution showcases the thorough nature of testing and performance evaluation. Initially, unit testing ensured that each algorithm handled transaction data accurately. Subsequently, integration testing verified the communication between predictive models and real-time analytics dashboards.

During performance testing, latency issues arose when processing a high volume of concurrent transactions. This prompted developers to refine data handling processes and optimize database queries for quicker execution. Moreover, user acceptance testing involved simulating fraud review processes with actual bank employees, ensuring that the system's alerts were concise and actionable, mitigating the risk of inundating staff with false positives.

Tools and Techniques

A variety of tools are available to developers to support comprehensive testing and performance evaluation:

- JUnit and PyTest: These frameworks automate unit testing in Java and Python, respectively, streamlining the process of verifying software components.
- Selenium: Ideal for testing web applications, Selenium ensures that user interactions with AI-driven interfaces are smooth and error-free.
- Apache JMeter: This tool is used for performance testing, specifically in assessing system behavior under heavy loads.
- TensorBoard: A powerful tool for visualizing machine learning experiments, TensorBoard helps developers understand model training dynamics and overall performance metrics.

Challenges and Best Practices

Despite the importance of rigorous testing and evaluation, several challenges need to be addressed. One common issue is overfitting, where a model performs exceptionally on test data but struggles in real-world applications. To counteract this, techniques such as cross-validation and regularization are essential.

To guarantee comprehensive testing and evaluation, teams should consider the following best practices:

- Establish feedback loops that encourage learning from errors and iterative refinement of system functionalities.
- Involve stakeholders in the test planning process to align testing efforts with both business objectives and user expectations.
- Implement version control and diligent documentation to track changes, ensuring

transparency throughout development cycles.

In conclusion, effective testing and performance evaluation are pivotal to delivering robust and reliable AI agents that meet the needs of users and stakeholders alike.

Harnessing Cross-Disciplinary Collaboration in AI Projects

The swift evolution of artificial intelligence (AI) is reshaping industries and presenting a wealth of opportunities that extend well beyond conventional boundaries. To fully unlock the capabilities of AI agents, cross-disciplinary collaboration emerges as a crucial driver of innovation, facilitating comprehensive, effective solutions.

The Power of Diverse Expertise

AI agents are not isolated constructs; their development relies heavily on a diverse range of specializations to optimize efficacy and user experience. For instance, consider the creation of an AI-enabled medical diagnostic tool. Its success is contingent upon the collaborative efforts of software developers—who craft the algorithms—medical professionals —who provide essential domain expertise—and regulatory specialists—who ensure adherence to healthcare standards. Each discipline contributes invaluable insights, ensuring that the AI functions accurately and ethically, while seamlessly integrating into existing healthcare frameworks.

Fostering Synergy Through Effective Communication

To achieve successful cross-disciplinary collaboration, robust communication channels must be established. Teams should cultivate environments where knowledge flows freely and the contributions of each expert are acknowledged and appreciated. Regular interdisciplinary meetings and collaborative workshops can be particularly effective in fostering open dialogue, aligning goals, and ensuring a shared understanding among team members.

Virtual collaboration platforms, such as Slack or Microsoft

Teams, can further enhance interactions, facilitating ongoing exchanges of ideas and feedback. For instance, when developing an AI agent for environmental monitoring, environmental scientists, data analysts, and software engineers might hold weekly sessions to discuss data interpretations and necessary system modifications. This continuous dialogue prevents misunderstandings and reinforces the scientific integrity of the project while enhancing its technical robustness.

Embracing Hybrid Models

Adopting hybrid models that integrate diverse methodologies can significantly enhance AI project outcomes. A compelling example is the intersection of machine learning and behavioral psychology in the development of AI-enhanced educational systems.

Within such hybrid environments, teams might align computational linguistics with pedagogy to refine natural language processing capabilities in educational applications. This collaboration ensures that the AI can understand nuanced student inquiries and deliver constructive feedback, ultimately enriching the educational journey.

Navigating Collaborative Challenges

Despite the advantages of cross-disciplinary collaboration, challenges can arise. Variations in terminology, differing problem-solving approaches, and contrasting project priorities may lead to misunderstandings or tension among team members. Fostering an environment of mutual respect and employing structured mediation techniques when conflicts surface are essential for effective teamwork. Clearly defined roles and accountability frameworks can clarify expectations and streamline collaborative efforts.

One illustrative scenario is found in AI ventures aimed at improving autonomous vehicle systems, where mechanical engineers, software developers, and urban planners must collaboratively navigate complex interdependencies. Recognizing and respecting each discipline's unique contributions fosters a cooperative atmosphere, enabling teams to pursue shared objectives rather than competing interests that could hinder progress.

Cultivating a Collaborative Culture

Sustaining a culture of cross-disciplinary teamwork requires a concerted effort to promote diversity of thought and encourage innovative approaches. Implementing team-building activities and cross-training sessions can help dismantle silos and foster empathy among team members from different backgrounds. Additionally, co-locating diverse teams and establishing innovation labs can create both physical and conceptual environments dedicated to collaborative exploration.

A noteworthy example arises from leading technology firms that create AI research hubs. These environments encourage partnerships between academicians and industry veterans, often yielding experimental breakthroughs that wouldn't occur in isolation.

Real-World Examples of Collaborative Success

Examining successful projects that embody cross-disciplinary collaboration can reveal valuable insights and best practices. For example, the development of AI-driven mental health applications often involves collaboration among AI developers, clinical psychologists, data scientists, and patient advocacy groups. Together, they work to create systems that are both technically robust and empathetic to users' needs.

These projects frequently adopt agile methodologies, allowing for an iterative cycle of feedback and refinement. Regular reviews and adaptive planning sessions empower interdisciplinary teams to respond swiftly to emerging insights, reinforcing the dynamism and resilience of their AI initiatives.

Cross-disciplinary collaboration is not merely advantageous —it is foundational to the effective advancement and implementation of sophisticated AI projects. Effective communication, the adoption of hybrid methodologies, and a culture that champions collaboration are essential in unlocking AI's transformative potential. Through this synergy, AI projects can overcome complex and multifaceted challenges, ultimately pioneering innovations that are as groundbreaking as they are inclusive.

Managing project timelines and resources is crucial for the success of AI agent development, serving as the cornerstone for effective strategic planning and operational execution. As organizations navigate the complexities of AI projects, the ability to harmonize time constraints with resource allocation is essential for achieving desired outcomes while maintaining high standards of quality and innovation.

Strategic Project Planning

Initiating an AI project begins with the establishment of clear and achievable objectives—a fundamental step that enables teams to define the project scope and identify the necessary resources for each developmental phase. For example, imagine an organization that intends to create an AI-driven customer service chatbot. The strategic plan should break down the project into distinct stages: research, design, development, testing, and deployment. Each stage should include specific timelines and resource requirements, forming a road map for success.

To visualize and manage these timelines effectively, project management tools such as Gantt charts or Agile boards can provide clear visual representations of progress against benchmarks. This not only enhances tracking capabilities but also empowers project managers to foresee potential bottlenecks, allowing for proactive resource allocation that keeps the project on course.

Resource Allocation

Effective resource management transcends simple budgetary concerns; it involves a strategic deployment of human talent, technological infrastructure, and material assets. For instance, when developing an AI model that demands significant computational power, selecting the right cloud services or computing infrastructure becomes vital to maintaining project momentum.

When allocating human resources, a nuanced understanding of team capabilities and workload distribution is essential. The use of cross-functional teams can leverage diverse expertise, but it also requires meticulous coordination to avoid overwhelming any single team member. Tools like Microsoft Project or Asana can help facilitate effective planning and scheduling, ensuring optimal engagement across different project components and maximizing both individual contributions and collective output.

Time Management Techniques

Time management is the backbone of any successful AI project. Employing Agile methodologies, such as Scrum, can be particularly advantageous. This approach fosters short development cycles—often referred to as sprints—and encourages iterative feedback loops. With this flexible framework, teams can quickly adapt to stakeholder input or unexpected market changes.

Employing time-boxing techniques can help maintain focus and prevent scope creep—the tendency for projects to expand beyond their original goals, which can result in delays and increased costs.

Managing Risks and Uncertainties

AI projects inevitably face risks associated with technological experimentation and fluctuating market demands. Identifying potential risks early in the project lifecycle and developing contingency plans is essential for mitigating adverse impacts. For example, in a collaborative AI research project prone to data privacy issues, conducting proactive ethical assessments and consulting legal experts can preempt costly setbacks.

Regular risk assessments, coupled with flexible leadership strategies, are crucial in navigating the complex dynamics of AI development. For projects with tight deadlines, incorporating buffer periods or overlapping resource allocations can provide the requisite flexibility to accommodate unforeseen delays or increases in workload without jeopardizing the overall timeline.

Leveraging Automation and Tools

Automation plays a pivotal role in enhancing both time and resource management, streamlining repetitive tasks and allowing team members to focus on activities that add higher value. Tools such as Trello or Jira can automate task allocation and progress reporting, simplifying administrative duties while ensuring transparency and accountability.

Moreover, harnessing AI-powered analytics can significantly enhance decision-making processes. Predictive algorithms can analyze historical performance data and current operational variables to provide more accurate forecasts of project timelines, leading to improved resource allocation and strategic adjustments.

Real-World Example: AI in Retail Logistics

A compelling case study can be drawn from the retail sector, where a company set out to leverage AI for enhancing logistics and inventory management. This multifaceted project required seamless collaboration among various teams—data scientists developing predictive algorithms, IT specialists configuring systems to manage vast datasets, and supply chain managers integrating operational processes. Automated inventory monitoring systems offered real-time data, enabling precise forecasting and resource management. Despite facing initial challenges, ongoing risk assessments and adaptive strategies ensured the project remained within budget and timeline constraints, ultimately leading to successful deployment that optimized inventory turnover and reduced overall costs.

Effectively managing project timelines and resources in AI development is a complex challenge that requires strategic planning, agile execution, and adaptive risk management. This holistic approach not only facilitates timely and cost-efficient AI agent development but also nurtures an environment that champions sustainable collaboration and inventive growth.

In exploring the successful development of AI agents, it's crucial to delve into a variety of case studies that exemplify the diverse strategies, challenges, and innovative solutions involved in their creation and deployment. These real-world scenarios not only highlight the multifaceted applications of AI agents but also illuminate the strategic expertise required to effectively manage intricate projects.

Case Study 1: Transportation and Autonomous Vehicles

A standout example of AI agent success can be observed in the realm of autonomous vehicles, particularly through the pioneering efforts of companies like Waymo and Tesla. These trailblazers have harnessed advanced AI algorithms to craft self-driving cars capable of navigating through a multitude of environments and traffic conditions.

Development Process:

- Sensor Integration and Data Processing: Autonomous vehicles depend on an array of sensors—such as LIDAR, radar, and cameras—to continuously gather data about their surroundings. The sheer volume of this incoming data necessitates real-time processing capabilities. Utilizing cutting-edge machine learning models, both Waymo and Tesla train their AI agents to recognize and react to various elements, including obstacles, traffic signals, and pedestrian movements.

- Simulation and Real-World Testing: The journey to real-world deployment begins in a virtual realm. Extensive simulations are conducted to test an array of scenarios, ensuring the systems are robust under different conditions. Only after these simulations yield satisfactory results do these vehicles proceed to controlled real-world testing, where further refinements of decision-making algorithms can occur.

Key Challenges and Solutions:

- Navigating Complex Urban Environments: One of the most significant challenges lies in maneuvering through bustling urban landscapes, which feature unpredictable pedestrian behavior and constantly shifting traffic dynamics. To tackle this, continuous learning algorithms are employed, allowing the AI to adapt to new data and situations as they arise.

- Regulatory Compliance and Public Trust: The path to success also involves navigating regulatory landscapes and building public trust.

Case Study 2: Healthcare and Personalized Medicine

In the healthcare sector, IBM Watson stands out as a transformative AI agent, revolutionizing personalized medicine. Its advanced capabilities have significantly altered how medical professionals diagnose and plan treatments for their patients.

Development Process:

- Data Aggregation and Processing: IBM Watson effectively synthesizes vast quantities of disparate medical literature, patient histories, and treatment outcomes into a cohesive data repository. Machine learning models trained on this comprehensive dataset enable Watson to generate valuable insights and propose tailored treatment options.

- Natural Language Processing (NLP): Vital to Watson's functionality, NLP algorithms empower the AI to interpret unstructured healthcare data, allowing it to parse complex medical jargon. This capacity equips physicians with actionable recommendations informed by the latest scientific research.

Key Challenges and Solutions:

- Data Privacy and Security: Dealing with sensitive patient information necessitates stringent compliance with privacy regulations such as HIPAA. IBM employs advanced encryption and data anonymization techniques to safeguard patient data while ensuring that AI-generated insights remain accurate and useful.

- Integration with Existing Systems: The initial integration of Watson with various electronic medical records (EMR) systems presented challenges. Strategic partnerships with healthcare technology vendors facilitated seamless interoperability, enhancing data exchange and usability.

Case Study 3: Finance and Fraud Detection

The financial sector has witnessed a profound transformation through the implementation of AI agents for fraud detection, as exemplified by banks like JPMorgan Chase. These institutions have adopted sophisticated AI models to monitor and identify fraudulent transactions.

Development Process:

- Machine Learning Models for Anomaly Detection: AI agents in this realm utilize machine learning models trained on historical transaction data to pinpoint anomalies indicative of potential fraud.

- Continuous Model Training: As the landscape of banking practices and fraudulent tactics evolves, constant retraining of these AI systems is imperative. This iterative approach ensures they remain effective in adapting to new threats, consistently maintaining high rates of detection accuracy.

Key Challenges and Solutions:

- Dynamic Nature of Threats: The ever-evolving tactics employed by fraudsters necessitate the use of robust machine learning algorithms capable of recognizing dynamic patterns. Incorporating ensemble methods, which merge predictions from multiple models, has proven instrumental in enhancing accuracy.

- Minimizing False Positives: Striking a balance between fraud detection and reducing false positives is critical to preserving customer satisfaction. Techniques such as adaptive thresholding and refined anomaly scoring help mitigate the risk of misclassifying legitimate transactions.

These case studies illuminate the diverse strategies and methodologies that have driven the successful deployment of AI agents across various sectors. From the rigorous simulation environments utilized in autonomous vehicles to the intricate natural language processing capabilities in healthcare and the agile anomaly detection systems in finance, these examples underscore the principles of adaptability, precision, and seamless integration essential for the effective use of AI technologies.

Design thinking has emerged as an essential methodology for driving innovation in artificial intelligence (AI), providing a structured yet adaptable framework for developing solutions centered on human needs. This approach emphasizes core principles such as empathy, ideation, and experimentation, empowering AI developers and researchers to create technologies that not only push the boundaries of what's possible but also resonate deeply with the end-users' experiences.

Understanding Design Thinking in AI Innovation

The design thinking process consists of five key stages: empathizing, defining, ideating, prototyping, and testing. Each stage is crucial for ensuring that AI solutions are not only technologically sound but also truly user-centric.

1. Empathizing with Users

Empathy lies at the core of design thinking and refers to the ability to genuinely understand and connect with the feelings and experiences of others. In AI development, this means immersing oneself in the environments and contexts of potential users.

Example: Take the development of AI health monitoring devices. Empathy is cultivated by engaging closely with both patients and healthcare professionals, uncovering their challenges such as the integration of devices within existing clinical workflows, and addressing concerns around data privacy and the overall reliability of these technologies.

2. Defining the Problem

The defining phase synthesizes insights gathered during the empathizing stage to create a clear and impactful problem statement. This serves as a vital focal point for the team, aligning their efforts and ensuring a common understanding of the goals at hand.

Example: For an AI customer service solution, the challenge

might be articulated as: "How might we effectively reduce customer wait times without compromising the quality of service?" Such a specific problem statement steers the design process toward refining algorithms for faster, more efficient responses that prioritize user satisfaction.

3. Ideation and Creative Exploration

Ideation fuels creativity by encouraging a fluid exchange of ideas, challenging conventions to explore a wide range of potential solutions. The ideation phase thrives on the input of diverse perspectives, enabling multi-disciplinary teams to brainstorm innovative concepts.

Example: During the ideation phase for smart home AI systems, teams may brainstorm various interaction models, weighing the pros and cons of voice recognition versus tactile interfaces. This exploration helps optimize user engagement while ensuring accessibility for all.

4. Prototyping and Iterative Development

Prototyping is where ideas transition from abstract concepts into tangible forms. Through rapid development of prototypes, teams can quickly test their assumptions and collect feedback, allowing them to refine solutions based on real-world user interactions.

Example: An AI-driven educational platform might begin with low-fidelity prototypes of its learning modules. These prototypes are tested in actual classroom settings, providing immediate feedback on which features captivate students most effectively and enhance learning outcomes.

5. Testing and Validation

The testing phase involves placing prototypes in the hands of users to observe their interactions with the solution. This phase is vital for validating hypotheses and ensuring that the technology truly meets user needs.

Example: In the development of AI-powered recommendation

engines for e-commerce sites, testing may include measuring user engagement and satisfaction across different recommendation models. This evaluation helps fine-tune the algorithms to deliver more relevant and accurate suggestions to users.

Cultivating a Design Thinking Mindset in AI

Embracing a design thinking mindset within the realm of AI innovation nurtures a culture of creative problem-solving, empathy, and user-focused design. This approach not only encourages iterative learning but also fosters an environment where failures are viewed as opportunities for growth and improvement.

Organizations can cultivate a robust design thinking culture by:

- Encouraging cross-disciplinary collaboration: Bringing together engineers, designers, and domain experts enriches the creative process, leading to a greater diversity of ideas.
- Promoting a fail-fast, learn-fast philosophy: Emphasizing rapid iteration and feedback loops accelerates both learning and innovation.
- Focusing on human-centered outcomes: Centering development efforts around user needs and experiences produces products that fulfill broader societal demands.

Integrating design thinking into AI innovation creates solutions that are not only at the forefront of technology but also deeply resonate with users and societal values. This holistic approach not only enhances the quality and relevance of AI technologies but also aligns them with ethical considerations. Embracing design thinking is a commitment to a journey where every step is evaluated by its impact on humanity, ultimately leading to AI solutions that enrich and enhance the human experience.

CHAPTER 6: ETHICAL AND SOCIAL IMPLICATIONS

Exploring the intricacies of AI ethics frameworks invites us to delve into the essential moral principles and guidelines that are becoming increasingly vital as artificial intelligence systems weave themselves into the fabric of our daily lives. These frameworks act as beacons for developers, policymakers, and users alike, guiding them through the complexities of ethical decision-making in the implementation of AI technologies.

Central to these AI ethics frameworks are key principles such as fairness, accountability, transparency, and privacy. Fairness is particularly critical, ensuring that AI systems do not reinforce or amplify existing biases. Instead, they advocate for equitable treatment across various demographics. A poignant illustration of this principle in action is found in the realm of hiring algorithms. Through rigorous fairness checks, these systems can be fine-tuned to mitigate the influence of historical biases, which may inadvertently favor candidates from particular backgrounds. Techniques such as algorithmic fairness auditing are essential in this regard, enabling the assessment and correction of biases to foster more equitable outcomes.

The principle of accountability underscores the importance of recognizing that those who create and operate AI systems must bear responsibility for the effects of their technologies. This concept was starkly highlighted in incidents involving self-driving cars, where an autonomous vehicle was implicated in a fatal accident. The ensuing discussions revolved around accountability: Who was responsible—the manufacturer, the software developers, or the operators? This emphasizes the critical need for well-defined accountability frameworks in AI ethics, ensuring that responsibility is traceable and actionable, rather than muddied within complex organizational hierarchies.

Transparency in AI systems is fundamentally about clarity and openness concerning their decision-making processes. For instance, in the credit scoring arena, both regulators and consumers demand a transparent view of why certain individuals are approved for loans while others are turned down. A lack of transparency, where users are unable to question the reasoning behind decisions, can breed distrust and resistance towards AI systems.

Privacy stands as a paramount concern in the discourse of AI ethics. With the sheer ability of AI systems to gather, analyze, and store vast quantities of personal data, the risk to individual privacy is significant. Ethical frameworks advocate for rigorous data protection practices. For example, principles like differential privacy can be employed to safeguard individual identities, even when data is aggregated for analysis, thus preserving privacy while still allowing for valuable insights.

Many of these frameworks draw from established ethical theories. Utilitarianism, which focuses on maximizing overall well-being, often guides AI systems aimed at improving public health outcomes. In contrast, a deontological approach emphasizes the importance of adhering to ethical guidelines, prioritizing patient consent and rights even if the outcome may not benefit the greatest number. This duality in ethical perspectives enriches the discussion, ensuring that technology does not merely advance but does so in a manner that respects human dignity.

Institutions and organizations worldwide are actively developing and refining AI ethics frameworks. These include the European Union's Ethics Guidelines for Trustworthy AI and the IEEE's Global Initiative on Ethics of Autonomous and Intelligent Systems, each bringing a unique perspective to the table. For example, the EU framework emphasizes the necessity of legal compliance and ethical scrutiny as prerequisites for fostering public trust in AI technologies. Such frameworks offer robust guidelines that can be tailored to specific organizational contexts while remaining aligned with global ethical standards.

Grasping the principles underlying AI ethics frameworks is crucial not just for those developing these technologies, but for society as a whole, which is increasingly dependent on them. This foundational understanding is essential for anticipating future ethical dilemmas as AI continues to evolve, ensuring that technological advancement aligns harmoniously with shared human values and societal progress.

Bias in AI represents one of the most formidable challenges in the journey of artificial intelligence development. This issue is not simply a technological obstacle but also an ethical conundrum that demands our attention to cultivate fair and impartial AI systems. It's imperative for developers, policymakers, and everyday users to understand the sources of bias and engage actively in finding solutions to ensure a beneficial future for AI technology.

One of the most significant contributors to bias in AI lies in the datasets used for training. AI systems learn from the information fed to them, and if this data is marred by historical prejudices or inaccuracies, the AI inevitably absorbs these biases. For example, an AI model trained on hiring data biased toward certain demographic groups may perpetuate these inequities, resulting in unjust hiring practices. This phenomenon has been starkly illustrated in recruitment tools employed by major corporations, where the biases embedded in the training data have led to notable gender imbalances in candidate selection.

In addition to biased data, the design of algorithms themselves can serve as a source of bias. The subjective decisions made by developers during the algorithm's creation can unintentionally introduce or exacerbate these biases if they are not diligently addressed. A poignant example of this issue is found in facial recognition technology, which has faced sharp criticism for its racial bias—often displaying significant inaccuracies when identifying people of color compared to their lighter-skinned counterparts. Such discrepancies are frequently rooted in training datasets that lack diversity, or in inadequate assessments of model performance across various demographic segments.

Moreover, societal norms and unconscious assumptions can subtly infiltrate AI systems, resulting in biases that shape how an AI agent interprets reality. This can lead to output decisions that mirror existing societal inequalities, often without the creators' recognition of these influences.

To effectively combat the sources of bias in AI, a comprehensive and multi-pronged approach is essential. One foundational step is to curate diverse and representative datasets for training AI models. For instance, stratified sampling can ensure that various demographic segments are accurately represented in the dataset, significantly promoting fairness within AI models.

Another critical strategy involves algorithmic fairness auditing. This process utilizes tools and methodologies designed to systematically assess AI systems for bias and discrimination. In the realm of facial recognition, this could entail retraining models on enriched datasets that include diverse representations while reassessing performance across different racial and gender identities.

Model interpretability is equally vital in the fight against bias. Designing AI systems that are transparent and comprehensible allows stakeholders to grasp how decisions are made, facilitating the identification of potential biases and enabling corrective measures. Techniques such as Local Interpretable Model-Agnostic Explanations (LIME) provide valuable insights into how models arrive at specific decisions, empowering stakeholders to recognize and rectify biased reasoning within the framework.

Finally, integrating ethical reviews and bias awareness training into the developmental process can illuminate hidden biases that might otherwise go unnoticed. Diverse interdisciplinary teams consisting of ethicists, sociologists, and technologists can provide a wider range of perspectives, ensuring that biases are identified and addressed in a collaborative manner.

Bias in AI agents transcends technical flaws; it is a pressing societal issue that reflects the inequalities pervasive in human decision-making. To address this challenge, a united effort from all stakeholders in AI development and deployment is crucial. By embedding these solutions throughout the AI development lifecycle, we can build systems that respect and uplift every individual, regardless of their background, steering our technological future toward one that embodies our collective ethical commitments.

The rise of AI agents has significantly reshaped the dynamics of modern workplaces, bringing with it a wave of opportunities and challenges. While the promise of enhanced efficiency and innovation is enticing, concerns about job displacement are pressing and must be addressed thoughtfully. Navigating this transformative landscape is essential for fostering a balanced environment where both technology and the human workforce can thrive.

At the heart of the anxiety surrounding AI is the automation of tasks traditionally performed by humans. This is particularly evident in sectors such as manufacturing, where repetitive processes are increasingly optimized by AI technologies. For example, robotic process automation (RPA) has minimized the need for certain low-skill manual roles, spotlighting the urgent need for companies to rethink their workforce strategies to mitigate the impact of these changes on employment.

Beyond the factory floor, AI's influence is palpable in customer service, with chatbots and virtual assistants swiftly taking over routine inquiries and interactions. In the telecommunications sector, AI-driven interfaces are now often the first point of contact for customers seeking assistance. While this transition enhances service efficiency, it also calls for strategic workforce planning to avoid significant job losses in a sector historically reliant on human interaction.

To counter these challenges, companies must place a strong emphasis on reskilling and upskilling their employees— strategies that not only equip vulnerable workers with relevant skills for the evolving job market but also cultivate a culture of continuous learning. In fields like healthcare, where AI is increasingly used for diagnostics and data management, training can focus on augmenting human roles with AI capabilities, centering on tasks that demand human empathy, judgment, and critical thinking.

A noteworthy example of successful reskilling can be seen in Germany's automotive industry, where collaboration between manufacturers and educational institutions has led to innovative training programs in mechatronics and AI system management. These initiatives are designed to empower current employees to transition into roles that necessitate a deeper understanding of emerging technologies, ensuring that advancements in the field do not lead to widespread job displacement.

Additionally, a number of tech companies are spearheading reskilling by providing free online platforms that offer courses in coding, machine learning, and data analysis. This democratization of education serves to empower individuals to enhance their skill sets independently, thereby increasing their marketability in an AI-driven job landscape.

Government and institutional support are vital in fostering a successful transition as well. Policymakers have the opportunity to facilitate this process by implementing programs that subsidize training for sectors most vulnerable to AI automation. For instance, Singapore's government has made substantial investments in lifelong learning initiatives, offering incentives for individuals seeking to retrain in digital skills.

However, an effective reskilling strategy cannot overlook the various barriers workers may encounter when adapting to new roles. Older employees, in particular, may face challenges in learning new technologies, which calls for a comprehensive approach to training that includes adaptability and resilience-building, along with mentorship programs pairing seasoned employees with those navigating transitional phases.

It is important to remember that reskilling should not solely aim to preserve existing jobs, but also to explore new opportunities that AI creates. This evolving environment can give rise to job titles previously unimagined, such as AI ethicists or machine learning trainers, indicating a profound transformation of the labor market rather than a simple reduction of available positions. Cultivating these new roles will require foresight and planning, highlighting the importance of interdisciplinary skills that marry technical expertise with ethical and managerial insights.

In conclusion, proactively addressing concerns surrounding job displacement serves as a safeguard against potential economic instability while also presenting opportunities for growth. This journey transcends mere survival; it represents a chance to harness the potential benefits of AI for human enhancement and societal progress.

The integration of artificial intelligence (AI) into decision-making processes presents significant challenges surrounding trust and transparency. As AI assumes roles once reserved for humans, it is essential that the decisions made by these systems are not only understandable but also justifiable. The foundation of trust in AI lies in its capacity to offer transparency in operations—this encompasses not just technical clarity but also effective communication and alignment with societal values.

One of the primary avenues for fostering trust is through the implementation of explainable AI (XAI). This approach seeks to render AI decision-making processes more interpretable for non-experts. For example, when an AI system assesses a loan application, XAI principles can provide a clear and detailed rationale behind its decision to approve or deny the request. In the financial sector, where consumers are keen to understand how elements like credit history and income influence decisions, such transparency is crucial.

In areas like healthcare, where AI is increasingly utilized for diagnostics, transparency takes on vital importance. This transparency extends beyond decision-making to include thorough documentation of the data sources and methodologies used in training AI models. The more accessible this information is to the public, the stronger the trust in AI outputs will become.

Ethical transparency is another critical dimension, particularly in addressing bias within AI systems. As AI is trained on historical data, it can inadvertently embed societal prejudices into its algorithms, leading to unintended discriminatory outcomes. A pertinent example can be found in AI recruitment tools, which have faced scrutiny due to biased decision-making linked to training data reflecting entrenched inequities. To combat bias, organizations must commit to ongoing audits and refinements of their algorithms, ensuring they meet ethical standards.

Corporate responsibility also plays a crucial role in fostering trust and transparency. There's a growing expectation for companies developing AI technologies to establish robust frameworks for accountability, allowing stakeholders— ranging from customers to regulatory bodies—to question and verify AI decisions. One effective strategy may involve creating independent review panels to oversee AI systems, providing an additional layer of trust through impartial external assessment.

To further cultivate transparency, some tech firms have begun to pursue open-source initiatives, allowing public access to their AI models and codebases. Such efforts not only facilitate peer review and collective improvement but also democratize AI development, encouraging broader community participation in refining these systems. However, open-sourcing alone is insufficient; these initiatives must be complemented by comprehensive documentation that educates users about model functionalities and limitations.

The issues of trust and transparency in AI extend beyond technical or corporate spheres—they represent social imperatives that require collaborative engagement from various sectors of society. Policymakers have a vital role in establishing standards for transparency, shaping regulations that require clear disclosures of AI decision criteria and accountable business practices. For instance, the European Union's General Data Protection Regulation (GDPR) enshrines explainability within data rights, setting a regulatory benchmark that other regions can adapt or emulate.

Education also serves as a fundamental pillar in building trust. Initiatives focused on data analytics and AI ethics empower users to engage critically with AI outputs, fostering informed trust in these systems.

In conclusion, the challenges of achieving trust and transparency in AI decision-making are multifaceted and necessitate collaboration across technological, corporate, and societal realms. This journey requires a steadfast commitment to transparency throughout the AI lifecycle, ensuring that AI becomes a positive force for transformation in society.

The regulatory landscape for AI agents is both intricate and rapidly evolving, aiming to strike a delicate balance between the swift advancements in technology and the essential societal, ethical, and legal standards that govern it. As AI systems play an increasingly pivotal role in critical decision-making across diverse sectors—from healthcare and finance to transportation and education—it has become imperative for regulatory frameworks to tackle a myriad of challenges, including transparency, accountability, fairness, and safety.

Central to these regulatory efforts is the urgent need to ensure that AI systems function in a manner that is both safe and just. This entails the formulation of legislation that imposes clear expectations on the design and implementation of AI technologies, similar to the way data protection laws, such as the European General Data Protection Regulation (GDPR), establish individual rights concerning personal data. For instance, the GDPR has served as a catalyst for the development of AI-specific regulations, mandating that operators elucidate the decision-making processes of their AI systems to promote transparency and accountability.

Countries across the globe are taking significant strides in defining regulatory guidelines tailored to the unique challenges of AI. The European Union is leading the charge with its proposed Artificial Intelligence Act, which categorizes AI applications based on their associated risk levels, ranging from minimal to unacceptable risk. High-risk applications—those involving critical infrastructure or potentially infringing on individual rights—are subjected to rigorous standards. These standards require comprehensive risk assessments and the systematic identification and mitigation of biases and errors.

In the United States, the approach to AI regulation has been more fragmented, with various states adopting differing policies on AI governance. Nonetheless, there is a growing momentum on the federal level to harmonize efforts to bolster innovation while protecting public interest. Organizations like the National Institute of Standards and Technology (NIST) are playing a crucial role in crafting frameworks that endorse trustworthy AI. These frameworks emphasize fairness, accountability, and resilience, providing industries with best practice guidelines while remaining adaptable to emergent technological developments.

Particular attention must also be paid to the field of autonomous vehicles, which presents its own set of unique risks and rewards. Regulatory bodies, including the U.S. Department of Transportation and the European Commission, are diligently working to develop standards ensuring that AI in vehicles can operate safely in various conditions.

Asia, too, is making strides in shaping regulatory paradigms. In China, new rules governing algorithm management and transparency emphasize strong state control and alignment with national interests. Conversely, Japan adopts a more industry-centered approach, promoting self-regulation alongside government oversight to foster innovation while upholding ethical standards.

The diverse regulatory landscapes across the globe raise important questions about the need for international consistency and cooperation. Disparate standards can complicate operations for companies working on a global scale, necessitating adaptable strategies that comply with local regulations. International organizations, such as the Organisation for Economic Co-operation and Development (OECD), are proactively working to develop cohesive principles for AI governance. The OECD's AI Principles prioritize human-centered values, fairness, and accountability, serving as a framework for nations aspiring to establish or refine their own regulatory measures.

Moreover, it is vital that these regulatory frameworks remain agile, capable of evolving in tandem with rapid advancements in AI technology. Policymakers face the challenge of crafting rules that are not only relevant today but will also stand the test of time as the technological landscape transforms. Innovative regulatory approaches, such as regulatory sandboxes, enable real-world experimentation with AI under controlled conditions, providing invaluable insights that can inform future policy decisions while fostering a climate of innovation.

Industry leaders play a crucial role in shaping this regulatory environment. Partnerships between industry stakeholders and regulatory agencies can create ecosystems where mutual interests—such as data privacy and the ethical use of AI—are harmoniously aligned with innovation objectives.

Ultimately, a collaborative approach between regulators, industry players, and academic institutions is essential for refining and advancing AI regulations that promote the beneficial integration of these technologies into society.

In conclusion, the regulatory landscape for AI agents reflects a concerted effort—both nationally and internationally—to forge standards that protect societal interests without stifling technological progress. This ongoing evolution in regulation promises to steer AI toward being a responsible and constructive force within the global community.

Understanding Social Impact Assessments of AI: A Path to Responsible Integration

As artificial intelligence increasingly permeates our daily lives and critical sectors, social impact assessments (SIAs) have emerged as vital instruments for comprehending and navigating the extensive implications of AI on societal frameworks. These assessments play a crucial role in ensuring that technological innovations not only advance progress but also foster positive outcomes while mitigating potential challenges.

What is a Social Impact Assessment?

A social impact assessment is a structured evaluation that focuses on understanding how AI technologies affect individuals, communities, and society as a whole, taking both immediate and long-term consequences into account.

The Process of Conducting a Social Impact Assessment

At the heart of an SIA lies a systematic exploration of the benefits and risks associated with deploying AI technologies. Consider the healthcare sector: AI-driven diagnostic tools have the potential to enhance efficiency and accuracy in medical practice, which can lead to better patient outcomes and lower costs. However, without careful assessment, these innovations could inadvertently widen the gap between communities, especially if underserved populations lack access to advanced technologies. A thorough SIA can identify such disparities and guide stakeholders in developing strategies to promote equitable access to these crucial healthcare advancements.

AI's Impact on Employment: A Dual Narrative

In the labor market, the implications of AI are both promising and challenging. While AI can boost productivity and create new job opportunities, it also poses the risk of job displacement in various industries. An SIA in this context sheds light on the dynamics at play, revealing that while automation may streamline manufacturing processes, it simultaneously underscores the need for upskilling initiatives to prepare workers for more complex tasks.

Cultural Shifts Driven by AI: Anticipating Change

In addition to economic impacts, SIAs are instrumental in forecasting cultural transformations stemming from AI integration. The ability of AI to deliver personalized media content can significantly alter consumption habits and influence societal perspectives. An effective SIA can analyze engagement patterns across diverse demographics, revealing how AI-curated content might reshape public opinion or modify cultural practices. Understanding these shifts is essential for developing strategies that ensure media consumption remains diverse and reflective of a broad spectrum of voices.

The Role of Smart Cities: A Case Study in SIA

A compelling example of SIA application is found in smart city projects, where urban environments incorporate AI technologies for improved traffic management, public safety, and energy efficiency. Here, SIAs can assess the social ramifications of these initiatives—evaluating whether AI implementations promote inclusivity in urban planning or whether they inadvertently exacerbate socioeconomic divides by favoring affluent areas. Engaging in thorough SIAs allows cities to align AI integration with broader goals of sustainable, equitable urban development.

Inclusive Stakeholder Engagement: A Key to Success

A holistic SIA is rooted in the active involvement of diverse stakeholders, including community members, industry specialists, and policymakers. For instance, including local voices in assessments related to AI in law enforcement—such as predictive policing—can illuminate critical concerns about privacy rights and civil liberties, leading to the design of fairer, more transparent practices that build public trust.

Methodological Rigor for Effective SIAs

To ensure the credibility and effectiveness of SIAs, a rigorous methodological framework is essential. This includes employing both qualitative and quantitative research methodologies—such as surveys, interviews, statistical analyses, and case studies—to capture a comprehensive array of impacts.

A Dynamic Approach: Adapting to Change

Moreover, SIAs should be viewed as ongoing processes, incorporating continuous monitoring and evaluation to adapt to the evolving nature of AI systems and user interactions. This iterative approach ensures that assessments remain relevant, allowing stakeholders to refine strategies that enhance benefits and mitigate adverse impacts over time.

In summary, social impact assessments of AI technology are indispensable for navigating the complexities of technological integration within society. Embracing this proactive approach enables societies to leverage the transformative power of AI, laying down robust foundations for sustainable economic growth, cultural enrichment, and the flourishing of human potential.

The Vital Role of Accountability in AI Actions

As artificial intelligence systems permeate various facets of our lives—from healthcare and finance to transportation and manufacturing—their influence is undeniable. However, alongside their growing prevalence comes the pressing need for accountability frameworks that ensure these technologies operate ethically and transparently. The significance of accountability in AI actions lies not only in safeguarding societal values and individual rights but also in fostering user trust in these rapidly evolving systems.

Understanding Accountability in the AI Landscape

Accountability in the context of AI encompasses a set of guidelines and practices designed to hold all parties involved responsible for the outcomes generated by artificial intelligence systems. This responsibility extends beyond the developers and operators of the technology; it includes the organizations that deploy these systems, requiring a collaborative effort to ensure that outcomes align with ethical standards. For instance, when an AI system is tasked with making decisions—be it for loan approvals, navigating autonomous vehicles, or diagnosing patients—there are numerous layers of decision-making that must be tracked and understood.

The Challenge of Defining Responsibility

One of the most critical aspects of accountability is the challenge of defining responsibility when AI systems produce unintended consequences or exhibit biases. Take, for example, an AI-driven hiring tool that inadvertently discriminates against minority candidates. In such cases, identifying where the fault lies—whether with developers who created the algorithm, the teams responsible for curating training data, or the organizations that implement the systems—can be complex yet essential. This necessitates thorough investigations into training datasets, algorithm design, and deployment practices to ensure fairness and transparency.

The Importance of AI Audits and Transparency

Regular audits of AI systems are crucial for enforcing accountability. These evaluations can verify adherence to ethical guidelines and assess whether algorithms operate as intended without perpetuating bias or discrimination. For instance, organizations that use AI for credit scoring should undergo audits to confirm that their systems evaluate customers fairly across all demographics.

Enhancing Interpretability to Uphold Accountability

Accountability is tightly knit with the interpretability of AI systems. Stakeholders, including users and developers, must comprehend how decisions are made for accountability to be meaningful. Emerging techniques in explainable AI (XAI) aim to unravel the complexities of sophisticated models, such as deep neural networks, providing insights into how these systems reach specific conclusions. In high-stakes contexts like healthcare, understanding the rationale behind an AI's decisions is crucial for medical professionals to provide informed patient care and ensure accountability in treatment outcomes.

Legal and Regulatory Frameworks

Governments and regulatory organizations have a pivotal role in developing legal frameworks that establish accountability standards for AI technologies. Regulations can mandate transparency regarding AI systems' functionalities and require organizations to provide mechanisms for redress in cases of malfunction or bias. The European Union's General Data Protection Regulation (GDPR), which includes the "right to explanation," empowers individuals to seek clarity on how AI-driven decisions affect them, thereby enhancing accountability measures.

Case Study: Accountable Autonomous Vehicles

The emergence of autonomous vehicles (AVs) underscores the complexities of assigning accountability in AI actions. When incidents involving AVs occur, the web of responsibility can extend to a range of stakeholders including hardware manufacturers, software developers, and vehicle operators. Determining fault in these situations often necessitates comprehensive investigations to understand whether failures stem from sensor issues, algorithmic errors, or operator mistakes. Thus, developing robust accountability frameworks that delineate responsibilities throughout the AV lifecycle becomes essential.

The Role of AI Ethics Committees

Creating AI ethics committees within organizations can also enhance accountability. Comprising interdisciplinary experts, these panels can provide oversight and ensure that AI initiatives align with ethical benchmarks and societal expectations. For example, a tech firm deploying AI technologies in facial recognition may engage its ethics committee to evaluate the potential impact on privacy and what measures have been taken to mitigate risks.

User Trust and the Necessity of Accountability

A lack of accountability can severely undermine user trust in AI systems and the entities that deploy them. On the other hand, a demonstrable commitment to accountability can significantly enhance an organization's reputation and consumer confidence. Users are more inclined to engage with technologies they perceive as reliable and respectful of their rights—qualities that are fostered through transparent and accountable actions.

Cultivating a Culture of Responsibility

Beyond formal structures, nurturing a culture of accountability within organizations is paramount. Encouraging ethical scrutiny and responsibility among AI developers, operators, and stakeholders at all levels contributes to an environment devoted to assessing the societal implications of AI technologies thoughtfully and proactively.

In summary, the significance of accountability in AI actions is immense. Establishing accountability not only addresses current challenges but also lays a firm foundation for navigating the dynamic AI landscape, enabling society to harness the benefits of AI while upholding essential human values. Embracing this responsibility is vital to shaping a future where AI can enhance lives ethically and equitably.

Understanding Public Perception of AI Agents

The public's perception of AI agents provides valuable insights into our societal readiness to embrace this transformative technology. As AI continues to revolutionize various sectors, the degree and speed of its adoption hinge significantly on public sentiment. Influenced by a myriad of factors —ranging from media portrayals to personal experiences and the transparency of AI applications—these perceptions must be comprehended and nurtured to create a welcoming environment for AI advancements.

The Role of Media in Shaping Public Opinion

One of the most significant influences on public perception is the portrayal of AI in the media. Often characterized by stark contrasts, media narratives can swing between highlighting the innovative potential of AI and amplifying apocalyptic warnings about job losses or superintelligent robots posing existential threats. For instance, blockbuster films like "The Matrix" or the anthology series "Black Mirror" frequently depict dystopian futures dominated by AI, feeding fear and skepticism among audiences.

These sensationalist stories, although fictional, can linger in the public consciousness, overshadowing the positive narratives surrounding AI's real-world applications. To counteract this polarization, it is essential to share accurate, balanced information that focuses on the tangible benefits and ethical considerations surrounding AI, helping to nurture a more informed public dialogue.

Building Trust Through Transparency

Trust emerges as a cornerstone in shaping public perception of AI agents. Generally, people are more likely to accept technologies that they understand and trust. For example, AI-driven recommendation systems on platforms like Netflix and Amazon have gained widespread acceptance because of their perceived benefits and the transparency surrounding their operation. These systems exemplify how openness about data usage and decision-making processes can cultivate trust, even when personal data is involved.

On the flip side, a lack of transparency can sow seeds of doubt and mistrust. Take, for example, predictive policing algorithms that have faced significant scrutiny due to their opaque decision-making processes and potential biases. Making AI systems more explainable and accessible to users is essential in fostering public confidence and promoting broader acceptance.

Case Study: AI's Role in Healthcare

Examining AI in the healthcare sector underscores the complexities of public perception. While AI's promise to revolutionize diagnostics and treatment is met with cautious optimism, concerns about data privacy and the accuracy of AI-driven diagnostics persist. IBM Watson for Oncology, an AI initiative designed to support cancer treatment decisions, faced criticism for its inconsistent results and lack of clear evidence validating its effectiveness.

To gain public trust, AI developers and healthcare providers must engage transparently with all stakeholders. Clear communication about the benefits, limitations, and safe deployment of AI technologies is vital for demystifying these tools and encouraging acceptance among patients.

The Essential Role of Education

Education functions as a powerful catalyst in shaping informed public perceptions of AI. Many misunderstandings stem from a lack of foundational knowledge about how AI systems operate. Broadening AI literacy initiatives— through public seminars, classroom integration, or hands-on workshops—can empower individuals to engage with AI critically. Collaborations between tech companies and educational institutions to offer open courses on AI fundamentals would play a crucial role in dismantling complex concepts and making them more accessible to the general population.

Confronting Ethical Concerns

Ethical issues surrounding privacy and autonomy also play a pivotal role in public sentiment. The Cambridge Analytica scandal, which highlighted the misuse of personal data for political manipulation, significantly damaged trust in digital platforms and AI. This stresses the urgent need for regulatory oversight and ethical guidelines to protect users.

Organizations must proactively confront potential ethical pitfalls by adopting transparent data practices and robust governance frameworks.

Creating Personalized User Experiences

Public perception of AI agents can shift positively when individuals directly experience their benefits in daily life. Virtual assistants like Siri, Alexa, and Google Assistant have gained widespread acceptance due to their user-friendly interfaces and usefulness—facilitating tasks such as setting reminders and controlling smart home devices. Nevertheless, privacy concerns must remain at the forefront; companies need to develop clear privacy policies and implement strong data protection measures to alleviate user apprehensions.

Closing the Perception Gap

Bridging the perception gap necessitates a collective effort from AI developers, policymakers, and community leaders.

In summary, public perception plays a crucial role in the successful integration of AI agents into society. Trust, transparency, and education are essential factors in aligning public sentiment with the abundant benefits AI technologies can provide.

Global Disparities in AI Access and Development: Navigating Challenges and Seizing Opportunities

As we stand on the brink of a new technological epoch driven by artificial intelligence (AI), it becomes increasingly clear that global disparities in access and development present both formidable challenges and unique opportunities. The promise of AI to revolutionize economies and enhance quality of life worldwide can only be realized if we address the inequalities that currently underpin the field—inequalities rooted in the uneven distribution of resources, expertise, and infrastructure.

The Uneven Distribution of Resources

At the heart of global disparities in AI lies a pronounced concentration of development in economically prosperous regions. Countries like the United States, China, and certain European nations have swiftly emerged as leaders in AI research, bolstered by substantial financial investment and a wealth of technical talent. Notably, iconic tech hubs such as Silicon Valley and Shenzhen are magnets for top-tier professionals, drawing investment that fuels innovation and propels these regions ahead in AI advancements.

This phenomenon has led to the rise of "AI superpowers" capable of deploying sophisticated technologies to tackle complex challenges. Unfortunately, this advancement comes at the cost of widening the gap with lower-income countries, which often grapple with limited resources and outdated technology. In many developing regions, insufficient access to reliable computing infrastructure and high-quality datasets stifles their ability to engage in AI research and development, leaving them at a stark disadvantage in an increasingly competitive global landscape.

Access to Education and Expertise: Bridging the Gap

Equally critical to understanding the disparity in AI access is the uneven availability of educational opportunities. In developed nations, high-quality educational institutions offer comprehensive courses and cutting-edge research facilities that prepare students for careers in AI. In contrast, many educational establishments in developing countries face systemic challenges, including outdated curricula and meager research funding, which inhibit the growth of a skilled workforce in technology.

To combat these gaps, innovative initiatives such as online learning platforms have emerged. Services like Coursera and edX provide courses developed by top-tier universities, democratizing access to valuable educational content for learners worldwide. However, the promise of these resources can be thwarted by issues surrounding digital literacy. Without foundational technical skills, many individuals find themselves unable to fully leverage the vast potential of these platforms.

AI for Development: A Case Study Approach

In response to these inequities, various initiatives have sought to harness AI for addressing developmental challenges in underrepresented regions. Take, for example, the transformative application of machine learning in agriculture, particularly in areas like Africa and South Asia. AI-driven platforms such as PlantVillage have emerged as vital tools for smallholder farmers, enabling them to diagnose pest infestations and manage diseases effectively—thus boosting crop yields and promoting food security.

Such applications exemplify the potential for developing tailored AI solutions that cater to the unique needs of diverse populations. Collaborative efforts involving international organizations, non-governmental organizations (NGOs), and local governments are crucial for scaling these initiatives and ensuring their sustainability over the long term.

Infrastructure and Digital Environments:
The Backbone of AI Deployment

The digital infrastructure essential for effective AI deployment varies significantly across regions. In many parts of Africa, Asia, and Latin America, inadequate electricity supply and limited internet bandwidth pose substantial barriers to the implementation of AI technologies. This lack of robust digital ecosystems not only stifles innovation but also hinders access to critically needed advancements in sectors such as healthcare, education, and governance.

To bridge this infrastructure gap, concerted efforts are essential. Expanding broadband access and investing in renewable energy sources are critical steps toward ensuring a stable power supply. Innovations like Google's Project Loon and SpaceX's Starlink, which aim to provide internet connectivity to underserved areas, could play a transformative role in reducing these disparities.

The Role of Policy and Regulation: Shaping the Future Landscape

The regulatory environment of a country greatly influences its ability to adopt and integrate AI technologies. Nations that establish clear guidelines and supportive policies tend to attract greater investment and innovation. In contrast, countries lacking coherent regulatory frameworks often struggle to realize their potential in AI, discouraging stakeholders from engaging with the local market.

For example, Estonia's success in digital governance underscores the importance of transparent policies in fostering an environment conducive to technological growth. To fully participate in the AI revolution, nations must prioritize the development of adaptable policies that encourage innovation while safeguarding ethical standards and data privacy.

Fostering Global Collaboration: A Path Forward

Global collaboration emerges as a promising solution to tackle the disparities in AI development and access. Frameworks like the Global AI Readiness Index, established by Oxford Insights, offer valuable insights into national capabilities concerning AI implementation.

Additionally, cross-border partnerships facilitate knowledge sharing and capacity-building initiatives, ensuring that successful strategies and lessons learned in one region can be effectively applied in others. Such cooperation nurtures a spirit of innovation that transcends borders, fostering an equitable distribution of AI benefits worldwide.

Confronting the uneven landscape of AI access and development necessitates a multifaceted and collaborative approach to ensure the advantages of AI technologies are accessible to all. In nurturing global partnerships and crafting inclusive policies, we can unlock the tremendous potential of AI, propelling a vision of technological progress that uplifts humanity as a whole.

Long-Term Implications of AI Agent Integration into Society

As artificial intelligence (AI) agents become increasingly woven into the tapestry of our everyday lives, we are compelled to consider their long-term effects on society. While the potential benefits of AI are vast—promising innovations across diverse sectors—we must also confront the significant ethical, social, and economic questions that arise from this technological evolution. A thoughtful exploration of these dimensions is essential to ensure a harmonious relationship between technology and humanity.

Economic Transformation and Workforce Evolution

One of the most striking consequences of AI agent integration is the anticipated transformation of labor markets. With AI capable of automating numerous repetitive and manual tasks, we stand on the brink of unprecedented productivity and economic efficiency. In manufacturing, for example, AI-driven robotics can execute intricate assembly processes, minimizing human error and facilitating rapid production scaling.

Yet, this automation comes with the potential for workforce displacement in sectors where routine tasks are prevalent. Retail cashiers and data entry clerks are among those whose roles may diminish as AI systems take over. Addressing the ramifications of this shift requires a proactive strategy focused on reskilling and upskilling the workforce.

Enhancing Human Potential Through Collaboration

AI agents possess remarkable potential to enhance, rather than replace, human capabilities. When employed as collaborative tools, they can significantly improve decision-making processes across various fields. In healthcare, for instance, AI-powered diagnostic systems analyze comprehensive datasets to provide clinicians with immediate insights, facilitating personalized treatment plans that lead to better patient outcomes. IBM Watson Health exemplifies this capability by delivering in-depth analyses of patient data, streamlining the healthcare process.

The education sector is also poised for substantial transformation through AI integration. Intelligent tutoring systems can provide personalized learning experiences that adapt to individual student needs, vastly improving engagement and achievement levels. For instance, platforms like Carnegie Learning harness AI to tailor educational content, illustrating how human oversight and machine efficiency can form a productive partnership.

Navigating Ethical and Moral Imperatives

As AI agents begin to assume duties formerly reserved for humans, the ethical implications of their decision-making processes cannot be overstated. Autonomous vehicles and AI systems in healthcare must operate in alignment with societal ethics and cultural values, ensuring that the choices made by these technologies uphold principles of fairness and non-discrimination. Furthermore, as we explore the use of AI in defense—such as autonomous drones—it is imperative to establish robust ethical frameworks to govern their deployment.

In matters of data privacy, AI agents must safeguard personal information, preventing misuse and potential breaches. Legislation such as the General Data Protection Regulation (GDPR) in Europe sets a high standard for data privacy worldwide, highlighting the vital importance of transparency and accountability in AI operations.

Shifting Social Dynamics and Public Perception

The integration of AI into daily life introduces new dimensions to social interactions, influencing how people perceive technology and each other. Virtual assistants like Amazon's Alexa and Google Assistant have become commonplace, fundamentally altering the way individuals manage daily tasks—from scheduling appointments to controlling home environments.

These interactions shape public perceptions of AI, impacting trust and acceptance. To foster confidence in AI technologies, it is essential to ensure transparency in decision-making processes. For instance, providing clear explanations for AI-driven outcomes in financial services can enhance user trust and engagement with these systems.

Evolving Regulatory and Governance Structures

The rapid expansion of AI technologies necessitates the development of regulatory frameworks that can adapt to emerging challenges while promoting innovation. Policymakers must strike a delicate balance between fostering technological growth and upholding citizens' rights. Countries like Singapore provide a compelling model, with AI-specific legislation designed to create a legislative framework that nurtures innovation while addressing associated risks.

On a global scale, international organizations such as the United Nations are crucial in advocating for harmonized standards and best practices for AI deployment. Collaborative efforts among nations can pave the way for guidelines that harness AI technologies for the collective benefit of humanity.

Cultural and Socioeconomic Evolution

The integration of AI agents is set to trigger broader cultural transformations that will reshape societal norms and values. As AI assumes roles traditionally filled by human beings, attitudes toward work, privacy, and interpersonal relationships are evolving. This transition calls for a reassessment of social contracts and ethical responsibilities to fully acknowledge AI's multifaceted impact on cultural identity.

Moreover, if deployed equitably, AI holds the promise of reducing socio-economic inequalities. For instance, intelligent systems can significantly enhance agricultural productivity in resource-limited regions, presenting opportunities for sustainable economic development. However, it is crucial to proactively identify and mitigate biases in AI systems to prevent the reinforcement of existing disparities.

Environmental Sustainability and Impact

AI agents can play a pivotal role in promoting environmental sustainability. Smart grid technologies, for example, utilize AI to dynamically allocate resources, thereby minimizing waste while promoting renewable energy integration. Additionally, AI's capabilities extend to climate modeling, enabling us to predict and address the impacts of climate change more effectively.

Nonetheless, we must remain cognizant of the environmental costs associated with AI, particularly regarding the energy consumption of data centers that support these advanced technologies. A commitment to sustainable AI development entails investing in energy-efficient infrastructure and exploring carbon-neutral technological solutions.

The long-term integration of AI agents into society presents an opportunity to reshape countless aspects of human life, from economic structures and ethical considerations to cultural paradigms and environmental strategies. Cultivating resilient frameworks and fostering a culture of continuous learning will empower societies to harness AI's vast potential while navigating the challenges it presents responsibly.

CHAPTER 7: THE FUTURE OF WORK WITH AI AGENTS

Throughout the course of industrial evolution, the interplay between humans and machines has consistently transformed, adapting to the needs of the time. Today, as artificial intelligence (AI) becomes an integral player across a multitude of professional landscapes, the study and implementation of human-AI collaboration models have emerged as critical areas of focus. This realm is rich with diverse frameworks, each presenting unique avenues to maximize the potential of human and artificial intelligence working in tandem.

Among these frameworks, the Collaborative Intelligence model stands out as a foundational concept. This approach envisions a seamless partnership between human intuition and AI's robust analytical capabilities. Specifically, AI excels at processing vast datasets at remarkable speeds, a strength that complements human attributes such as empathy, ethical reasoning, and nuanced judgment. A practical application of this model can be seen in the customer service sector: chatbots efficiently handle common queries, allowing human agents to address intricate cases that necessitate the subtleties of human understanding. Consequently, this collaboration empowers agents to engage more meaningfully with customers, enhancing both satisfaction and resolution rates.

Another significant model is the Human-on-the-Loop

approach. Unlike fully autonomous systems, this model emphasizes human oversight while leveraging AI's capabilities for complex tasks. For example, in the realm of finance, AI monitors real-time transactions and analyzes market data. However, humans are indispensable in this model, ready to step in during irregularities to avert potential crises. Such oversight is crucial to maintaining ethical standards and regulatory compliance, illustrating how human intuition remains vital even in highly automated environments.

On the flip side, the AI-on-the-Loop model is particularly relevant in contexts where AI serves to enhance human decision-making. The healthcare sector provides a telling example; here, AI analyzes patient data to propose possible diagnoses and treatment options. Nevertheless, the physician's role remains paramount, as they interpret AI-generated insights through the lens of their clinical expertise and patient interactions. This synergy boosts diagnostic accuracy while preserving the human touch that is essential for compassionate patient care.

Moreover, the Human-in-the-Loop systems are gaining traction as organizations seek to refine and enhance AI training cycles. In such setups, human experts play an active role in validating and correcting AI outputs, thereby increasing overall accuracy. A clear illustration of this is found in language translation services, where skilled editors review and adjust initial AI-generated translations to ensure they are linguistically and culturally appropriate. This collaborative process not only improves the AI's performance but also fosters a learning feedback loop that benefits both the technology and its users.

In the realm of manufacturing, collaborative robotics—colloquially known as cobots—highlight the importance of human-AI partnerships. Cobots work alongside human operators on assembly lines, taking on repetitive and ergonomically challenging tasks. This collaboration releases human workers from mundane chores, allowing them to engage in more complex, cognitively demanding work that requires problem-solving and creativity. As a result, this integration enhances job satisfaction and fosters an environment ripe for innovation.

The educational landscape is also being transformed through the AI as Co-Educator model, which utilizes AI platforms to create personalized learning experiences tailored to individual student needs. AI systems analyze performance data to identify learning obstacles and propose customized interventions, all while educators provide essential guidance and support. This partnership nurtures critical thinking and social learning, creating an enriching educational atmosphere.

While these diverse collaboration models showcase remarkable potential, they also prompt essential conversations about their seamless integration into daily practices. Establishing mutual trust between human participants and AI systems is paramount. This requires transparent AI mechanisms that clearly communicate their decision-making processes to users, thereby fostering understanding and confidence. Striking a balance between the efficiency of AI and the empathy inherent to human interaction is crucial for successfully implementing these models.

The exploration of human-AI collaboration extends into broader societal discussions about the future of work. We are challenged to envision environments where AI augments rather than replaces human efforts, recognizing AI for its potential to enhance human capabilities. These models exemplify a future where technology and humanity intertwine, shaping workplaces that not only maximize productivity but also honor human-centric values and ethical considerations. Ultimately, the future of intelligent collaboration represents not merely a technological frontier but a paradigm shift in both professional and personal interactions, reimagining how we coexist and thrive alongside advanced intelligent systems.

As technology increasingly integrates itself into the very fabric of our daily lives, the conversation surrounding automation versus augmentation takes center stage with growing urgency. This debate lies at the heart of how artificial intelligence (AI) is utilized across various sectors and its profound implications for the workforce and society. Though both automation and augmentation fundamentally alter the workplace landscape, they diverge significantly in their impact and implementation strategies.

Automation involves completely transferring specific tasks to machines, effectively absolving humans of certain responsibilities. Throughout history, automation has been motivated by the quest for efficiency and cost savings. In industrial environments, for instance, machines have taken over manual labor for tasks that are repetitive, dangerous, or demand endurance beyond human capability. A notable example can be found in the automotive industry, where automated assembly lines produce intricate components with speed and precision far beyond what human workers can achieve.

In contrast, augmentation emphasizes the enhancement of human capabilities through AI, enabling individuals to execute tasks more effectively. Rather than replacing human input, augmentation seeks to complement and elevate it, fostering symbiotic relationships between technology and the workforce. Take the medical field as an example: AI-powered diagnostic tools enhance the abilities of radiologists by analyzing vast arrays of imaging data, resulting in earlier and more accurate diagnoses without removing the human element from clinical decision-making.

At the heart of the automation versus augmentation debate lies the question of the future of work. Automation, while presenting concerns about job displacement, also opens the door to substantial economic growth and innovation. As AI systems undertake mundane and labor-intensive tasks, human resources are freed for activities that demand higher-level cognitive skills, creativity, and emotional intelligence. Industries such as logistics and supply chain management have reaped the rewards of automated systems that streamline operations, reduce errors, and enhance service delivery, showcasing the dual potential of automation.

On the flip side, the augmentation model paints a more optimistic picture, viewing technology as a collaborative partner rather than an adversary. Central to this philosophy is the concept of Collaborative Intelligence, where AI and humans partner to amplify each other's strengths. For instance, in journalism, AI tools can quickly analyze vast amounts of data to identify trends, allowing journalists to devote their efforts to narrative construction, contextual analysis, and investigative reporting—areas that rely heavily on human insight and intuition.

Moreover, the educational sector exemplifies the positive ramifications of augmentation. AI systems can create personalized learning pathways adapted to each student's unique needs, helping educators pinpoint learning gaps and devise more targeted interventions. This partnership enriches the educational landscape, making learning both more effective and inclusive.

As organizations and societies navigate this complex terrain, several critical factors must be considered. Workforce transformation necessitates not just technical skill development but also a mindset geared toward adaptability and the embrace of new roles. Policymakers and institutions have a vital role in developing frameworks that support workers making transitions from automated tasks and help those integrating augmentation into their workflows.

In summary, while automation may threaten the displacement of existing roles, it also paves the way for new opportunities in job creation and economic progress. Concurrently, augmentation cultivates a collaborative environment that enhances human potential rather than usurping it. As we move forward, the dialogue surrounding these approaches will evolve, shaped by emerging technologies and changing societal priorities. Navigating this intricate landscape effectively may well determine the successful integration of AI into future work settings, guiding us toward a more harmonious coexistence with technology.

As we navigate the ever-evolving landscape of the workforce, driven by the dual forces of artificial intelligence and cutting-edge technologies, the emergence of new skill sets is becoming increasingly pivotal. This shift is not merely a response to changing job requirements; it is essential for flourishing in an ecosystem where human cognition and machine intelligence coalesce. The skills necessary for tomorrow's workforce can be discerned by fostering a harmonious balance between technical expertise, emotional intelligence, and an ethos of continuous adaptation.

Technical Proficiency forms the cornerstone of this evolution, representing the expertise needed to thrive amidst technological advancements. As companies incorporate increasingly sophisticated tools, a solid grasp of digital technologies becomes imperative across various sectors. Skills such as data analysis, coding, and AI literacy serve as foundational pillars. For instance, proficiency in programming languages like Python or R is not only critical for software developers; it is also invaluable for professionals in marketing and logistics, where making data-driven decisions is essential.

The ability to engage with machine learning models and comprehend their implications is rapidly becoming essential across multiple industries. Take the example of a financial analyst who utilizes AI to forecast market fluctuations —having a deep understanding of algorithms and their applications is crucial for success in this role. To meet this escalating demand, educational institutions and professional development programs are increasingly embedding machine learning fundamentals into their offerings, preparing the workforce for a future where these skills are in high demand.

Complementing technical skills is Emotional Intelligence (EI) —an irreplaceable asset in a world of automation. As machines excel at performing structured tasks, the value of human attributes such as complex problem-solving, empathy, and effective communication gains prominence. These skills are particularly vital in leadership roles, especially within technology-driven organizations, where cultivating team dynamics and fostering collaboration can be the difference between success and stagnation.

In the healthcare industry, for example, while AI can significantly enhance diagnostic accuracy, the essence of patient care hinges on robust emotional intelligence. The ability to connect with patients empathetically, convey complex medical information transparently, and address emotional and psychological needs are essential components of care that technology cannot replicate.

Adaptability and Lifelong Learning stand out as arguably the most crucial skills in our fast-paced technological landscape. The relentless advancement of AI and related fields demands a workforce that not only recognizes the importance of staying informed but actively seeks out opportunities for continuous professional development. As job roles evolve, so too must the knowledge and competencies of individuals. Initiatives like massive open online courses (MOOCs) and in-house training programs play a vital role in facilitating this lifelong learning journey.

Consider the transformation occurring in the retail sector, where augmented reality is revolutionizing the customer experience. Employees must be equipped not only to utilize these innovative tools but also to understand the strategic implications behind their use, necessitating a mindset geared toward ongoing education and flexibility in embracing new technologies.

Beyond individual skill sets, there is a growing need for competencies that effectively connect people with technology. Cross-disciplinary collaboration is becoming the norm, requiring professionals from diverse backgrounds to merge their expertise in tackling complex challenges. This collaborative environment calls for skills in cultural competence, effective communication, and project management, empowering teams to harness diverse perspectives to achieve shared objectives.

Lastly, ethical reasoning and decision-making have never been more critical, particularly as AI systems gain autonomy. Navigating the ethical implications of AI's impact demands a workforce adept at thoughtfully assessing moral dimensions and making decisions that align with societal values. This skill is especially crucial for roles that directly influence AI system design and deployment, such as data scientists or product managers in the tech sector.

In conclusion, the future workforce must be equipped with a rich tapestry of skills, including technical mastery, emotional awareness, adaptability, and ethical consideration. These competencies will not only help individuals keep pace with rapid technological advancements but also empower them to leverage these innovations for meaningful and sustainable progress. As educational institutions and industry leaders increasingly recognize the necessity of these skills, revamping curricula and implementing forward-thinking training initiatives will be vital in nurturing a capable and resilient workforce ready to meet the challenges of tomorrow.

The workplace is undergoing a remarkable transformation driven by the rise of AI agents, a change that is particularly striking in the context of remote work. This trend has gained extraordinary momentum in recent years, reflecting a profound shift in how organizations operate and manage their workforce beyond the confines of traditional office environments.

AI agents are not merely technological advancements; they represent a paradigm shift that enhances the remote work experience by automating routine tasks. This automation allows professionals to redirect their energies toward strategic and creative endeavors, thereby enriching the quality of work dynamics. For instance, consider AI-powered virtual assistants deployed within remote teams. These agents take on the responsibility of task management, scheduling, and follow-ups, significantly alleviating the cognitive burden carried by human employees.

A striking example of AI's transformative power in remote settings can be found in the customer service sector. Here, AI-driven chatbots can autonomously handle basic inquiries at any hour, liberating remote customer service representatives to address more complicated issues that require personal attention and empathy. This shift not only boosts operational efficiency but also enhances customer satisfaction by ensuring that complex queries receive the thoughtful engagement they deserve.

Moreover, AI agents facilitate collaborative efforts among distributed teams, ensuring seamless communication and data sharing among members located in diverse geographical locations. Advanced technologies, such as natural language processing (NLP) chatbots, can transcribe meetings, summarize discussions, and even provide recommendations based on historical data. This functionality not only sustains productivity but also fosters continuity in collaborative projects, regardless of the physical distance separating team members. Additionally, sentiment analysis features allow these intelligent agents to gauge team morale and engagement, offering managers valuable insights to cultivate a positive work culture, even amidst predominantly virtual interactions.

The impact of AI in remote work extends well beyond enhancing productivity. It significantly influences corporate culture and team dynamics. AI-driven analytics equip remote managers with insights into work patterns, enabling them to identify employees who may be either overburdened or underutilized. This capability facilitates the equitable distribution of workloads and promotes a healthier work-life balance—an essential consideration in remote environments, where the absence of direct, face-to-face interactions can often obscure workload imbalances.

The realm of cybersecurity exemplifies another critical area where AI agents play a vital role in securing remote work environments. As organizations increasingly rely on cloud platforms and virtual networks, the potential for cybersecurity threats grows. AI agents bolster organizational defenses by continuously monitoring network traffic, identifying anomalies, and neutralizing potential breaches before they escalate into serious threats. These protective measures are indispensable for safeguarding sensitive corporate data, maintaining trust, and ensuring business continuity, particularly when the workforce is predominantly operating remotely.

Despite their myriad benefits, the integration of AI agents into remote work settings does present challenges. Concerns around surveillance and data privacy can arise, necessitating a careful balance between operational efficiency and employee trust. To navigate this delicate landscape, organizations must prioritize transparency.

As these changes ripple through the workplace, educational institutions are responding by equipping the workforce with essential skills for thriving in AI-enhanced and remote environments. Professional development programs increasingly emphasize digital literacy, data analysis, and technology ethics—skills that are becoming indispensable in the modern work landscape.

In summary, AI agents are reshaping the remote work experience by blending automation with human collaboration, paving the way for flexible, efficient, and secure work environments. As these trends continue to evolve, the future of work is poised to be increasingly decentralized and digitally supported, driven by an inspiring synergy between human intellect and artificial intelligence.

AI agents are not merely enhancing existing workflows; they are actively creating a wealth of new roles and career pathways that were once relegated to the realm of science fiction. As these technologies evolve and expand their capabilities, they catalyze innovative ecosystems that harbor jobs reflecting a unique blend of human creativity and artificial intelligence. This dynamic relationship paves the way for transformative change across various industries, symbolizing a new era of work that calls for adaptability, vision, and collaboration.

Among the most captivating new positions is that of the AI Trainer. Just as humans learn through experience, AI systems depend on rigorous training to enhance their performance and precision. AI Trainers curate and annotate expansive datasets, playing a vital role in refining algorithms. Their expertise ensures that AI agents can accurately interpret and respond to data. Take, for instance, the intricacies involved in developing language models; AI Trainers guide these systems in understanding the subtleties of human language, significantly advancing natural language processing capabilities. Their work is essential in ensuring that AI applications are both effective and contextually aware, bridging the gap between machine responsiveness and human expectation.

Another fascinating role that has emerged is the AI Interaction Designer. As we witness an increasing demand for seamless human-AI collaboration, the design of interactive experiences becomes crucial. These professionals are tasked with crafting intuitive user interfaces that facilitate smooth and effective interactions with AI agents. They draw upon a diverse skill set that encompasses human-computer interaction, psychology, and design principles. Imagine a healthcare virtual assistant that helps patients navigate the often daunting process of scheduling appointments; AI Interaction Designers ensure that each conversation is natural, fluid, and adaptable to a variety of user needs, enhancing patient engagement and satisfaction.

Amid the rapid advancements in AI, the role of the Ethics Consultant has emerged as vital. In sectors heavily reliant on AI, these professionals work diligently to ensure that implementations align with ethical standards and do not inadvertently cause harm to individuals or communities. They address pressing issues such as bias in algorithmic decision-making and safeguarding consumer privacy, advocating for responsible AI practices that prioritize societal welfare.

The growing influence of AI on decision-making processes has led to the rise of AI Forensic Analysts—a critical role in the realms of cybersecurity and legal compliance. As organizations increasingly automate complex decisions, understanding the roots of errors becomes essential. AI Forensic Analysts investigate data trails and operational methodologies, reconstructing the decision-making pathways of AI agents. In the event of system malfunctions or breaches, they seek forensic evidence to establish accountability and formulate strategies to prevent recurrence, thereby bolstering trust in AI systems.

Furthermore, organizations are now recognizing the importance of AI Systems Managers, who serve as the vital link between technical teams and operational objectives. These professionals oversee the integration of AI into workflow processes, ensuring that technological solutions align with business goals while also adhering to regulatory standards. Balancing technical expertise with strategic foresight, AI Systems Managers optimize AI applications in diverse environments. For example, in a manufacturing facility, they might calibrate AI-enabled machinery to maximize efficiency and output, all while ensuring compliance with industry regulations that protect worker safety and product quality.

Lastly, the rapid evolution of AI technology has given rise to the need for AI Policy Advisors. Both governments and corporations now seek insightful analysis regarding the policy implications of AI advancements. These advisors track global AI trends and regulatory developments, helping organizations navigate complex political landscapes. Their input can shape policies that harmonize innovation with public interests, whether advising multinational corporations on strategic initiatives or assisting lawmakers in crafting legislation that balances the benefits of AI with ethical governance.

These emerging roles illuminate the expansive possibilities AI brings to the job market, underscoring the necessity for new skill sets that integrate technical expertise with creative thinking, ethics, and strategic insight. As the workforce adapts to accommodate these roles, educational systems that emphasize interdisciplinary learning will play a crucial part in preparing future professionals to thrive in environments enriched by AI.

In summary, AI agents are not just reshaping the workforce; they are paving the path for diverse and transformative career opportunities across industries. Embracing these evolving roles is vital for individuals and organizations aiming to excel in an AI-driven future—one filled with unprecedented advancements and societal progress. As these careers continue to develop, they represent an exhilarating intersection of technology, creativity, and human aspiration, inviting us to explore the limitless potential of what lies ahead.

The integration of AI agents into the workplace has catalyzed a profound transformation in employee sentiment, revealing a complex tapestry of reactions that blend hope and skepticism. As organizations increasingly adopt AI technologies, the relationships between human workers and machines are evolving, necessitating a deeper examination of how employees perceive and adapt to this technological revolution.

At the outset, the introduction of AI in work environments sparks a diverse range of emotions. On one hand, there's palpable enthusiasm for the potential of AI to drive efficiency and innovation. Many employees welcome the opportunity to relinquish tedious, repetitive tasks, thus redirecting their focus towards more strategic and creative engagements. For example, in a customer service context, AI-powered chatbots can adeptly manage routine inquiries, freeing human agents to tackle complex customer situations that necessitate empathy and nuanced understanding—areas where human expertise remains irreplaceable.

Conversely, concerns about job loss due to automation persist as a significant anxiety for employees. Those in roles heavily reliant on repetitive tasks often view AI as an existential threat to their job security. This fear, while not without merit —as certain tasks are indeed ripe for automation—can be mitigated by proactive measures. Innovative organizations are stepping up, actively reskilling and upskilling their workforce to prepare them for more advanced, fulfilling roles. For instance, in a manufacturing setting embracing automation, robots may handle assembly line duties, yet the company simultaneously invests in training its workforce to oversee these robotic processes, troubleshoot issues, and enhance production efficiency.

The perception of AI as a collaborator rather than a competitor is critical in shaping employee sentiment. How AI systems are designed and integrated significantly influences whether workers view these technologies as complementary tools or as replacements that devalue their contributions. When AI is introduced transparently and inclusively, employees are more likely to embrace it as an ally. A case in point can be seen in the financial sector, where AI-driven data analytics provide insightful market forecasts. This allows employees to make informed, strategic decisions rather than getting bogged down in time-consuming data mining.

Communication serves as another essential element in molding employee attitudes towards AI integration. Open discussions regarding the goals of AI deployment, its anticipated impacts, and the measures in place to preserve jobs can significantly reduce uncertainty and build trust among the workforce. Organizations that actively involve employees in the AI adoption process cultivate a culture of innovation and collaboration, decreasing resistance and uniting the workforce around a shared vision of harnessing technology for positive outcomes. For example, a retail company that employs AI to optimize inventory management can enhance accuracy while ensuring employees feel a sense of ownership by inviting them to participate in selecting and testing AI solutions.

Moreover, the ethical implementation of AI profoundly impacts employee sentiment. Concerns regarding data privacy and surveillance can erode trust if employees feel their personal information is at risk or may be used without their consent. It is crucial for organizations to adopt proactive strategies, such as implementing comprehensive data privacy policies and securing employee consent, to maintain trust and reinforce the notion of AI as a responsible partner within the workplace.

Success stories from organizations that have effectively navigated AI integration highlight the significance of creating a working environment where human intelligence and AI capabilities coexist harmoniously rather than in opposition. When technology is seen as a catalyst for professional growth, rather than a disruptive force, employee sentiment tends to shift positively. For instance, in healthcare, AI systems that swiftly analyze medical images allow doctors to allocate more time to patient care—an adjustment that not only enriches job satisfaction but also significantly enhances patient outcomes.

In conclusion, employee sentiment toward AI integration is inherently intricate, influenced by individual experiences, organizational contexts, and the broader ramifications of technological progress. Embracing this technological shift not only enhances operational efficiency but also aligns human and artificial capabilities toward a shared aspiration: achieving increased productivity and satisfaction in a world enhanced by AI.

As the workplace undergoes profound transformations with the advent of AI agents, the necessity for continuous learning and adaptation has surfaced as a fundamental driver of success for both individuals and organizations. This imperative resonates across all sectors, revolutionizing traditional career trajectories and introducing fresh dynamics within various industries.

In today's fast-paced environment, continuous learning has become essential for remaining relevant. Employees are no longer simply required to acquire new skills; they must also foster a mindset that embraces change and innovation in the face of unexpected challenges. A thriving learning culture— one that prioritizes curiosity and encourages experimentation —fuels this adaptability. Consequently, conventional educational frameworks are increasingly being enhanced by cutting-edge training methodologies designed to keep pace with technological advancements.

Take the software development industry, for example. With programming languages and development frameworks consistently evolving, engineers find themselves in a constant state of professional growth. Leading tech companies, such as Google and Microsoft, recognize this critical need and provide their teams with versatile learning opportunities. This proactive approach ensures that developers are equipped not just to meet today's demands but also to anticipate tomorrow's challenges.

Beyond individual skill enhancement, organizations must also revisit and reshape their structures, workflows, and strategies to fully harness the potential of AI integration. In sectors like finance, the shift toward machine learning algorithms has ushered in a new era of data-driven decision-making. Here, employees are encouraged to refine their analytical and problem-solving abilities to complement the capabilities of AI systems. This evolution not only enhances productivity but also elevates the role of employees, enabling them to become facilitators of AI-generated insights and strategic recommendations.

The healthcare sector provides another compelling illustration of the importance of continuous learning. With the integration of AI innovations—such as predictive diagnostics and personalized treatment plans—medical professionals are actively engaging in ongoing education to effectively utilize these advanced tools. For instance, AI-driven platforms that sift through extensive patient data require clinicians to hone their data literacy in addition to their medical expertise. To bridge the gap between technology and traditional practice, many healthcare institutions frequently organize workshops and simulated scenarios, enabling physicians to practice incorporating AI findings into their patient consultations.

Leadership plays a pivotal role in fostering an environment conducive to continuous learning. Visionary leaders understand the significance of cultivating a growth mindset within their teams and often establish policies that support and incentivize learning initiatives. This support not only encompasses formal training programs but also encourages informal knowledge sharing, creating a culture where employees feel empowered to exchange insights and innovative breakthroughs. Organizations implementing such strategies tend to exhibit greater agility and resilience when faced with technological disruptions.

Of course, the journey toward a culture of continuous learning is not without its challenges. Companies must address issues such as resource allocation for training programs and resistance from individuals hesitant to embrace change. Creating a supportive infrastructure that provides dedicated time and access to educational opportunities can help mitigate these challenges. Cisco's "Learning@Cisco" program serves as a noteworthy example of this approach, granting employees specific hours for skill development, coupled with expert guidance and a comprehensive library of learning materials.

Importantly, the concept of continuous learning extends to AI systems themselves, underscoring the need for adaptable design. Machine learning models, for instance, require ongoing refinement to maintain efficacy, typically achieved through processes like reinforcement learning, wherein AI systems evolve by learning from real-world feedback. This need for growth mirrors the human experience; both the workforce and AI agents must continually adapt to unlock their full potential.

In summary, the narrative surrounding continuous learning and adaptation highlights the symbiotic relationship between humans and AI agents. This proactive approach not only enhances operational capabilities but also strengthens an organization's capacity for innovation, paving the way for transformative growth in an AI-augmented future.

In today's rapidly evolving organizational landscape, effective leadership strategies for teams augmented by artificial intelligence (AI) have become essential for achieving sustainable success. As AI technologies transform traditional workplace roles and enhance operational efficiencies, leaders are challenged to create an integrated environment where human ingenuity and machine intelligence work in concert. This intricate balance demands a deep understanding of both technological advancements and the invaluable human element that drives innovation.

One of the foremost strategies for leaders is to foster a collaborative culture that views AI as a partner rather than a competitor. This begins with reshaping perceptions of AI among team members, promoting the idea that these technologies empower rather than displace human talent. Leaders can showcase how AI enhances human roles by automating mundane tasks, thereby liberating employees to engage in more creative and strategic endeavors. A noteworthy example is Google's approach to optimizing its advertising operations, where machine learning algorithms handle extensive data analysis. This not only improves efficiency but allows talented teams to channel their energies into crafting compelling ad campaigns.

Transparency is another foundational element of effective leadership when deploying AI technologies. In sectors like finance, where AI-powered risk assessment tools are becoming commonplace, it is critical for leaders to elucidate how these technologies enhance, rather than undermine, decision-making processes. Such clarity encourages team members to embrace AI systems enthusiastically, leading to improved performance and collaboration.

In addition, inclusive decision-making can significantly

enhance AI-enhanced teams by capitalizing on diverse viewpoints. Leaders should actively cultivate cross-functional teams and stimulate open discussions that incorporate a range of perspectives. IBM exemplifies this approach with its commitment to multidisciplinary teams in developing AI solutions.

Continuous learning is a vital pillar in the strategies employed by leaders of AI-augmented teams. Leaders must champion lifelong education by promoting ongoing skill development initiatives and providing access to resources that foster AI-related competencies. Pfizer, for example, has instituted internal training programs that empower its research teams to leverage AI in drug discovery, significantly accelerating the innovation process and enhancing competitive advantage.

Additionally, creating an agile organizational structure is paramount in adapting to the fast-paced nature of AI technologies. Flexibility in team configurations and project scopes enables organizations to swiftly respond to emerging AI capabilities and market fluctuations. Agile methodologies are increasingly adopted by innovative companies like Spotify, which utilizes squad-based teams to seamlessly integrate AI tools into personalized music experiences.

Encouraging a culture of experimentation is another effective strategy for enhancing team dynamics in AI environments. A prime example is 3M's "15% Time" policy, which encourages employees to dedicate a portion of their workweek to pursuing experimental projects, resulting in groundbreaking innovations that often incorporate AI technologies.

Moreover, emotional intelligence and clear communication are crucial qualities for leaders managing AI-enhanced teams. Recognizing and addressing employees' emotional responses to AI integration can play a vital role in reducing resistance. Leaders should employ coaching and feedback mechanisms to align team motivations with organizational AI strategies

—an approach effectively utilized by Salesforce through its executive mentoring programs.

Finally, leaders must commit to continuously evaluating and recalibrating their AI strategies to stay in harmony with evolving business objectives and ethical considerations. This entails remaining vigilant about technological advancements and assessing how AI implementations align with the organization's mission. Leaders who engage with external discussions and policy frameworks are better positioned to guide their teams in responsibly leveraging AI's capabilities.

In summary, leading AI-enhanced teams is a multifaceted endeavor that marries technological proficiency with the human spirit of innovation. Through these strategies, organizations unlock the full potential of their AI initiatives while cultivating resilient teams poised to thrive in an ever-evolving future.

As artificial intelligence continues to weave its way into workplaces around the globe, prioritizing safety and promoting ethical practices have become crucial in navigating this transformative landscape. The challenge lies not only in leveraging AI to enhance operational efficiency but also ensuring its alignment with core ethical principles. This combined focus presents a unique opportunity to foster work environments where innovation flourishes in tandem with essential human values.

To effectively maintain workplace safety in the context of AI adoption, it is vital to conduct thorough risk assessments of AI systems. This process should begin during the design and deployment stages, identifying potential failure points and vulnerabilities. For example, consider the manufacturing sector, where AI-driven robots are increasingly used to automate repetitive tasks. In such environments, it is essential to implement robust safety measures that prevent collisions and equipment failures. Regular safety drills and alignment checks can play a significant role in minimizing risks and creating a safer work environment for all employees.

Alongside safety measures, the integration of ethical principles into organizational AI policies is paramount. Establishing frameworks for transparency and accountability helps build trust among employees and stakeholders alike. Take, for example, the rise of AI-powered performance monitoring tools across various industries. While these tools can provide valuable insights into productivity, they must be accompanied by clear guidelines to prevent misuse and protect employee privacy. Organizations embracing AI in performance evaluation must delineate transparent policies that balance the need for operational efficiency with respect for individual privacy rights.

In sensitive sectors such as healthcare, the need for ethical rigor becomes even more pronounced. AI algorithms used in diagnostics and patient management must adhere to the highest ethical standards. The risk of bias arising from skewed training data can result in misguided recommendations, potentially harming vulnerable patient groups. Consequently, healthcare organizations must establish extensive validation mechanisms and conduct ongoing audits of their AI systems to ensure equitable and non-discriminatory care delivery.

To successfully uphold both safety and ethical standards, organizations should promote the involvement of diverse perspectives in AI development. Engaging a wide range of stakeholders—including technologists, ethicists, and frontline employees—can lead to comprehensive risk assessments and informed ethical guidelines. Microsoft's AI, Ethics, and Effects in Engineering and Research (AETHER) Committee is a prime example of this collaborative approach.

Moreover, nurturing a culture of continuous ethical education is essential. As AI technologies evolve, so too should the ethical understanding of those who design and manage them. Implementing training initiatives focused on ethical AI practices and safety protocols empowers team members to identify and confront emerging ethical challenges proactively. These educational efforts could include workshops or e-learning modules exploring case studies relevant to the industry context, effectively preparing employees for the complexities that come with AI integration.

Regulatory compliance is another critical facet of ensuring workplace safety and ethical AI deployment. Organizations must stay updated on shifting legal standards and weave compliance measures into their AI strategies. For instance, the European Union's General Data Protection Regulation (GDPR) imposes stringent requirements on data protection and privacy, particularly for AI systems handling personal data. Companies operating within or alongside the EU must ensure their AI implementations are compliant with GDPR, safeguarding data integrity and promoting ethical conduct.

An innovative approach involves continuously monitoring and adapting to technological advancements that bolster safety and ethical compliance. Emerging innovations such as explainable AI (XAI) can significantly enhance transparency in AI systems, illuminating decision-making processes and fostering user trust.

Ultimately, the quest for workplace safety and ethical AI integration requires a cohesive strategy that merges technical expertise with ethical foresight. Empowering teams to prioritize these dimensions is fundamental to preserving the integrity of AI systems, creating environments where technology not only enhances human capabilities but also steadfastly safeguards well-being and core values. Through intentional actions and dedicated leadership, organizations can unlock the transformative potential of AI while upholding safety and benefiting society at large.

As we look ahead to the rapidly evolving job market shaped

by artificial intelligence (AI), several transformative trends are coming into focus. These trends are not only reshaping industries but also redefining the roles within them. To successfully navigate this seismic shift, it is essential to understand the underlying forces at work and to leverage the principles guiding this evolution.

The integration of AI across various sectors is set to redefine traditional job roles while also creating entirely new career paths. Take, for example, the healthcare industry: while conventional diagnostic methods continue to be vital, AI is revolutionizing patient care through telemedicine. This shift has given rise to specialized positions such as AI-driven health consultants, who are adept at interpreting complex data outputs and providing remote patient advice. These roles require a unique blend of medical knowledge and technical expertise, underscoring the growing demand for professionals who can bridge healthcare and data analytics.

In the manufacturing sector, AI's impact is equally profound. The rise of smart factories marks a significant transition from manual labor to sophisticated oversight of AI-powered machinery. Workers are evolving into roles that emphasize data analysis and machine maintenance rather than traditional manufacturing tasks. Technicians are now becoming data scientists and AI specialists, focusing on optimizing production processes through predictive maintenance and real-time analytics. To thrive in this new environment, training programs aimed at reskilling the workforce are essential, empowering employees to adapt and excel alongside evolving technologies.

The financial services industry illustrates another facet of this transformation, as algorithmic trading and AI-driven credit scoring reshape the landscape. Financial analysts, who once focused primarily on data collection and interpretation, are increasingly expected to wield AI tools to refine decision-making processes and generate strategic insights from advanced data analysis. This shift necessitates professionals who possess both financial literacy and a solid understanding of machine learning principles.

In this evolving landscape, organizations must prioritize the development of soft skills among their workforce. Abilities such as empathy, communication, and leadership will increasingly set human workers apart in an AI-driven environment. As AI takes over technical and routine tasks, the demand for human intelligence in areas that require emotional connection and critical thought becomes more pronounced. This presents an invaluable opportunity for fostering continuous learning initiatives that emphasize these essential skills and promote holistic skill development.

Education systems will play a pivotal role in preparing individuals for this dynamic job market. Curricula must integrate AI literacy, encouraging students to engage with technology as creators rather than mere consumers. Both K-12 and higher education programs should strive to blend STEM (Science, Technology, Engineering, and Mathematics) education with the humanities. This interdisciplinary approach will help cultivate graduates who are well-equipped to address the complex challenges of the future workforce.

Furthermore, the rise of AI may give birth to entirely new sectors, such as AI ethics management. As AI becomes increasingly ubiquitous, organizations will need individuals who can navigate the delicate ethical considerations surrounding AI deployment—ensuring that technology is used responsibly while maximizing its potential benefits. This burgeoning field presents significant opportunities for those with expertise in technology and ethics.

A collective effort from governments, educational institutions, and organizations will be essential to facilitate these transitions smoothly. Policy frameworks designed to foster skill development and ensure equitable access to reskilling resources are critical. For example, initiatives in countries like Singapore that promote lifelong learning and professional development serve as strong models for effectively adapting to this transformative era, allowing the workforce to embrace new job roles that incorporate AI seamlessly.

In the broader socio-economic context, the implications of AI on job markets could prompt a rethink of economic structures. Concepts such as universal basic income, initially conceived to address potential job displacement, are gaining traction as feasible strategies for ensuring livelihoods in an AI-enhanced world. Engaging with these ideas reflects a proactive and adaptive approach to policymaking—one that seeks to construct an environment where technological advances contribute to human flourishing.

In conclusion, anticipating the future job market amidst the evolution of AI demands a nuanced understanding of these intersecting domains. The synergy between artificial intelligence and human creativity holds the promise of an employment landscape transformed, filled with opportunities for innovation and growth. Successfully navigating this new terrain will require flexibility, a commitment to continuous learning, and adherence to ethical practices, ensuring that the future is characterized by a harmonious collaboration between humans and machines for shared advancement.

CHAPTER 8: INNOVATIONS DRIVING AI AGENT EVOLUTION

The rapid evolution of artificial intelligence owes much to significant advancements in algorithm development, which serve as the foundation for AI agents' growing capabilities. Each breakthrough not only enhances these agents' functionalities but also empowers them to tackle increasingly sophisticated tasks with remarkable precision and efficiency. To truly appreciate the impact of these innovations, it's essential to explore several pivotal areas that have shaped the landscape of AI.

A transformative leap has been made in the realm of deep learning, facilitated by the emergence of advanced neural network architectures. Convolutional Neural Networks (CNNs), for instance, have revolutionized computer vision, equipping AI agents with the ability to recognize and classify images almost with human-like accuracy. This evolution is particularly evident in fields like medical imaging, where algorithms can detect abnormalities in X-rays or MRIs with impressive proficiency. A standout example is Google's DeepMind, which showcased a deep learning system capable of identifying over 50 types of eye diseases with a level of accuracy that surpasses that of seasoned ophthalmologists.

Natural Language Processing (NLP) has also undergone a remarkable transformation, driven by innovative algorithms. The inception of transformer models, such as BERT (Bidirectional Encoder Representations from Transformers) and GPT (Generative Pre-trained Transformer), has fundamentally altered the way AI agents interpret and generate human language. These models employ attention mechanisms that allow them to evaluate the significance of each word within a sentence, enabling the production of coherent, contextually aware text. In practical terms, consider a customer service AI agent powered by a GPT-like model. This smart assistant not only engages users with conversational ease but also comprehends nuanced inquiries and delivers personalized responses, thus significantly elevating customer satisfaction and overall user experience.

Reinforcement learning algorithms stand out for their capacity to emulate behavioral psychology principles in optimizing decision-making through trial and error. A prime illustration of this capability can be found in AlphaGo, developed by DeepMind, which utilized reinforcement learning to triumph over world champions in the ancient board game Go. This innovative approach allows algorithms to learn from extensive gameplay data, refining strategies by simulating the outcomes of various moves. The implications of reinforcement learning stretch beyond gaming; they are now being integrated into autonomous vehicle navigation systems, where real-time assessments of driving strategies adapts to varied road conditions and challenges.

The introduction of Generative Adversarial Networks (GANs) has ushered in a new era of creative AI. In the creative industries, GANs are being harnessed to generate artistic designs or produce high-quality synthetic data for training models, effectively addressing data privacy concerns and ethical considerations.

Moreover, the exploration of neuromorphic computing is pushing the boundaries of algorithmic advancements. This innovative field seeks to replicate the human brain's architecture, offering the potential to significantly enhance the processing efficiency of AI agents. Such advancements are particularly vital in applications requiring instantaneous responses, like robotics or Internet of Things (IoT) devices. Algorithms tailored for neuromorphic systems may pave the way for AI agents with lower energy consumption while executing complex computations—an essential development in the quest for sustainable technology.

In conclusion, the recent breakthroughs in algorithm development are inextricably linked to the capabilities of AI agents. Through innovations in deep learning, natural language processing, reinforcement learning, and generative models, the spectrum of applications continues to broaden across healthcare, customer service, entertainment, and various other sectors. These advancements are far from theoretical; they are yielding substantial enhancements in efficiency, accuracy, and user engagement. As the realm of algorithms continues to advance, we can anticipate even more groundbreaking innovations that will refine and deepen the sophistication of AI, shaping the future of intelligent agents in ways we can scarcely imagine today.

Advancements in computer vision mark an exhilarating era in the realm of artificial intelligence, empowering machines to interpret and understand visual data with unparalleled accuracy and versatility. At the heart of this exciting evolution are several groundbreaking techniques that have radically transformed the way AI systems perceive their surroundings. These innovations have permeated various industries— including healthcare, automotive, retail, and entertainment— creating a ripple effect that changes how we interact with technology.

A cornerstone of this evolution is the enhancement of convolutional neural networks (CNNs). These sophisticated deep learning models have been a game-changer in image recognition tasks. Unlike traditional methods that rely on manual feature extraction, CNNs are designed to automatically learn from and interpret the input data, allowing for the identification of intricate patterns with remarkable efficiency. For instance, in the realm of autonomous vehicles, industry leaders such as Tesla and Waymo utilize cutting-edge vision systems powered by CNNs. These systems enable cars to interpret their real-time environments—detecting road signs, recognizing pedestrians, and assessing the behaviors of other vehicles.

Another significant leap in computer vision is the rise of real-time video analysis. Innovative tools have emerged that can recognize and track objects in motion, offering transformative applications in diverse fields. A prime example can be observed in sports analytics, where companies like Second Spectrum provide teams and coaches with intricate insights derived from live game footage. Their computer vision algorithms meticulously monitor player movements, ball trajectories, and tactical formations, delivering crucial analytics that inform coaching strategies and training regimens. This level of analysis not only enriches the understanding of sports performance but also sets a new standard for coaching precision.

The synergy between computer vision and augmented reality (AR) is also dramatically reshaping user interactions across various platforms. Take IKEA's mobile app, for example, which utilizes AR technology to enhance customer engagement. This innovative application allows users to visualize furniture within their own homes before making a purchase. This immersive experience not only empowers customers to make informed buying decisions but also enhances overall satisfaction, illustrating how computer vision can elevate the retail experience.

Face recognition technology is another prominent area showcasing significant advancements within computer vision. Improvements in algorithms now enable more reliable identification, even under challenging conditions such as low light or unusual angles. This technology has been adopted by airports and security agencies to expedite passenger processing without compromising safety protocols. However, its extensive use—especially in countries like China—raises important questions about privacy and ethical considerations surrounding surveillance and data management. This highlights a complex interplay between efficiency and ethical dilemmas, underscoring the dual-edged nature of these advancements.

The introduction of unsupervised learning methodologies has further redefined traditional data labeling and training approaches within computer vision. As manually labeled datasets can be labor-intensive and sparse, algorithms that leverage unstructured data are opening new avenues for model training. Researchers are increasingly exploring self-supervised learning techniques, where models autonomously discern patterns and characteristics from unlabeled images. This innovation has the potential to significantly expand the scope of computer vision applications, particularly in areas where traditional labeling proves cumbersome, such as satellite imagery analysis or the interpretation of surveillance footage.

Lastly, the integration of computer vision with edge computing is enhancing the responsiveness and efficiency of AI agents in real-time applications. For example, smart cameras equipped with built-in processing capabilities can analyze video feeds for anomalies or recognize specific events without relying on remote cloud processing. In retail environments, these intelligent cameras can monitor inventory levels and customer behavior instantaneously, providing actionable insights that empower swift decision-making and operational optimizations.

As we navigate these monumental advancements in computer vision, it is crucial to recognize their broader societal and ethical implications. From enhancing healthcare diagnostics to optimizing athletic performance through live analytics, the potential applications are vast and varied. Striking a balance between technological innovation and ethical responsibility will be essential as we forge ahead in this dynamic field.

Speech recognition technology has evolved dramatically, fundamentally reshaping the dynamics of communication between humans and machines. This rapid progression is largely attributed to breakthroughs in deep learning, marked by the implementation of recurrent neural networks (RNNs) and more recently, transformer architectures. As a result, artificial intelligence (AI) systems have become significantly more adept at interpreting spoken language, responding in increasingly natural and intuitive ways that facilitate smoother interactions.

One of the most significant advances in speech recognition has been the transition from traditional Gaussian Mixture Models (GMMs) to sophisticated neural network-based approaches. Initially, GMMs depended heavily on predefined acoustic models, which constrained their ability to adapt to variations in accents, intonation, and background noise. In contrast, contemporary neural network systems, particularly those employing long short-term memory (LSTM) networks, thrive on sequential data processing and accurately capture the temporal dependencies inherent in speech. This adaptability allows these systems to learn from diverse datasets, culminating in improved recognition rates across various speakers and environments. Industry leaders such as Google and Microsoft are harnessing these advancements in their virtual assistants, providing users with increasingly precise transcriptions and contexts during interactions.

The real-world implications of these technological enhancements are profound. In the healthcare sector, integrated voice recognition systems are revolutionizing patient documentation by seamlessly transcribing spoken language into electronic health records (EHR). This innovative approach not only accelerates the documentation process but also minimizes the errors often associated with manual data input. Technologies like Nuance's Dragon Medical One utilize advanced speech recognition algorithms specifically tailored for clinical language, empowering healthcare professionals to efficiently dictate notes and focus more on patient care rather than administrative burdens.

Beyond healthcare, the influence of voice-activated AI extends into customer service, where automated conversational agents are enhancing user experiences. Notably, Amazon's Alexa exemplifies this evolution, delivering accurate responses to a wide range of user inquiries—whether it's fetching information, playing music, or controlling smart home devices.

Moreover, the advancements in speech recognition technology are significantly improving accessibility for individuals with disabilities. Speech-to-text applications allow those with hearing impairments to communicate more effectively by transforming spoken language into written text in real-time. Innovations like Ava exemplify this mission, enabling users to participate in conversations without barriers. Such technological applications highlight the transformative power of AI in creating more inclusive environments.

Furthermore, the integration of context-aware capabilities marks a notable progression in speech recognition. Modern AI systems are designed not only to recognize individual words but also to comprehend contextual cues. For instance, in noisy environments such as bustling cafes or crowded conferences, advanced noise-cancellation techniques come into play.

Companies like Apple have incorporated these technologies in Siri, utilizing multiple microphones to enhance directionality and filter out ambient sounds, resulting in clearer communication even in challenging settings.

In an increasingly interconnected world, tech giants are also prioritizing multilingual and cross-language functionalities to broaden accessibility. Google Translate, for example, has made significant strides in real-time translation, enabling smooth communication between speakers of different languages. Through the employment of sophisticated neural networks, these applications facilitate seamless conversational exchanges, fostering richer connections and collaborations across diverse cultures.

However, alongside these remarkable advancements, the ethical considerations surrounding speech recognition technology are paramount. The pervasive use of such systems raises legitimate concerns regarding privacy and data security. As speech recognition technologies often gather substantial amounts of audio data, there is a risk of unintentionally storing sensitive information. To address these challenges, it is essential to establish stringent privacy protocols and maintain transparency in data handling, ensuring protection against potential misuse.

As speech recognition technology continues to advance, we are entering an era where voice may become the primary interface for technology interaction. The future is brimming with possibilities, with AI agents poised to engage in more fluid dialogues and interpret human emotions through tonal variations and speech patterns. These capabilities could revolutionize various industries, from entertainment to mental health, offering tailored experiences that resonate deeply with individual users.

As we navigate the evolving landscape of speech recognition, it is evident that the sophistication of AI systems is advancing rapidly, guided by both scientific innovations and a commitment to human-centered design principles. The potential for more interactive and responsive systems is ever-growing, underscoring the importance of recognizing both the technical and social ramifications of these technologies. Ultimately, the goal is to ensure that speech recognition remains a tool for empowerment—fostering meaningful connections, elevating everyday interactions, and championing inclusivity in our diverse and interconnected society.

Quantum computing is on the brink of revolutionizing a multitude of fields, particularly artificial intelligence (AI), by introducing capabilities far beyond the reach of conventional computers. Harnessing the principles of quantum mechanics, these advanced machines possess the ability to process and analyze enormous volumes of data at unparalleled speeds, opening up new avenues for problem-solving and optimization. As we explore the intersection of quantum computing and AI more deeply, it becomes increasingly evident that this technological evolution could drastically enhance the abilities of AI agents across various applications.

One of the most captivating features of quantum computing is its use of qubits, which represent a significant departure from traditional bits. While a classical bit can either be a 0 or a 1, a qubit can exist in a state of superposition, embodying both values simultaneously until it is measured. This extraordinary property enables quantum computers to conduct multiple calculations in parallel, allowing AI systems to tackle complex tasks with remarkable efficiency.

Take, for example, the optimization challenges that frequently arise in logistics and supply chain management. Classical algorithms often falter in these scenarios, primarily due to the exponential increase in potential solutions as the problem's scale grows. Quantum algorithms, such as the Quantum Approximate Optimization Algorithm (QAOA), leverage the principles of superposition and entanglement to traverse vast solution spaces concurrently. Imagine a delivery company aiming to optimize its routes across a sprawling network of destinations—while a classical system may require extensive time and resources, a quantum computer could swiftly pinpoint the most efficient route, leading to significant savings in both fuel and time, thereby enhancing overall customer satisfaction.

Moreover, the potential of quantum computing to elevate machine learning algorithms is substantial. Quantum machine learning (QML) holds the promise of accelerating data processing speeds and improving the accuracy of predictive models. Algorithms like the Quantum Support Vector Machine (QSVM) can analyze and classify large datasets with greater efficacy than their classical counterparts. When trained on quantum data, these QML algorithms can surpass traditional methods, particularly excelling in complex pattern recognition tasks such as image classification and natural language processing.

Prominent tech giants like Google and IBM are pioneering efforts to integrate quantum computing with AI. Google's Quantum AI team has made strides in scaling their quantum processors, demonstrating that quantum algorithms may lead to groundbreaking advances across various domains, including drug discovery and climate modeling. Meanwhile, IBM's Quantum Experience platform empowers researchers to experiment with quantum algorithms, fostering a deeper understanding of how these novel computational techniques can be applied to AI.

However, the convergence of quantum computing and AI does not come without challenges. Constructing a scalable quantum computer is an engineering feat of monumental proportions, primarily due to the fragile nature of qubits, which are susceptible to environmental interference. Quantum decoherence—the loss of quantum information—

represents a significant obstacle to stable calculations. While advancements are underway, ensuring that quantum systems can function reliably in real-world applications is critical for their effective integration with AI technologies.

Additionally, as quantum-enhanced AI capabilities expand, ethical considerations must be taken into account. The unprecedented speed at which quantum computers can process and analyze data raises significant concerns regarding privacy and security. The potential for creating powerful AI systems that could inadvertently act against societal interests highlights the necessity for a robust ethical framework. It is imperative that the development of quantum-enhanced AI prioritizes these ethical risks while fostering innovation.

In summary, the synergy between quantum computing and artificial intelligence presents a promising frontier, with the potential to transform numerous industries. As researchers and industry leaders delve into this exciting relationship, they must remain vigilant in addressing both the technical hurdles and ethical dilemmas that may arise. The potential benefits are vast—ranging from the optimization of intricate systems to the enhancement of data analysis capabilities—quantum-enhanced AI could reshape the technological landscape in ways that resonate with humanistic values. Embracing this transformative potential requires a collaborative approach involving academia, industry, and regulatory agencies, ensuring that the evolution of AI is not only innovative but also responsible and equitable.

Advancements in AI Ethics Technology: Navigating the Future of Responsible Innovation

As artificial intelligence continues to evolve at a rapid pace, the integration of ethical considerations into AI systems has transitioned from a supplementary concern to a vital foundation. In a world where AI permeates diverse sectors —ranging from healthcare and finance to the arts—there is a heightened urgency for robust ethical frameworks. This discussion takes an in-depth look at the innovative practices that are defining ethical governance in AI, emphasizing practical applications and the need for interdisciplinary collaboration to ensure that technology resonates with societal values.

Ethical Algorithms: A Paradigm Shift in Decision-Making

One of the most significant innovations in AI ethics technology is the emergence of ethical algorithms. These algorithms not only analyze data but are consciously designed to incorporate ethical considerations into their decision-making processes. For instance, in the realm of law enforcement, facial recognition systems can be programmed to reduce biases against specific demographic groups.

Extensive research, such as those conducted by experts at MIT, has revealed alarming disparities in error rates when traditional algorithms are employed, especially across different demographic groups. The implementation of fairness-aware algorithms thus marks a transformative step toward cultivating more just AI systems that actively challenge societal biases.

The Rise of Explainable AI (XAI)

Another noteworthy advancement is the development of explainable AI (XAI). As AI assumes increasingly critical roles across various domains, the ability of these systems to provide transparent and comprehensible justifications for their decisions becomes paramount. For example, when a healthcare AI system analyzes medical images to diagnose conditions, it's essential for the technology to articulate its reasoning in terms understandable by medical professionals. This transparency not only promotes trust among users but also fortifies ethical adherence.

Techniques like attention mechanisms or feature visualization allow AI systems to pinpoint specific attributes of medical images that contributed to a diagnosis. This fosters accountability in clinical decision-making and helps healthcare providers better understand and trust the technology that guides their practices.

Bias Detection and Mitigation: Proactive Ethical Tools

Alongside these technical innovations, an increasing number of organizations are adopting tools designed for bias detection and mitigation within AI workflows. For example, Microsoft's Fairness Toolkit plays a critical role by enabling developers to audit AI applications for imbalances in treatment across diverse populations prior to deployment. Utilizing statistical analyses and algorithm adjustments based on audit findings allows organizations to proactively address ethical concerns. This proactive stance mitigates the risk of unintended harm before the AI system is introduced to end-users.

Establishing Ethical Governance: A Comprehensive Approach

In addition to technical advancements, there is a growing recognition of the importance of robust ethical governance frameworks within organizations. Companies such as Google have established AI ethics boards to scrutinize projects and ensure compliance with established ethical standards. These boards typically feature a diverse mix of stakeholders, including ethicists, technologists, and community representatives, whose varied perspectives are invaluable for informed decision-making. This multifaceted approach empowers organizations not only to innovate responsibly but also to hold themselves accountable when faced with ethical dilemmas.

Navigating the Challenges of Rapid Innovation

However, the rapid ascent of AI ethics technology does not come without its challenges. A key hurdle lies in striking the right balance between innovation and regulatory oversight. As AI technologies evolve swiftly, regulatory frameworks often find themselves lagging behind, leading to guidelines that can feel fragmented or ill-suited to address emerging ethical complexities. Industry leaders advocate for a collaborative engagement between technologists and policymakers to create flexible regulations that maintain ethical integrity amid ongoing advancements.

As AI systems increasingly operate with a degree of autonomy, questions surrounding accountability and liability become more intricate. In the case of a self-driving car involved in an accident, determining whether the manufacturer, software developers, or even the user holds responsibility is a contentious issue. This emphasizes the urgent need for clear legal and ethical standards to navigate accountability in AI, especially as these technologies integrate into critical societal functions.

Promoting Continuous Education and Ethical Awareness

Continuous education surrounding AI ethics is paramount. As these systems become integral to everyday life, fostering a culture of ethical awareness and ongoing learning within organizations is essential. Incorporating regular training on AI ethics, alongside discussions of ethical dilemmas, into corporate strategies prepares teams to effectively tackle the challenges that lie ahead.

In summary, the strides made in AI ethics technology are fundamentally transforming how organizations approach the development and deployment of AI systems. As AI continues its upward trajectory, the commitment to embedding ethical considerations will be crucial in ensuring that technology serves humanity positively and constructively. This intersection of technology and ethics is not merely a responsibility; it is a profound opportunity to redefine success in the era of intelligent systems.

Innovative Human-Computer Interfaces: Revolutionizing Interaction in the AI Era

The realm of human-computer interaction (HCI) is

experiencing a dynamic and transformative shift, significantly influenced by advancements in artificial intelligence. As AI becomes deeply woven into the fabric of our daily lives, these innovative interfaces are setting the stage for a new kind of interaction—one that is not just aesthetically pleasing or user-friendly, but fundamentally alters our relationship with technology. This evolution aims to create experiences that are more intuitive, inclusive, and highly responsive; an exploration of these pioneering interfaces unveils insights into the future of human-computer collaboration, one in which technology serves to enrich and enhance the human experience rather than complicate it.

Voice Interfaces: The Rise of Conversational Agents

One of the most notable advancements in HCI is the emergence of voice interfaces and conversational agents. Technologies like Amazon's Alexa, Google Assistant, and Apple's Siri illustrate the profound capabilities of natural language processing, allowing users to engage with devices using their own words. Gone are the days of sifting through complex menus; now, users can ask questions or issue commands fluidly, minimizing barriers and creating a seamless connection with technology.

For example, envision a scenario in a smart home. A user might simply say, "Set the thermostat to 72 degrees." The AI not only comprehends the command but connects to the appropriate device, executing the command without any manual input. This represents a revolutionary departure from traditional interfaces—a paradigm shift where technology molds itself to fit the user's natural preferences and behaviors instead of requiring users to conform to rigid systems.

Augmented Reality (AR) and Virtual Reality (VR): Immersive Experiences

The integration of augmented reality (AR) and virtual reality (VR) is redefining user interactions by creating deeply immersive experiences. These technologies blend the digital with the physical, opening doors to unprecedented levels of engagement. For instance, AR applications like Google Lens empower users to uncover information about their surroundings in real time—by merely pointing their smartphone cameras at objects, users can instantly learn about plant species, get navigation assistance, or even view product prices. Such functionalities enrich user understanding, making information not just available but engagingly interactive.

VR, meanwhile, is transforming domains such as education and training. Imagine medical students participating in simulated surgeries through VR, acquiring skills without the inherent risks of live procedures. This approach not only enhances their educational journey but also provides immediate feedback, aligning theoretical knowledge more closely with practical application.

Gesture-Based Interfaces: A Natural Evolution

The advent of gesture-based technology marks another exciting frontier in HCI. As exemplified by systems like Microsoft's Kinect, touchless interfaces allow users to control gadgets through their physical movements and facial recognition. This advancement is particularly significant in settings where conventional input methods may be impractical—such as operating rooms or for individuals with disabilities.

Consider a surgeon working in a hospital; with a gesture-based interface, they could manipulate surgical imaging software without compromising sterile conditions. This innovation highlights the power of collaboration between software developers and healthcare experts, showcasing how their combined efforts can yield solutions that genuinely cater to users' needs in complex environments.

Brain-Computer Interfaces (BCI): Bridging the Gap

Perhaps the most groundbreaking development in HCI is the emergence of brain-computer interfaces (BCI), which facilitate direct communication between the human brain and machines. Companies like Neuralink are at the forefront of this technology, focusing on assisting individuals with mobility impairments or neurological disorders. With carefully implanted sensors, these interfaces allow patients to control devices simply by contemplating desired movements, such as moving a cursor or navigating a robotic arm.

Imagine a person living with amyotrophic lateral sclerosis (ALS) using a BCI to create messages or adjust their living environment just by thinking about it. This astonishing advancement breaks through traditional barriers, opening up new avenues for independence and interaction. While the technology is still largely experimental, its potential to reshape human interaction with devices is extraordinary.

Emphasizing Inclusivity and Accessibility

As we delve deeper into the realm of innovative human-computer interfaces, prioritizing inclusivity and accessibility is imperative. Every new technology should serve a diverse array of users, especially those with disabilities or neurodiverse conditions. Adhering to user-centered design principles is essential; technologies must be developed with the unique needs of varied user populations in mind to ensure equitable access.

For instance, initiatives like SignAll are pioneering AI-powered systems that translate sign language into text and speech, effectively bridging communication gaps for the deaf and hard-of-hearing communities. These innovations are not only technically impressive; they are also socially impactful—fostering inclusivity and connection in an increasingly digital landscape.

Integrating Emotional Intelligence into Interfaces

The trend of integrating emotional intelligence into user interfaces represents yet another transformative shift, enhancing how systems interpret and respond to human behavior. Emotionally intelligent interfaces can assess visual, auditory, and textual cues to discern user sentiment. A striking example is found in customer service applications where AI can recognize frustration in a caller's tone and adapt its responses accordingly, fostering a more empathetic interaction.

In telehealth platforms, for example, AI can evaluate a patient's emotional state during a consultation and modify its approach to align with the patient's needs. This level of responsiveness not only elevates the quality of care but also paves the way for better patient outcomes, illustrating the potential of user-centric technologies in sensitive contexts.

Innovative human-computer interfaces are ushering in a new era of interaction that is increasingly accessible, intuitive, and aligned with human needs. From the simplicity of voice interfaces to the groundbreaking potential of brain-computer interfaces, these advancements are forging novel pathways for collaboration between humans and AI. As we envisage the future, integrating values of inclusivity, emotional intelligence, and interdisciplinary collaboration will be crucial in harnessing the full promise of these technologies. Ultimately, our commitment to enhancing the human experience through thoughtful design and application will shape the trajectory of interaction in the age of artificial intelligence, ensuring that innovation uplifts and empowers every user.

The intersection of artificial intelligence and creativity ushers in a thrilling new era, vividly illustrated by the concept of exploratory AI. This innovative category of AI goes beyond mere computation, venturing boldly into domains that have long been the playgrounds of human creativity and artistic expression. The implications of this evolution extend across various fields—impacting design, science, entertainment, and business strategy alike.

At the heart of exploratory AI lies the belief that creativity can be both formalized and enhanced through data-driven methodologies. Generative algorithms, which are central to this technology, are designed to create new content by learning from a wealth of existing data. This capability is perhaps most strikingly exemplified in the realm of art. Consider tools like OpenAI's DALL-E, which harness exploratory AI principles to generate stunning visual art from textual prompts. When presented with a prompt such as "a two-headed flamingo in a surreal landscape," the AI skillfully combines style and imagination, producing unique images that challenge our traditional notions of creativity.

In product design, companies like Autodesk are seamlessly integrating exploratory AI into their design processes. Their generative design software empowers engineers to set specific parameters—such as materials, spatial constraints, and desired performance outcomes. The AI then explores a multitude of design variations, often uncovering patterns and solutions that would elude human design teams. For instance, when tasked with creating a lightweight yet sturdy component, the AI might propose designs that mimic organic forms found in nature. This has profound implications for innovation in critical sectors such as aerospace and automotive engineering, where efficiency and creativity are paramount.

When it comes to pharmaceutical development, exploratory AI's potential is equally transformative. Traditionally, drug discovery has been a labor-intensive endeavor laden with trial and error. However, platforms like BenevolentAI are revolutionizing this field by applying machine learning to vast datasets that encompass scientific literature and clinical trial results.

Music composition presents another fascinating application of exploratory AI. Algorithms like AIVA (Artificial Intelligence Virtual Artist) are trained on expansive libraries of classical music, enabling them to generate original compositions across an array of styles. When tasked with evoking specific emotions or themes, AIVA skillfully blends genres and suggests variations, fostering collaboration with human musicians. This dynamic interplay between human creativity and artificial intelligence not only expands the boundaries of musical expression but also equips artists with unique tools for enhancing their creative endeavors.

As these examples demonstrate, the true potential of exploratory AI lies in its ability to enhance and complement human creativity. When individuals engage with AI, they can transcend cognitive barriers and explore uncharted territories. In the fashion industry, for example, designers are increasingly relying on AI for trend forecasting. This provides designers with actionable insights, enabling them to curate collections that are both stylish and data-informed, harmonizing artistic vision with market trends.

The impact of exploratory AI manifests vividly in problem-solving scenarios that demand adaptability and innovation. In the business arena, AI can scrutinize operational inefficiencies by analyzing data from various departments. Through sophisticated simulations, exploratory AI can propose novel strategies to optimize supply chains or enhance customer experiences. For instance, a retail chain struggling with declining sales might employ AI to model different pricing strategies based on comprehensive consumer behavior analytics, resulting in tailored promotional campaigns that engage specific demographics effectively.

However, as we celebrate the advancements in exploratory AI and its transformative potential, it is essential to confront the ethical questions they raise. For example, when an AI-generated artwork sells for thousands of dollars, who should receive credit for that creativity? Is it the artist, the programmer, or the AI itself? Engaging with these questions is vital for ensuring that our technological advancements are harmonized with ethical considerations.

As we navigate the evolving landscape of exploratory AI, one guiding principle becomes clear: we must foster a spirit of collaboration that views AI as a thought partner rather than a mere tool. The synergy between human intuition and exploratory AI could pave the way for unprecedented breakthroughs, revolutionizing our approach to challenges across diverse sectors. This amalgamation of creativity and technology promises not only to enrich industries but also to drive transformative change, reshaping our relationship with innovation.

Ultimately, exploratory AI stands at a pivotal crossroads, merging creativity and problem-solving to redefine how artificial intelligence can co-create alongside us. The ramifications for industries and personal creativity are far-reaching, necessitating a mindful exploration of its vast potential and inherent responsibilities. As we delve deeper into an era defined by AI's transformative capabilities, embracing its possibilities while upholding ethical integrity will be crucial in shaping the future of human-AI collaboration in creative pursuits.

Swarm intelligence and collective behavior represent an enthralling area of artificial intelligence, where intricate patterns and solutions emerge from the collaboration of relatively simple individual agents. This concept draws inspiration from natural phenomena, highlighting how numerous independent actors can come together to form a coherent and efficient system.

The roots of swarm intelligence can be traced to the behavior of social insects such as ants, bees, and termites, each of which exhibits a remarkable ability to collaborate while utilizing local knowledge to achieve shared objectives. Take, for instance, the behavior of ants: they communicate through pheromones, creating chemical trails that guide others to optimal food sources. This simple yet effective communication enables the colony to efficiently navigate its environment, inspiring the development of algorithms that address optimization problems across a spectrum of applications.

One notable breakthrough in swarm intelligence is Particle Swarm Optimization (PSO), a computational technique that involves a group of potential solutions—referred to as particles —navigating a solution space. Each particle updates its position based on personal experience and the experiences of its neighbors, gradually converging toward the most favorable solution. PSO has been effectively implemented across various fields, including engineering, finance, and machine learning, to optimize complex functions and enhance decision-making processes.

Imagine a logistics company striving to streamline delivery routes for its fleet of vehicles. As these vehicles update their positions and share information about their routes, the entire fleet synergizes to identify the most efficient routing options, significantly reducing fuel consumption and delivery times.

Ant Colony Optimization (ACO) algorithms provide another striking example of swarm intelligence in action. Inspired by the foraging patterns of ants, ACO is particularly effective for solving combinatorial optimization problems, such as the traveling salesman problem or network routing challenges. In an ACO model, artificial ants navigate a graphed landscape, depositing pheromones along their routes to guide others. As shorter paths accumulate higher pheromone levels, they attract more artificial ants, thereby enhancing the system's capability to discover optimal or near-optimal solutions.

The telecommunications industry, for instance, has

successfully leveraged ACO to optimize network traffic routing.

Beyond optimization, the concept of swarm intelligence is making significant inroads into robotics through the deployment of swarm robotics, which involves multiple robots working together to accomplish complex tasks. Researchers at Harvard University, for instance, have created robotic swarms capable of executing a variety of missions, including environmental monitoring and search-and-rescue operations. Each robot operates independently yet relies on shared information and collective behavior to tackle challenges, such as efficiently deploying sensors over extensive areas to gather crucial environmental data.

A prominent initiative showcasing the potential of swarm robotics is the Swarmanoid project. This ambitious undertaking aims to improve robotic capabilities by integrating aerial, ground, and climbing robots into a unified operation. These diverse robotic agents can share information, coordinate their movements, and tackle missions more effectively than isolated units. In practical scenarios, this could involve coordinating a search in disaster-stricken areas, where ground robots traverse rugged terrain while aerial robots provide situational awareness from above.

Moreover, the decision-making capabilities stemming from swarm intelligence offer exciting possibilities for enhancing human-AI collaboration.

However, the integration of swarm intelligence into AI systems is not without its challenges. A primary concern is ensuring that individual agents communicate effectively to avoid information overload or confusion within the group. Miscommunication can lead to erratic behaviors or suboptimal problem-solving. To address this, researchers meticulously model agent interactions, establishing clear communication protocols that promote coherent collective behavior.

Ethical considerations also arise when employing swarm intelligence in sensitive domains. For example, in military applications, the autonomous nature of swarm algorithms raises critical questions about accountability and decision-making in combat situations. It is crucial for researchers and policymakers to navigate these ethical dilemmas as swarm intelligence becomes increasingly prevalent across various sectors.

The investigation of swarm intelligence and collective behavior in AI represents an exhilarating frontier in technological innovation. As organizations continue to explore these groundbreaking approaches, the potential for transformative breakthroughs rooted in collective intelligence will reshape industries, inspire innovative solutions, and encourage deeper discussions about the implications of autonomous decision-making.

In conclusion, as swarm intelligence matures, its capacity to adapt and respond to real-world complexities positions it as a vital force driving the future of AI advancements.

The integration of artificial intelligence (AI) and blockchain technology marks a significant breakthrough in the way data is handled, shared, and leveraged across diverse industries. This collaboration not only transforms data governance but also ushers in exciting new possibilities for innovation and excellence.

Take the healthcare sector, for instance. In conventional systems, patient data is often siloed across multiple platforms, which can make accessing and sharing vital information both challenging and risky. Leveraging AI algorithms to analyze this aggregated data in real-time allows for the identification of critical trends and patterns that can lead to improved patient outcomes.

Imagine a hospital that adopts a blockchain-enabled electronic health record (EHR) system to store comprehensive patient information, including treatment histories and real-time health metrics. With AI analyzing this extensive dataset, healthcare professionals can utilize predictive analytics to spot patients at risk for conditions such as diabetes or heart disease, based on their medical history and lifestyle factors. This powerful integration provides timely insights that not only facilitates early intervention but also supports personalized treatment plans tailored to individual needs.

The financial services sector also stands to gain immensely from the fusion of AI and blockchain. With transparency being a key priority—especially for fraud detection—this combination is particularly advantageous. For example, banks can use blockchain to securely and transparently record each transaction. AI can enhance these security measures by continuously analyzing transactional data for anomalies that might signal fraudulent activity. When AI detects irregular patterns, such as unusual withdrawal behaviors across multiple accounts, it can promptly flag these transactions for further investigation, significantly speeding up the response to potential threats.

A noteworthy example is JPMorgan Chase's innovative use of blockchain through its Interbank Information Network (IIN). This system not only provides a secure infrastructure for cross-border payments but also integrates AI-driven analytics that bolster compliance and risk assessment efforts.

Similarly, supply chain management presents a compelling arena for the integration of AI and blockchain. Here, enhanced visibility and traceability are essential, especially in tracking the origins and journeys of goods. Blockchain acts as a comprehensive ledger, documenting every transaction along the supply chain, from raw material sourcing to final delivery. AI can then analyze this continuous data flow to optimize logistics, foresee potential supply chain disruptions, and enhance inventory management.

Consider a global apparel brand that harnesses blockchain to trace its clothing production processes from initial materials to retail. Additionally, in the event of product recalls, the brand can track defective items precisely to their source, significantly reducing risks to consumer safety and improving response measures.

However, integrating AI and blockchain is not without its challenges. Technical limitations may surface, particularly around the scalability of blockchain solutions in accommodating the vast amounts of data that AI generates. Additionally, the decentralized nature of blockchain can slow down data processing speeds, posing a hurdle for real-time applications. Balancing the need for swift data access with the security offered by blockchain requires innovative architectural approaches.

Regulatory and governance considerations add another layer of complexity. Navigating compliance with data protection regulations, such as the General Data Protection Regulation (GDPR), can become intricate when managing data across decentralized networks. Organizations must craft clear policies regarding data ownership, consent, and usage to ensure compliance and protect user rights.

Ethics also play a crucial role in this discourse. The combination of AI and blockchain raises important questions about accountability and transparency, especially in critical sectors like finance and healthcare. As these technologies evolve and systems become increasingly autonomous, adhering to ethical standards will be fundamental in maintaining public trust.

In conclusion, the convergence of AI and blockchain technology heralds a transformative era characterized by enhanced security, improved transparency, and optimized efficiency across various sectors. Examples from healthcare, finance, and supply chain management illustrate the practical applications and enormous potential of this partnership. Nevertheless, organizations must skillfully navigate the inherent challenges and ethical considerations to responsibly harness the advantages offered by this powerful convergence. As we progress, the dual promise of AI and blockchain will continue to pave the way for innovative solutions that elevate industries and redefine standards of excellence.

As the field of artificial intelligence continues to evolve at a rapid pace, several emerging technologies are poised to transform the capabilities and functionalities of AI agents. Staying ahead of these trends is essential, as they are set to reshape industries, redefine job roles, and enhance the interactions between humans and machines. In this exploration, we will delve into the future technologies that promise to empower AI agents, examining their potential impacts and showcasing real-world applications.

Quantum Computing: The Next Frontier

At the forefront of AI innovation lies quantum computing. Unlike traditional computers that process information in binary form—using bits represented as zeros and ones—quantum computers utilize qubits. This allows them to perform intricate calculations at speeds previously deemed unattainable. The implications for AI are profound, particularly in complex fields like drug discovery and intricate simulations. For example, a pharmaceutical company might leverage quantum AI agents to analyze molecular interactions, rapidly identifying viable drug candidates and significantly accelerating the journey from concept to market.

Edge Computing: Bringing Intelligence Closer

Another transformative technology on the horizon is edge computing, which processes data at or near its source instead of relying solely on centralized data centers. This shift not only minimizes latency but also boosts speed and enhances user privacy, creating an environment where AI agents operate more efficiently. Consider the application in autonomous vehicles. An AI agent, empowered by edge computing, can analyze surrounding data in real-time to make instantaneous decisions crucial for safety, such as avoiding obstacles.

Natural Language Processing: Elevating Human Interaction

Natural Language Processing (NLP) is also undergoing a transformation, spurred by advancements in deep learning and neural networks. Next-generation NLP technologies will enhance AI agents' ability to understand and generate human languages with remarkable nuance and context. Picture an AI-driven customer service agent capable of not merely responding to inquiries but also detecting a customer's emotional state through tone of voice or word choice. This advanced capability allows the agent to customize responses in an empathetic manner, enriching the customer experience and fostering brand loyalty. Moreover, the evolution of these technologies opens new avenues for AI-driven conversational agents to engage in therapeutic settings, offering mental health support that feels genuinely human and responsive.

Explainable AI: Building Trust through Transparency

In conjunction with NLP advancements, the rise of Explainable AI (XAI) is crucial for maintaining user trust. XAI aims to demystify the processes and decisions of AI systems, making them comprehensible to non-experts. This is especially vital in high-stakes sectors such as finance and healthcare, where understanding the rationale behind AI-driven decisions is paramount. For example, when an AI agent proposes a specific investment strategy, it should articulate clear reasoning grounded in data analytics and predictive modeling.

Augmented and Virtual Reality: Immersive Learning Experiences

The integration of AI with augmented reality (AR) and virtual reality (VR) heralds an exciting era of exploration. Imagine a VR educational AI agent tailored to personalize learning experiences based on student interactions. As learners grapple with complex scientific concepts through interactive AR overlays or simulated environments, the AI agent assesses their understanding and adapts the curriculum accordingly in real-time. This immersive approach not only transforms education but also enhances training in fields like medicine or emergency response, preparing individuals for real-world scenarios in a safe, simulated setting.

Brain-Computer Interfaces: A New Realm of Interaction

The advancement of brain-computer interfaces (BCIs) offers a glimpse into a future where direct communication between the human brain and external devices is possible. As AI agents become adept in this space, they may enable individuals to control systems simply by thinking about their actions. For instance, a person with mobility challenges could use an AI agent to operate a smart home environment by imagining the task at hand, such as turning on lights or adjusting temperature settings. The maturation of this technology has the potential to redefine accessibility, significantly enhancing independence and quality of life for many individuals.

Harnessing the Internet of Things: A Connected Future

With the advent of the Internet of Things (IoT), a vast network of connected devices opens doors for AI agents to enhance decision-making and automation. For example, smart cities powered by IoT data can deploy AI agents to optimize traffic flow, conserve energy, and bolster public safety. As these agents analyze real-time inputs from various sensors— traffic cameras, environmental monitors, and public transport systems—they can implement proactive adjustments that elevate urban living standards in unprecedented ways.

Navigating Data Privacy and Security: The Need for Innovation

The landscape of data privacy and security is also undergoing significant transformation. As user consent and data protection regulations like GDPR gain prominence, AI agents must adopt innovative technological safeguards. Techniques such as secure multi-party computation (SMPC) allow AI agents to process data while keeping sensitive information private. This capability paves the way for collaborative learning models that respect user privacy. For instance, banks could gain insights from shared data patterns without compromising individual customer information, fostering trust while enhancing algorithmic learning.

In conclusion, the future of AI agents brims with transformative technologies that promise to elevate their capabilities and foster deeper, more meaningful interactions with human users. From quantum computing and edge computing to next-generation NLP, explainable AI, AR/VR, brain-computer interfaces, IoT innovations, and advanced privacy techniques, these advancements signal not just incremental change but monumental shifts in how we engage with technology. As we move forward, the vision of AI as a vital ally in everyday life becomes increasingly tangible, promising a future that champions innovation and humanity.

CHAPTER 9: INTEGRATING AI AGENTS INTO EXISTING SYSTEMS

Integrating AI agents into existing systems is a complex journey that demands meticulous planning and execution. Legacy systems, often constructed during eras long before AI technologies became prevalent, typically embody architectures that were once cutting-edge but now present significant compatibility dilemmas. The real challenge lies not only in bridging the technological divide but also in strategically aligning organizational objectives with the innovative capabilities offered by AI. Neglecting these challenges can result in increased costs, operational inefficiencies, and widespread frustration across an organization.

Technological Incompatibility: Bridging the Gap

A primary concern in the integration process is the technological mismatch between AI agents and legacy systems. Many of these systems are rooted in outdated frameworks and programming languages, which can struggle to interface effectively with contemporary AI solutions. Take, for example, a financial institution relying on a legacy mainframe for its core banking operations, potentially programmed in COBOL, a language that predates AI's rise. The task of incorporating AI-driven predictive analytics into such a framework can be monumental. It often requires bespoke middleware solutions and intricate API mappings to facilitate seamless communication and data exchange between the established system and new AI capabilities.

To overcome these technological barriers, organizations may adopt a phased integration strategy. This approach could involve the development of dedicated AI modules that can function autonomously while interfacing with legacy systems through specialized gateways. For instance, in the retail sector, businesses are increasingly deploying AI agents to manage dynamic pricing based on consumer behavior data without necessitating significant revisions to their core inventory management systems. This not only enhances efficiency but also respects the integrity of the original architecture.

Cultural and Structural Resistance: Fostering Acceptance

Another pivotal aspect that organizations must navigate is the cultural and structural resistance that often accompanies technological change. Operators of legacy systems, who may possess decades of invaluable knowledge, might view AI integration as a potential threat to their expertise and job security. Such apprehension can impede even the most promising integration plans. To counteract this resistance and foster acceptance, organizations should prioritize change management initiatives. Implementing comprehensive training programs that highlight the collaborative nature of AI—as supportive agents enhancing human skill rather than replacing it—can significantly alleviate concerns. For example, a healthcare institution introducing AI for patient data analysis might offer workshops demonstrating how AI insights can enrich patient care, rather than undermining the essential role of healthcare professionals.

Data Migration: Transforming Legacy Databases

Data migration is another intricate component of successfully merging AI with legacy systems. Often, legacy databases are structured in ways that render them ill-suited for the real-time processing demands of AI. The transition to a more AI-friendly environment requires not only the migration of data but also its transformation into accessible formats. For instance, a legacy logistics management system primarily focused on record-keeping might house data in silos, making it challenging to implement AI for route optimization. Organizations must first unify and normalize their disparate data sources before they can effectively leverage AI's capabilities.

Ensuring Reliability and Performance: A Focus on Stability

Maintaining system reliability and performance is critical throughout the integration process. The introduction of AI agents should enhance, not compromise, the stability of existing systems. To achieve this, organizations must implement rigorous testing and monitoring strategies, assessing system performance both before and after integration. Utilizing cloud-based infrastructures temporarily to test AI functions against mirrored datasets can minimize the risk of disruptions in production environments, ensuring a smooth transition.

A Holistic Approach to Integration

Ultimately, integrating AI agents into legacy systems is more than just a technical upgrade; it is a comprehensive undertaking that requires thoughtful planning and strategic alignment across technological, operational, and cultural dimensions. This balance between innovation and tradition can empower organizations to thrive in an increasingly competitive landscape, unlocking new efficiencies and capabilities that drive success.

Unlocking the Power of Integration: APIs and Interoperability in the Age of AI

In today's rapidly evolving technological landscape, the ability to integrate AI agents with legacy systems hinges on the development of robust APIs and seamless interoperability. As organizations pursue innovative AI solutions, bridging the gap between outdated infrastructure and modern technology is essential. Well-designed APIs not only facilitate smooth communication and data exchange but also ensure operational synergy across diverse systems. Therefore, strategic API development and interoperability are critical factors in enabling successful digital transformation.

API Architecture: Crafting Interfaces for Today's Needs

The effectiveness of an API is rooted in its architecture, which must meet the unique demands of both legacy systems and sophisticated AI applications. Choosing the right architectural style is paramount. RESTful APIs, with their stateless operations and scalability, are commonly preferred for AI applications that require swift and efficient data interactions. On the other hand, GraphQL presents a more versatile option, allowing clients to specify their exact data needs. This capability can significantly enhance performance and reduce bandwidth consumption—particularly valuable when processing large datasets in AI systems.

Consider the scenario of an e-commerce company that wishes to infuse AI-driven customer personalization into its legacy order management system. This integration requires an API that intelligently translates customer interaction data into actionable insights without overwhelming legacy operations.

Achieving Seamless Interoperability: Connecting Diverse Systems

Interoperability is vital for enabling AI agents to function cohesively within heterogeneous systems. To achieve this integration, organizations must address challenges like data format disparities, which often involve converting between structured, semi-structured, and unstructured data types.

One effective solution is utilizing middleware that mediates interactions between AI applications and legacy systems.

For instance, a financial institution could implement an Enterprise Service Bus (ESB) to streamline data exchanges between AI-driven risk assessment tools and conventional account management software. The ESB acts as a facilitator, dynamically translating data formats and protocols for smoother cross-platform communication.

Additionally, adopting language-agnostic technologies, such as JSON or XML, for data interchange can substantially mitigate interoperability issues. For example, in a healthcare environment, these formats enable AI analytics systems to access patient records seamlessly, ultimately leading to improved diagnostic accuracy and patient outcomes.

Ensuring Security: The Role of API Gateways

In an era where data breaches and security threats are rampant, safeguarding API access is of paramount importance, especially when sensitive company information is involved. Implementing an API gateway introduces a vital layer of security that manages access control, request authentication, usage monitoring, and rate limiting. This is particularly critical in sectors like finance and healthcare, where unauthorized access could result in catastrophic repercussions. For instance, an AI-driven predictive maintenance application connecting with a legacy manufacturing system would greatly benefit from these robust security measures, protecting sensitive operational data from potential intrusions.

Rigorous Testing and Optimization:
Guaranteeing API Performance

The backbone of seamless integration lies in well-performing APIs, which necessitate thorough testing and optimization processes. This includes functional testing to confirm that APIs execute their intended operations correctly and load testing to evaluate their capacity to manage surges in data requests, a common scenario for AI-driven analytics.

Automated testing tools like Postman or JMeter can simulate high data volume operations, helping to identify bottlenecks or vulnerabilities. Organizations should commit to routinely conducting these tests, updating schemas in line with evolving AI models, and optimizing code for peak efficiency. This ongoing diligence ensures sustained high API performance.

Strategic Implementation: Maximizing Business Value

Implementing APIs strategically can transform legacy systems, unlocking significant new business value. For example, a transportation company may deploy AI for route optimization to enhance operational efficiency. An effectively designed API can facilitate real-time access to traffic data from external sources, integrating this information into legacy navigation tools to yield cost savings and boost customer satisfaction.

Ultimately, the goal of API development and interoperability extends beyond technological integration; it seeks to advance an organization's overall capacity for innovation. This thoughtful integration places companies on a path toward sustained growth and competitiveness in an AI-driven future, fully leveraging the potential of new technologies while preserving the value of existing infrastructure.

Evaluating Deployment Strategies: Cloud vs. On-Premises for AI Agents

Choosing the appropriate environment for deploying AI agents is more than just a technical decision—it's a pivotal choice that can fundamentally shape an organization's agility, security, and scalability. As AI technologies become increasingly integral across diverse industries, understanding whether to opt for cloud-based or on-premises deployment is more crucial than ever. Each option comes with its own set of advantages and challenges, and organizations must conduct a meticulous evaluation tailored to their specific needs, objectives, and existing infrastructure.

Cloud Deployment: Embracing Flexibility and Scalability

The appeal of cloud-based deployment lies in its remarkable flexibility and scalability. This adaptability proves invaluable in environments where workloads may fluctuate or during periods of rapid growth.

Imagine a digital marketing agency that employs AI to dissect consumer behavior patterns across numerous channels. Utilizing platforms like AWS, Google Cloud, or Azure, this firm can process immense volumes of real-time data, seamlessly scaling its operations during peak marketing periods without sacrificing performance.

Moreover, cloud deployment fosters enhanced collaboration among geographically distributed teams. Data scientists and engineers can access shared environments from virtually anywhere, streamlining workflows and driving innovation. This advantage is particularly significant for multinational corporations, where effective cross-border collaboration is essential.

However, the reliance on third-party cloud providers does carry inherent risks related to data privacy and compliance. With sensitive information traversing organizational firewalls, the potential for vulnerabilities increases. Therefore, implementing stringent security measures and adhering to industry regulations is paramount to safeguarding data against breaches.

On-Premises Deployment: Prioritizing Control and Security

For organizations that prioritize meticulous control over their IT infrastructure, on-premises deployment can provide a strong alternative. This approach ensures that all data processing occurs within the confines of the organization's security perimeter, significantly reducing exposure to external threats. Industries like government defense or healthcare, where confidentiality is non-negotiable, often lean toward this model to comply with rigorous data security mandates.

Choosing an on-premises setup also allows for extensive customization of hardware and software, optimizing performance for specific AI workloads. For instance, a financial firm engaged in real-time trading can benefit from tailored servers designed for minimal latency and dedicated processing power, facilitating rapid decision-making.

Nevertheless, this approach is not without its drawbacks. Organizations may face substantial upfront capital expenditures and ongoing maintenance costs, alongside potential challenges in scalability. Establishing and maintaining physical infrastructure demands continuous investment and skilled technical teams, which can lead to higher operational costs and delays in scaling capabilities compared to cloud alternatives.

Hybrid Models: Balancing Advantages

Given the unique strengths and challenges associated with both cloud and on-premises deployments, hybrid models emerge as a compelling solution.

For example, an enterprise that manages a public-facing e-commerce site might deploy customer analytics applications in the cloud to efficiently handle varying online traffic, while keeping mission-critical functions reliant on an on-premises setup to ensure compliance with stringent data security regulations.

Hybrid models allow organizations to blend the best of both worlds, ensuring compatibility with legacy systems while leveraging the cloud's scalability for non-sensitive operations. This creates an optimal equilibrium between resource utilization and operational security.

Strategic Decision-Making: Tailoring
Deployment to Business Goals

Ultimately, the choice between cloud and on-premises deployment should reflect the organization's strategic objectives and operational nuances. Factors such as data sensitivity, regulatory compliance, budgetary constraints, and growth projections must all play a central role in the decision-making process.

For instance, startups might favor cloud deployment to minimize initial investment and facilitate quick scaling in alignment with their evolving business model. Conversely, well-established enterprises with significant existing infrastructure assets may opt for on-premises solutions to maximize the utilization of their resources while ensuring the integrity of their data.

Emerging sectors leveraging AI, such as autonomous driving technologies, often require dedicated, high-performance local systems to handle real-time data processing. In such scenarios, an on-premises or hybrid strategy may prove crucial for meeting the computational demands of machine learning algorithms that enable rapid decision-making on the road. This strategic approach not only aligns AI capabilities with overarching business goals but also addresses operational needs and regulatory requirements.

Empowering organizations to unlock the transformative potential of AI technologies, these informed decisions provide a pathway to enhanced business value while ensuring stringent security and control. In navigating the rapidly evolving landscape of AI agents, mastering deployment strategies is essential for capitalizing on the myriad opportunities these technologies present.

Ensuring Seamless User Experiences in AI Agents

Delivering a seamless user experience is a fundamental goal in the deployment of AI agents, significantly impacting user adoption, satisfaction, and engagement levels. Achieving this involves not only the technical capabilities of AI systems but also a thoughtful approach to designing interactions and interfaces.

Understanding the User Journey

At the heart of a seamless user experience is a comprehensive understanding of the user journey. This entails diligently mapping out the various touchpoints where users engage with AI agents, pinpointing pain points, and identifying opportunities for improvement. Collecting data through user feedback, surveys, and analytics can provide invaluable insights into user behaviors and preferences.

For example, take a virtual customer service assistant powered by AI. These insights enable iterative improvements, enhancing the agent's comprehension and responsiveness, ultimately enriching the overall user experience.

Designing Intuitive Interfaces

Creating a user-friendly interface is essential to ensure that interactions with AI agents are straightforward and effective. Prioritizing simplicity, clarity, and navigability is crucial. The interface should facilitate key tasks while minimizing cognitive load, and visual elements—such as intuitive icons and clearly labeled buttons—should guide users through processes without unnecessary complexity.

Consider a predictive analytics tool for financial analysts. A well-designed dashboard displaying real-time trends and customizable widgets empowers users to tailor their interface according to their analytical needs, boosting both efficiency and satisfaction.

Personalization for Individualized Experiences

Personalization significantly enhances user experiences by tailoring interactions to match individual preferences and behaviors. AI agents utilize machine learning algorithms to deliver customized responses and relevant content, fostering a sense of value and understanding for users.

On e-commerce platforms, for instance, AI agents can recommend products based on a user's previous searches and purchase history. This not only simplifies the shopping experience by reducing search time but also cultivates customer loyalty through enhanced relevance and convenience.

Ensuring Consistent Performance

Maintaining consistency in performance is crucial for building user trust and reliability. AI agents must operate predictably across a range of environments and under varied load conditions. Implementing robust testing and quality assurance processes ensures that AI systems remain reliable, delivering expected outcomes without crashes or unexpected behavior.

For instance, consider a real-time language translation AI deployed in a global business environment. It is essential for the AI to provide consistent, high-quality translations regardless of varying network conditions or languages, facilitating seamless communication among multicultural teams.

Responding to User Feedback

Incorporating mechanisms for gathering and acting on user feedback is vital for continuous improvement. Establishing user feedback loops—through direct surveys or passive observation of user behavior—illuminates areas needing enhancement and adaptation.

Take a healthcare chatbot, for example. Feedback on the accuracy and clarity of its responses can be used to refine the chatbot's algorithms, improving its understanding of medical terminology and enhancing future interactions.

Comprehensive Training and Support

Equipping users with extensive training resources and support is crucial for integrating AI agents into everyday workflows. Comprehensive manuals, instructional videos, and responsive support teams empower users to leverage the full potential of AI capabilities.

For instance, a CRM system augmented with AI to automate client communication might benefit from offering onboarding webinars and an intuitive knowledge base. This enables users to effectively utilize features such as automated scheduling and sentiment analysis, thereby boosting overall productivity.

Balancing Automation and Human Touch

As organizations increasingly automate tasks, striking the right balance between automation and human interaction remains critical. Retaining a human touch in AI interactions is vital for tasks that require emotional intelligence or complex decision-making.

In customer service scenarios, for instance, an AI-powered system may autonomously manage routine inquiries while escalating more nuanced or sensitive issues to human agents. This approach enhances efficiency without sacrificing the quality of personalized care in more complex situations.

Ultimately, creating seamless user experiences necessitates a holistic approach that integrates technical, design, and human elements.

The commitment to excellence in user experience is an ongoing journey, requiring continual iteration and responsiveness to evolving user needs and technological advancements. Successfully deploying AI agents that deliver seamless experiences empowers users to achieve their goals more efficiently and effectively, unlocking the full potential of AI-driven transformation.

Embracing Change: Navigating the Integration of AI in Organizations

In today's rapidly evolving technological landscape, change is not just an option—it's a necessity. The introduction of artificial intelligence (AI) agents into established systems presents organizations with both exciting opportunities and significant challenges. For organizations to reap the full benefits of AI technology while minimizing disruptions, effective change management is crucial. This discipline not only facilitates a smooth transition but also aligns all stakeholders with the new processes, ensuring that the shift towards AI is both strategic and sustainable.

Cultivating a Culture of Adaptability

At the heart of successful change management lies the cultivation of a culture that embraces adaptability. Leadership plays a pivotal role in fostering an environment where change is seen as an opportunity for innovation rather than a threat.

Transparent communication is essential in this process. When organizations outline the potential impacts and benefits of AI systems—both for the company and the workforce—employees are more inclined to embrace the change. Hosting workshops and open forums can demystify AI, making the technology more relatable and less intimidating, thereby encouraging a collective enthusiasm for the future.

Engaging Stakeholders from the Start

Involving stakeholders—including employees, clients, and partners—early in the change process is vital for success. Their insights can help identify challenges and craft tailored solutions that reflect the organization's diverse needs.

For instance, a retail company implementing an AI-driven inventory management system should actively include input from store managers, supply chain partners, and IT staff during the planning phase. This collaborative effort ensures that the technological solution aligns with real-world operational requirements, leading to smoother implementation and increased chances of success.

A Phased Approach: Pilot Programs for Testing

One effective strategy for integrating AI technologies is to adopt a phased approach through pilot programs. This method allows organizations to test new technologies in controlled environments, enabling them to evaluate performance and identify any issues before a full-scale rollout.

Take the example of a healthcare provider introducing AI for managing patient data. The insights derived from such pilots serve as a blueprint for broader deployments, significantly reducing disruptions in critical operations.

Empowering the Workforce Through Training

As organizations transition to AI-driven processes, comprehensive training programs become indispensable. Tailoring training to meet the specific needs of different job roles ensures that every team member can confidently and effectively utilize new systems.

For example, when deploying an AI-enhanced customer relationship management (CRM) tool, sales representatives may need to hone their skills in leveraging AI-generated insights during customer interactions. Interactive training sessions, continuous learning resources, and hands-on practice not only alleviate anxiety surrounding new technologies but also build employees' confidence in their capabilities.

Continuous Monitoring and Evaluation

After integrating AI systems, ongoing monitoring and evaluation are paramount to ensure alignment with organizational goals.

For instance, a financial institution that has deployed an AI-based fraud detection system might monitor metrics such as transaction clearance times, false-positive rates, and customer satisfaction. Regular evaluations and feedback loops enable the organization to respond nimbly to emerging challenges, reinforcing a commitment to continuous improvement.

Celebrating Success and Incorporating Feedback

Throughout the change process, recognizing and celebrating milestones reinforces a positive perception of AI integration. Sharing success stories and showcasing tangible benefits fosters a supportive atmosphere, emphasizing the advantages of embracing change.

Equally important is the constructive handling of feedback— whether it points to areas needing improvement or introduces fresh perspectives on existing strategies. Establishing a robust feedback mechanism, such as an internal online platform or regular meetings, allows employees to voice their experiences and suggestions. Proactively responding to this feedback not only enhances AI implementations but also nurtures trust and engagement among stakeholders.

Building Resilience for Continuous Change

As AI and other technologies continue to evolve, organizations must foster resilience to navigate future changes effectively. This involves embedding change management practices into the organizational culture, continuously refining strategies based on lessons learned, and maintaining agility in the face of unexpected developments.

Successful change management necessitates a holistic approach that integrates leadership vision, strategic planning, stakeholder engagement, and ongoing evaluation. The ability to navigate the complexities of AI systems hinges on understanding and addressing the human elements intertwined with technological advancements. This proactive approach paves the way for not just acceptance, but enthusiastic adoption of AI-driven innovations, setting the stage for ongoing growth and transformative advancements.

Ensuring Data Synchronization and Integrity in AI Systems

The successful integration of AI systems into existing infrastructures hinges on two interrelated principles: data synchronization and data integrity. Together, they form the foundation for AI agents to operate using the most current and accurate information, which is essential for informed decision-making and enhanced operational efficiency. As companies increasingly adopt AI into their workflows, maintaining reliable and synchronized data flows becomes vital for achieving successful AI outcomes.

The Significance of Data Synchronization

Data synchronization is the process that ensures consistency in data across various systems and platforms, guaranteeing that all users operate with the same real-time information. Within the context of AI systems, this consistency is crucial for ensuring that the insights and decisions generated by AI agents are grounded in reliable and coherent data.

Imagine a logistics company leveraging AI for route optimization. If fleet location data is not synchronized across their various systems, AI models may end up making routing decisions based on outdated or incomplete information. This lapse could increase delivery times and fuel costs, ultimately undermining the very benefits that AI is intended to provide. Therefore, synchronization transcends mere alignment of data feeds; it fosters operational coherence and enhances overall effectiveness.

Strategies for Effective Data Synchronization

To achieve effective data synchronization, several strategies can be employed, including batch processing, streaming, and real-time synchronization:

1. Batch Processing: This method collects data over a predefined period before processing it as a single batch. While not suitable for real-time requirements, it can be effective in scenarios where immediate updates are less critical. For example, a retail chain might employ batch processing to sync daily sales

data overnight, refreshing inventory systems with the day's transactions.

2. Streaming: In this approach, data is processed and synchronized continuously as it is generated. It is particularly important for applications that necessitate immediate insights, such as financial trading platforms, where any delay could result in considerable monetary losses.

3. Real-Time Synchronization: This occurs through the integration of APIs, ensuring that data updates are reflected instantly across all platforms. A pertinent example can be found in healthcare, where a patient's medical records must be updated in real-time—such as when new lab test results are added—to ensure that healthcare providers always have access to the most current information.

Upholding Data Integrity

Data integrity pertains to the accuracy and consistency of data throughout its lifecycle. It is paramount for AI systems, as upholding integrity is essential for yielding valid results and fostering trust in AI outputs. Without a commitment to data integrity, even a well-synchronized system can lead to misleading conclusions.

For instance, consider the dataset preparation for training machine learning models. Ensuring data integrity necessitates robust validation checks to identify and rectify inaccuracies or anomalies. If a sales prediction model is trained on erroneous data—say, inaccurate sales figures due to manual entry errors—the reliability of that model will be compromised, which could result in misguided business strategies.

Techniques to Preserve Data Integrity

To maintain high standards of data integrity throughout AI operations, organizations can employ several techniques:

1. Validation and Verification: Rigorous data validation processes are essential for preventing inaccurate or corrupted data from infiltrating the system. Verification checks ensure that manually entered data adheres to predefined formats and logical structures.

2. Access Control and Audit Trails: Limiting data access to authorized personnel reduces the risk of unauthorized changes. Audit trails provide critical transparency, allowing organizations to monitor data modifications and assess their implications.

3. Regular Testing and Updates: Continuous testing not only helps identify data integrity issues early on but also ensures that AI models are recalibrated using high-quality data inputs. Regular system updates to accommodate new data standards or rectify identified errors are essential to maintaining data integrity.

Real-World Applications and Challenges

In the realm of financial services, ensuring both synchronized and integral data is vital for effective fraud detection systems. Real-time synchronization enables the identification of fraudulent activities as they occur, while data integrity guarantees that alerts are based on accurate transaction data, thereby minimizing false positives and false negatives.

However, organizations often face challenges such as data silos, complex infrastructures, and disparate data formats that can obstruct both synchronization and integrity. Addressing these challenges commonly requires a multi-faceted approach, including advanced data engineering, investment in comprehensive integration platforms, and the adoption of standardized data formats across all systems.

Data synchronization and integrity are not mere technical

necessities; they serve as the backbone of reliable and effective AI systems. This strategic alignment of data management practices not only enhances the accuracy and timeliness of AI-driven decisions but also positions companies to remain competitive and utilize AI innovations as transformative catalysts for business growth.

Performance Metrics for Integrated Systems: Navigating Success and Efficiency

The integration of AI agents into established systems is a transformative venture, yet its success hinges on meticulous evaluation processes. Performance metrics serve as vital tools in this landscape, enabling organizations to assess operational efficiency, user satisfaction, and overall effectiveness.

Decoding Performance Metrics

At their core, performance metrics are quantifiable indicators designed to gauge the effectiveness of integrated AI systems. They provide insights into how effectively these systems perform their intended functions and highlight opportunities for improvement. When defining metrics, it's essential to ensure they align closely with organizational goals and the specific objectives underlying the AI deployment.

Essential Key Performance Indicators (KPIs)

To accurately measure performance, organizations typically employ a tailored set of Key Performance Indicators (KPIs). Here are a few critical KPIs to consider:

1. Accuracy and Precision: These measures assess the correctness of AI outputs. For example, in an AI-driven fraud detection system, accuracy reflects the percentage of correctly identified fraudulent transactions. Precision, on the other hand, indicates the proportion of actual frauds among those flagged, providing a deeper insight into the system's efficacy.

2. Response Time: This metric evaluates how quickly the AI system processes data and delivers results. In customer service settings, swift response times are instrumental for maintaining high levels of customer satisfaction and ensuring fluid interactions.

3. System Uptime and Reliability: Uptime metrics gauge the availability and dependability of the AI system. In sectors like healthcare—where AI supports life-critical functions—high availability and reliability are non-negotiable.

4. User Satisfaction: Obtained via direct feedback and comprehensive surveys, this metric reflects end-users' perceptions of the AI system's effectiveness and efficiency. High user satisfaction not only drives increased adoption rates but also promotes sustained engagement.

5. Resource Utilization: This involves measuring CPU, memory, and network usage to optimize system efficiency. Identifying performance bottlenecks through resource utilization metrics allows organizations to adjust resources strategically.

Best Practices for Establishing Meaningful Metrics

To ensure that performance measurement yields valuable insights, organizations should adhere to several best practices:

1. Alignment with Strategic Goals: Each metric should reflect the organization's overarching objectives. For instance, an e-commerce platform integrating AI for personalized shopping experiences might focus metrics on conversion rates, customer satisfaction, and retention.

2. Dynamic Adaptability: As both AI systems and the business environment evolve, so too must

the metrics. Flexibility in measurement allows organizations to keep pace with changing objectives and advancements in technology.

3. Robust Data Collection: Effective metric evaluation relies on comprehensive data gathering. Organizations should deploy robust data pipelines and advanced analytics tools to ensure meticulous tracking and thorough evaluation of performance-related data.

4. Visual Reporting Tools: Employing visual dashboards can significantly enhance the interpretation of performance data. For example, a graphical dashboard displaying response times and accuracy rates of an AI-driven customer support tool allows stakeholders to swiftly grasp insights and make informed decisions.

Case Study Illustration

Let's consider an AI-enhanced supply chain management system tasked with optimizing inventory and delivery logistics. For instance, high inventory accuracy coupled with lagging order fulfillment times might indicate bottlenecks in logistics coordination. Armed with these insights, the company can implement precise interventions to streamline logistics processes and enhance overall efficiency.

The Importance of Comparative Analysis

Engaging in comparative analysis enables organizations to benchmark their AI systems against industry standards or competitors' performances.

Final Thoughts: Fostering Innovation Through Performance Metrics

Performance metrics transcend mere retrospective analysis; they are essential instruments for driving innovation within AI systems. This proactive approach not only amplifies the operational performance of integrated systems but also aligns with broader strategic goals, fostering sustainable growth and ensuring that AI agents remain invaluable assets in an increasingly competitive technological landscape.

Case Studies of Successful AI Integrations: Insights from Real-World Implementations

The successful incorporation of AI agents into existing systems not only demonstrates the potential for innovation but also provides a wellspring of lessons for businesses aiming to elevate their operations. These examples reveal common pitfalls to avoid and highlight pathways for success, effectively serving as a blueprint for businesses embarking on their AI journeys.

Case Study 1: Transforming Healthcare with AI-Enhanced Diagnostics

In the realm of healthcare, the integration of AI technologies has ushered in significant advancements, particularly in diagnostic accuracy. A notable example can be found in a major hospital network in Europe, where an AI-driven imaging analysis tool was deployed to elevate the precision and efficiency of radiological evaluations.

Implementation Strategy:

The hospital collaborated with a cutting-edge AI technology provider to implement a neural network-based image recognition system. This innovative tool was specifically designed to analyze radiological images for abnormalities, augmenting the expertise of trained radiologists.

Key Metrics for Success:

1. Enhanced Diagnostic Accuracy: The AI system achieved an impressive accuracy rate exceeding 95% in identifying medical conditions within images.
2. Time Efficiency: The integration resulted in a remarkable 40% reduction in the time taken to

process and analyze radiological images.

3. Radiologist Confidence: Subsequent feedback highlighted increased confidence among radiologists, who viewed AI as a reliable second opinion rather than a replacement for human judgment.

Lessons Learned:

One crucial lesson from this integration process was the necessity for transparent communication between AI developers and healthcare professionals. Ongoing training sessions were instrumental in ensuring that radiologists were fully informed about the capabilities and limitations of the AI tool, fostering a collaborative atmosphere that harmonized human expertise with AI insights.

Case Study 2: Revolutionizing Retail Customer Experiences with AI

In the retail sector, AI integration has transformed the way businesses engage with their customers, exemplified by a leading global retail chain's implementation of AI-powered recommendation engines.

Implementation Strategy:

The retailer harnessed sophisticated machine learning algorithms to analyze customer data from various touchpoints, including online browsing habits, purchasing patterns, and in-store interactions. This comprehensive data formed the backbone of a recommendation engine that provided personalized product suggestions to shoppers.

Key Metrics for Success:

1. Boosted Conversion Rates: The tailored recommendations led to a 15% increase in online conversion rates, demonstrating the effectiveness of personalization.

2. Elevated Customer Satisfaction: Surveys indicated a marked improvement in customer satisfaction,

with clients appreciating the bespoke shopping experience.

3. Increased Average Order Value: Targeted cross-selling and upselling initiatives driven by AI insights lifted the average order value by 12%.

Lessons Learned:

A critical takeaway from this case was the paramount importance of data quality and integration. The accuracy of AI-driven recommendations relies heavily on well-managed datasets. Additionally, safeguarding customer data privacy emerged as a vital consideration, reinforcing the need for robust security protocols to protect sensitive information.

Case Study 3: Enhancing Manufacturing Operations through Predictive Maintenance

The manufacturing industry stands to gain significantly from AI, particularly through the adoption of predictive maintenance strategies. A leading automotive manufacturer exemplifies this with its successful integration of AI, which aimed to minimize equipment downtime and boost operational efficiency.

Implementation Strategy:

The manufacturer installed AI sensors across its production machinery, collecting real-time data to feed into machine learning models designed to predict potential equipment malfunctions before they occurred.

Key Metrics for Success:

1. Downtime Reduction: The implementation of predictive maintenance strategies led to a 30% decrease in unplanned downtime, dramatically enhancing production efficiency.
2. Cost Savings: Proactive identification of potential equipment issues resulted in a notable 20% reduction in maintenance costs.

3. Improved Worker Safety: Anticipating machinery failures not only optimized operations but also enhanced safety measures in the workplace, decreasing the likelihood of accidents related to equipment malfunction.

Lessons Learned:

A pivotal insight from this case was the necessity for cross-disciplinary collaboration.

Each of these case studies offers valuable insights that can guide future AI integrations across various sectors. From enhancing diagnostic accuracy in healthcare to personalizing the retail experience and improving operational efficiency in manufacturing, these examples underscore the transformational power of AI. However, successful integration hinges on meticulous strategic planning, careful alignment with organizational objectives, and a steadfast commitment to balancing technological advancements with human factors.

Empowering End-Users Through Training and Support in AI Agent Integration

Crafting Tailored Training Programs

Empowering end-users begins with the creation of tailored training programs that cater to the diverse needs and skill levels of the workforce. These programs must blend theoretical instruction with practical, hands-on experiences to cultivate a rich understanding of AI systems.

Real-World Application: A global logistics leader successfully rolled out an AI-powered supply chain optimization tool by executing a phased training strategy. The initial sessions provided a foundational overview of AI concepts and their specific applications within the industry. Building on this groundwork, subsequent workshops introduced interactive simulations that allowed employees to engage directly with the tool, immersing themselves in its features and functionalities through real-world scenarios. This structured approach not only ensured technical proficiency but also nurtured employees' confidence in integrating AI insights into their everyday tasks.

Embracing E-Learning and Remote Training Solutions

The rise of digital learning platforms offers organizations an opportunity to transcend conventional classroom training. E-learning modules and remote training sessions present flexible, scalable solutions that can accommodate varying user needs and geographical limitations.

Case in Point: A prominent financial institution that adopted an AI-driven customer service platform recognized the value of online training. They provided a mix of interactive e-learning modules and webinars tailored for their global workforce. This approach allowed employees to learn at their own pace, with the option to revisit complex subjects as needed. Live Q&A sessions facilitated real-time engagement with subject matter experts, promoting a collaborative learning experience that reinforced understanding.

Building Sustainable Support Networks

Training should not be viewed as a one-off event. Organizations must establish sustained support mechanisms that address users' evolving needs and help troubleshoot challenges that may arise post-implementation. Creating effective support networks fosters a culture of ongoing learning and adaptability.

Illustrative Example: A healthcare provider implementing AI in patient management systems developed an extensive support structure to aid their staff. This included a dedicated helpdesk for immediate assistance with technical issues, online forums for peer-to-peer exchanges, and regular feedback sessions with AI system developers. This multi-faceted support system not only provided quick resolutions to immediate concerns but also served as a platform for users to voice their experiences, ultimately leading to enhancements in the technology itself.

Fostering Collaborative Learning Environments

Encouraging collaborative learning is essential for promoting the exchange of best practices among users and igniting innovation within the organization. Programs that emphasize peer mentoring and workshops can create an informal but enriching learning environment.

Example of Success: In an automotive manufacturing firm, employees who excelled in utilizing AI-driven quality control systems were designated as 'AI Champions.' These champions conducted regular workshops to share their firsthand insights and strategies for optimizing the AI system's use. This initiative not only facilitated knowledge transfer but also fostered a collective sense of ownership and encouraged a culture of innovation within the organization.

Monitoring and Evaluating Training Effectiveness

To truly gauge the success of training initiatives, organizations must systematically monitor and assess their effectiveness. This involves setting clear objectives, gathering relevant performance data, and using user feedback to continuously refine training strategies.

Practical Example: A retail enterprise leveraging AI for inventory management established performance metrics as part of its training program. Routine surveys collected employee feedback, providing invaluable insights into the training's relevance and effectiveness from the end-user perspective.

A strategic, well-rounded approach to training and user support is paramount for maximizing the benefits of AI agent integration. Through these concerted efforts, the true potential of AI technologies can be unlocked, driving operational excellence and fostering innovation across various industries.

The Evolving Landscape: Future Trends in
System Integration with AI Agents

As organizations increasingly weave AI agents into their operational frameworks, they are witnessing a transformative shift that promises to enhance integration, efficiency, and innovation across diverse applications. The trends emerging in this space not only reflect technological advancements but also signify evolving methodologies and organizational attitudes toward AI. Below, we explore the most promising trends and strategic considerations that will shape the future of system integration across various industries.

Trend 1: Advanced Interoperability and Unified Platforms

A pivotal trend is the drive toward enhanced interoperability and the creation of unified digital platforms. The demand for AI agents to communicate seamlessly across disparate systems has led to the advancement of sophisticated Application Programming Interfaces (APIs) and middleware solutions that facilitate smooth interactions between different software environments.

Example: In the public transportation arena, cities are increasingly seeking to integrate AI-driven traffic management systems with existing municipal infrastructure.

Trend 2: Edge Computing for Agile Decision-Making

Edge computing is emerging as a cornerstone of future system integration, allowing AI agents to process data closer to its source rather than depending solely on centralized data centers. This strategy minimizes latency, empowering real-time decision-making and enhancing system resilience.

Real-World Application: Manufacturing enterprises leveraging AI for quality assurance are implementing edge computing solutions to boost operational efficiency.

Trend 3: Strengthened Cybersecurity Measures

As the integration of AI agents becomes more prevalent, organizations are recognizing the urgent need to bolster cybersecurity. Future system integrations will increasingly incorporate advanced security protocols specifically designed for AI applications, addressing inherent vulnerabilities and safeguarding sensitive information.

Case Illustration: Financial institutions, known for their susceptibility to cyber threats, are investing heavily in AI-driven cybersecurity systems.

Trend 4: Modular and Scalable Architectures

Modular and scalable architectures are becoming indispensable for adapting to the evolving needs of AI applications.

Practical Example: Healthcare providers that employ AI-driven diagnostic tools are increasingly adopting modular architectures that allow for the seamless addition of new functionalities, such as updated algorithms, without requiring a complete overhaul of existing systems. This adaptability keeps systems current and enhances their ability to provide advanced medical insights.

Trend 5: Human-Centric Design and UX Optimization

With the proliferation of AI agents, there is a growing emphasis on human-centric design and optimizing user experiences. Future system integration initiatives will prioritize creating intuitive interfaces and interactions that resonate with user needs, thereby enhancing engagement and productivity.

Illustrative Scenario: In the customer service sector, AI-powered chatbots are evolving to deliver more human-like interactions. Organizations are investing in user experience research to ensure that AI agents can effectively manage complex customer inquiries while maintaining a natural conversational flow, ultimately boosting customer satisfaction and loyalty.

Trend 6: Synergizing AI with the Internet of Things (IoT)

The convergence of AI and IoT is poised to revolutionize system integrations, allowing AI agents to analyze vast streams of data from IoT devices. This synergy creates opportunities for smarter environments in homes, cities, and industrial settings.

Practical Example: Smart city initiatives are tapping into the potential of AI and IoT integration to improve urban living. AI systems are analyzing data collected from IoT sensors to optimize waste management, enhance energy efficiency, and bolster public safety, turning real-time insights into actionable strategies for urban development.

The future of system integration with AI agents is an expansive landscape brimming with opportunities, shaped by technological advancements and innovative approaches. Organizations that embrace these trends will be well-equipped to unlock the full potential of AI, facilitating seamless interactions, informed decision-making, and robust security measures.

CHAPTER 10: GLOBAL PERSPECTIVES ON AI AGENTS

Regional variations in artificial intelligence (AI) adoption reveal a rich and intricate landscape where innovation, economic priorities, and cultural influences intertwine. Each region showcases distinct attributes that shape the embrace and implementation of AI technologies. To appreciate these variations, we must explore the socio-economic factors, governmental strategies, and cultural attitudes that drive AI adoption around the globe.

In North America, particularly the United States, the AI landscape is marked by significant investment and a dynamic entrepreneurial spirit. The U.S. solidifies its role as a global leader through technology hotspots like Silicon Valley, where substantial venture capital fuels groundbreaking AI innovations. Key sectors such as healthcare benefit from advanced predictive analytics, enhancing patient care and outcomes, while the financial industry leverages algorithmic trading to optimize market dynamics. The cultural embrace of innovation and a willingness to take risks, paired with strong collaborations between universities and industry leaders, further accelerate AI developments.

Across the Atlantic, Europe's approach to AI adoption emphasizes the importance of regulatory measures. The European Union is at the forefront of advocating for ethical AI practices, with a strong focus on data privacy and protection, notably through the widely recognized General Data Protection Regulation (GDPR). This careful yet progressive stance shapes AI development, ensuring that ethical considerations are firmly embedded in the growth of technology. Countries like Germany and France integrate AI into manufacturing and automotive sectors, driving initiatives related to Industry 4.0. This commitment to ethical standards frequently contrasts with the more commercially inclined strategies seen in North America, highlighting Europe's dedication to balancing technological progress with respect for individual rights and societal norms.

In Asia, China's trajectory in AI adoption is marked by rapid integration driven by robust governmental support and substantial investment. The Chinese national strategy positions AI as a cornerstone of future economic growth, resulting in extensive funding and proactive policy initiatives aimed at advancing research and deployment. The enormous data generated by its vast population equips China with a significant advantage in developing data-driven AI models. Applications of AI are pervasive, ranging from smart city innovations that enhance urban management to facial recognition systems utilized for public safety. While concerns about surveillance and data privacy are growing, China's state-led approach enables it to excel in certain AI sectors, often outpacing Western nations in the scale of implementation.

Japan, adjacent to China, presents a unique perspective on AI integration, with a pronounced focus on robotics and human-centered applications. The societal acceptance of robots as helpful companions has positioned Japan as a frontrunner in the development of service robots, especially in healthcare and eldercare, where AI is instrumental in addressing challenges associated with an aging population. This seamless fusion of AI into everyday life illustrates how cultural perceptions can deeply influence the adoption and practical application of technology.

Conversely, regions such as Africa and parts of Latin America face significant hurdles in AI adoption, often stemming from limited infrastructure and investment. Nevertheless, there are promising developments, as local innovators adapt AI technologies to tackle specific challenges. In the agricultural sector, for example, AI-driven tools enhance crop management and improve yield outcomes. Despite existing infrastructural challenges, the transformative potential of AI to foster social good is immense, with emerging frameworks for using AI in social services and sustainable development.

Ultimately, the diverse landscape of AI adoption across regions underscores the complex interplay of cultural perspectives, economic aspirations, and regulatory contexts. As these elements continue to evolve, they will define the unique pathways through which AI technologies are perceived and implemented globally. Recognizing this diversity is crucial; it emphasizes the necessity for a nuanced understanding of how AI can effectively serve varied populations while honoring local values and addressing specific regional needs.

The landscape of artificial intelligence (AI) initiatives across emerging markets presents a vibrant and multifaceted picture, marked by remarkable innovation and significant challenges. These regions, rich in untapped potential and distinct socio-economic conditions, are increasingly harnessing AI to foster development and reshape industries in profound ways.

In Africa, AI initiatives are showcasing the transformative power of technology in tackling persistent developmental issues. Agriculture, a vital sector for many African nations, has seen groundbreaking applications of AI that significantly improve farming practices. For instance, Aerobotics, a South African startup, employs AI-driven drones to capture high-resolution aerial imagery. This innovative approach to precision agriculture not only boosts productivity but also plays a crucial role in enhancing food security—a pressing concern across the continent.

The healthcare sector in these emerging markets is another area where AI is making a substantial impact. In various parts of Asia, where equitable access to quality healthcare remains a challenge, AI-driven diagnostic tools are emerging as both cost-effective and accessible solutions. Take Qure.ai in India, for example; this company utilizes deep learning algorithms to analyze radiological images, facilitating rapid and accurate diagnoses for conditions like tuberculosis and brain injuries. Such AI innovations are indispensable in regions with limited healthcare infrastructure, providing scalable solutions that far surpass traditional approaches.

Latin America is also actively engaging with AI to address local needs while aligning with global technological trends. In Brazil, for instance, initiatives focusing on natural resource management harness AI to protect biodiversity while promoting sustainable practices. Companies like Olho do Dono are integrating AI into cattle management systems, which enhance productivity and encourage environmental stewardship by optimizing grazing patterns to prevent overgrazing and mitigate deforestation.

Southeast Asia is witnessing a surge in e-commerce, an industry ripe for AI enhancements. Companies are deploying advanced algorithms to streamline supply chain logistics, tailor customer experiences, and automate customer service through chatbots. Take Go-Jek in Indonesia: this innovative company utilizes AI not only to improve their ride-hailing services but also to expand into financial services, thereby fostering greater financial inclusion in a country with a notable unbanked population.

However, the road to realizing AI's full potential in emerging markets is fraught with obstacles. Many of these regions struggle with limited digital infrastructure, a shortage of skilled AI professionals, and inconsistent policy environments. Issues such as inadequate internet connectivity can hinder the deployment of AI solutions reliant on cloud computing and real-time data processing. Overcoming these challenges necessitates a comprehensive approach that combines infrastructure investments with educational initiatives aimed at cultivating a skilled AI workforce.

International collaboration is essential in strengthening AI development within these regions. Programs like the African Masters in Machine Intelligence (AMMI) are paving the way for improved AI education across Africa, helping to build networks of talent dedicated to cutting-edge research and practical applications. Additionally, partnerships with global tech firms provide essential resources and support, enabling local startups to innovate and compete effectively on a global scale.

The potential for AI in emerging markets is vast, presenting not only prospects for economic advancement but also avenues for societal transformation. As these initiatives continue to evolve, they hold the promise of not only redefining industries locally but also contributing significantly to the global dialogue on AI as a catalyst for inclusive and sustainable development.

Governments across the globe hold a crucial position in shaping the future of artificial intelligence (AI), significantly impacting both the speed of technological advancement and the ethical frameworks that guide its implementation. Their involvement is comprehensive, encompassing the creation of regulatory standards, funding for research, skill development, and fostering partnerships with private sector players. This multifaceted engagement is vital for effectively navigating the rapid evolution of AI, ensuring its growth aligns with both national interests and global needs.

A central pillar of governmental responsibility in AI

development is the establishment of robust regulatory frameworks that promote safe and ethical usage of these technologies. The European Union stands as a notable example, having made strides with the implementation of the General Data Protection Regulation (GDPR). This legislation emphasizes the imperatives of data privacy and protection —critical elements given that AI systems often depend on extensive datasets. The GDPR has not only influenced regulatory practices in Europe but has also set a benchmark for other nations striving to craft their own data protection policies.

In addition to regulation, governments invest substantially in AI research and development to fuel innovation while ensuring oversight over the direction of technological progress. For instance, China's ambitious "New Generation Artificial Intelligence Development Plan" highlights the nation's commitment to AI, allocating significant resources for education, research, and infrastructure development. This strategic investment not only accelerates domestic innovation but also positions China as a formidable player in the global AI landscape, demonstrating how government funding can unlock both economic and strategic advantages.

Talent cultivation is another critical area where governments wield influence. Developing a skilled workforce proficient in AI technologies is essential for maintaining competitiveness in an increasingly technology-driven world. Initiatives like the United States' AI Institutes focus on supporting AI-related research across universities, illustrating a national strategy aimed at building a resilient workforce. Similarly, India's Skill India initiative emphasizes training programs in AI, data science, and machine learning, ensuring that the country's population is equipped to tackle future challenges in a fast-evolving field.

Governments are also key facilitators of collaboration between the public and private sectors, creating environments conducive to innovation. In emerging economies, where tech ecosystems are still taking shape, governmental support is pivotal in organizing partnerships that drive technological adoption. Singapore's Smart Nation initiative exemplifies this effort by promoting public-private collaborations, facilitating the integration of AI into urban planning and public services to create smarter, more efficient cities.

International cooperation, spearheaded by governments, is essential in addressing transnational concerns such as cybersecurity and the ethical dimensions of AI in surveillance. Initiatives like the Global Partnership on AI (GPAI) provide vital platforms for countries to share best practices and establish common guidelines, ensuring that AI serves as a catalyst for global progress rather than a battleground for geopolitical rivalry.

Despite these promising initiatives, governments encounter significant challenges in keeping pace with the rapid pace of technological advancements while balancing the need for innovation with regulatory oversight. To effectively guide AI development, they must adopt a nimble approach, continually revising policies to align with emerging technologies and evolving societal demands. Striking the right balance is crucial —over-regulation can inhibit innovation, whereas under-regulation might lead to unethical practices and a decline in public trust.

Furthermore, effective governance in AI must tackle issues of bias and inclusivity, ensuring that technology benefits diverse populations and does not exacerbate existing inequalities. This entails crafting transparent policies that welcome stakeholder input and emphasize fairness and equity —an endeavor that is both challenging and essential as AI increasingly permeates all aspects of life.

As AI technologies mature and evolve, the role of governments will be instrumental in steering these innovations toward positive outcomes. Ultimately, this will lead to a trajectory of progress that is ethical, inclusive, and sustainable for all stakeholders involved.

In today's rapidly evolving world of artificial intelligence (AI), international collaborations and partnerships have become essential to harnessing technological advancements while upholding ethical standards on a global scale. The intricate nature and swift pace of AI development require a unified, cross-border approach that emphasizes shared knowledge, collective resources, and cohesive policies.

A shining example of this spirit of cooperation is the Global Partnership on AI (GPAI). Comprising nations such as the United States, Canada, France, and the United Kingdom, the GPAI serves as a vital platform where member countries can share insights, strategies, and best practices. This collaborative environment is crucial for tackling pressing global challenges, including AI ethics, data privacy, and equitable access to technology.

International partnerships often extend into research and development, transcending the limitations often faced within individual countries. The EU's Horizon Europe program exemplifies this by promoting transnational collaborations among AI researchers.

Regulatory collaboration is another critical aspect of international AI partnerships. Initiatives like the joint testbed for autonomous vehicles developed by Singapore and Germany illustrate how countries can collectively explore and refine international guidelines.

Moreover, the intersection of public and private sectors in AI deployment is increasingly important. The AI4EU project exemplifies this dynamic, seamlessly connecting European AI companies with academic institutions. This collaboration not only bridges innovation with practical application but also accelerates the market integration of AI solutions, ensuring they cater to both technological advancements and societal needs.

Educational institutions also greatly benefit from international AI partnerships. Initiatives like the MIT-SenseTime Alliance on Artificial Intelligence highlight how academia can unite globally to push the boundaries of AI research and education.

However, the path to successful international collaborations is not without its challenges. Disparities in technological readiness, cultural variations in ethical perspectives, and differing levels of resource access can create hurdles in synchronizing AI initiatives. To overcome these issues, fostering a continuous and inclusive dialogue among international organizations and consortia is crucial. This dialogue must prioritize transparency and shared objectives, ensuring that all stakeholders, particularly those from underrepresented regions, have a voice in shaping policies.

Additionally, addressing geopolitical tensions is essential as AI technologies increasingly intertwine with national security concerns. Initiatives such as the OECD's Recommendation on Artificial Intelligence offer guiding principles to nurture cooperation among member countries, helping to bridge divides and promote a collaborative governance framework. Sustaining this cooperative spirit requires a concerted effort from all stakeholders to prioritize shared interests over national competition.

Ultimately, advancing successful international collaborations in AI involves a visionary approach that balances technological innovation with ethical considerations and cultural diversity.

The integration of artificial intelligence (AI) across varying cultural landscapes significantly transforms not only technological applications but also the foundational social norms and value systems of societies. To truly grasp the cultural impacts on AI, it's essential to delve into the intricacies of how regional traditions, societal structures, and local sensibilities influence the reception and implementation of AI technologies.

A particularly illustrative example can be found in the healthcare sector. In Western nations, AI-driven diagnostic tools are typically lauded for their efficiency and precision, enhancing traditional medical practices with advanced data algorithms that predict outcomes and recommend treatment plans based on extensive datasets. However, when these technologies are introduced in different cultural contexts, they often encounter varied levels of acceptance. For instance, in many East Asian countries, there exists a strong communal ethos and a notable trust in technological advancements. This cultural backdrop facilitates a smoother adoption of AI in healthcare, as communities are inclined towards innovations that promise collective benefits. In contrast, regions where individual privacy holds paramount importance may display significant reluctance toward AI systems that necessitate extensive sharing of personal data.

The interplay between AI and cultural norms is further evident in customer service and retail environments. In Japan, the concept of omotenashi—an embodiment of gracious hospitality—shapes the design of AI-driven customer service agents, which are meticulously programmed to engage with customers through a lens of politeness and attentive service, mirroring human interactions. These AI systems integrate culturally specific etiquette, enhancing user experience and fostering acceptance by aligning with local traditions.

Conversely, in nations like Germany, where a strong emphasis is placed on privacy and individuality, the approach to AI in customer service is notably more conservative. Here, AI applications are designed to prioritize user autonomy over the data shared with these systems, in alignment with stringent privacy legislation such as the General Data Protection Regulation (GDPR). This cultural commitment to data protection significantly influences the design and deployment of AI technologies, ensuring that they resonate with societal values surrounding privacy.

Further illustrating the influence of cultural perspectives on AI applications is the education sector. In Turkey, for example, AI tools are being tailored for language learning, integrating cultural references like idioms and historical context to enrich the educational experience. This adjustment signifies a growing recognition that AI applications in education must align with local educational philosophies and practices, crafting learning tools that are both effective and culturally resonant.

AI also plays a pivotal role in the preservation of cultural heritage. Initiatives such as the digitization of indigenous languages or the reconstruction of ancient artifacts through AI highlight technology's potential to safeguard and celebrate cultural identities. These projects underscore the dual nature of AI: serving not only as a utility for cultural preservation but also as a bridge fostering a global appreciation of diverse heritages.

Yet, the cultural implications of AI are not without challenges. The widespread adoption of AI technologies can sometimes perpetuate cultural homogenization, where dominant cultural norms overshadow local traditions and practices. This concern necessitates a conscientious approach to AI development, emphasizing the importance of cultural sensitivity and diversity. Developers and technologists should actively engage with cultural experts and community leaders to ensure that AI applications are crafted in ways that honor and enrich local customs rather than supplanting them.

Moreover, the effects of AI on cultural narratives extend deeply into the realms of media and entertainment. In influential centers like Hollywood, AI algorithms increasingly shape content creation and distribution, prompting critical discussions on representation and the risk of reinforcing cultural stereotypes. This reality highlights the urgent need for thoughtful design in AI systems employed in media, incorporating safeguards to ensure diverse cultural representation and narrative authenticity.

In conclusion, the cultural implications of AI are profound and multifaceted, demanding an insightful approach that harmonizes technological innovation with the preservation of cultural integrity.

The impact of artificial intelligence (AI) agents on global supply chains represents a transformative evolution, fundamentally altering traditional models into agile, data-driven ecosystems that prioritize efficiency and responsiveness. As supply chains become increasingly intricate—spanning continents and involving a web of suppliers, manufacturers, and distributors—the integration of AI agents is crucial, yielding far-reaching benefits across multiple dimensions of supply chain management.

One of the most remarkable contributions of AI agents lies in their ability to enhance predictive analytics, which allows businesses to forecast demand fluctuations with extraordinary precision. This is particularly evident in sectors like consumer electronics, where the unpredictable demand for products such as smartphones poses significant challenges. This empowers supply chain managers to refine procurement strategies and optimize inventory levels, effectively curbing both surpluses and shortages while increasing responsiveness to market shifts.

In logistics, AI agents excel at optimizing routing and transportation efficiency—an essential component of effective supply chain management. These intelligent systems analyze real-time data, encompassing traffic conditions, weather patterns, fuel prices, and transportation schedules, to recommend the most efficient shipping routes. This sophisticated decision-making process is already being employed by logistics leaders like DHL and UPS, who leverage AI-driven platforms to manage their expansive fleets and streamline warehouse operations. Through minimizing idle time and consolidating deliveries, AI agents not only cut costs but also promote sustainability, helping to lower carbon footprints in an era increasingly focused on environmental responsibility.

Moreover, AI agents are indispensable in supplier relationship management, especially in today's complex global networks vulnerable to disruptions from geopolitical tensions, natural disasters, or market volatility. This allows firms to create contingency plans, diversify their supplier networks, and ensure continuity amid unforeseen challenges. For instance, automotive manufacturers—who heavily depend on a vast array of global suppliers—utilize AI agents to facilitate proactive risk management. These agents aggregate data from supplier reports, news outlets, and market analysis, promptly flagging risks like political instability or a supplier's financial difficulties, enabling manufacturers to swiftly adjust their operations and maintain production schedules.

Inventory management also sees remarkable advancements through the application of AI agents. Traditional systems often struggle to balance high service levels with minimal holding costs. Yet, AI agents resolve this challenge by utilizing sophisticated algorithms to predict reorder points and optimal stock levels, taking into account lead times, demand variability, and seasonal trends. This capability is particularly beneficial in fast-moving consumer goods sectors, where maintaining product freshness and navigating shelf-life constraints are crucial.

Additionally, AI integration in supply chains revolutionizes quality control, particularly in industries that demand stringent component integrity, such as aerospace. Advanced computer vision and machine learning technologies empower

AI agents to automate inspection processes along production lines, analyzing high-resolution images to detect minute defects that might go unnoticed by the human eye. This ensures that only components of the highest quality progress through the manufacturing pipeline, significantly enhancing overall product reliability.

However, the implementation of AI agents in global supply chains is not without its challenges. Concerns around data security and privacy arise, especially given the interconnected nature of these networks that often cross national boundaries. Implementing robust cybersecurity measures is essential to safeguard sensitive information from unauthorized access and potential breaches. Additionally, the rise of automation in roles traditionally held by humans may raise questions about workforce displacement in areas such as inventory management and logistics coordination.

Despite these challenges, the advantages of deploying AI agents across global supply chains are compelling and abundant. They yield unprecedented levels of transparency, efficiency, and agility, compelling businesses to reimagine operational strategies and embrace innovation. As these technologies evolve, they promise the potential for resilient and responsive supply chains that not only meet changing global demands but also proactively address emerging trends. The strategic incorporation of AI agents signifies more than a technological enhancement; it heralds a fundamental shift towards more intelligent, sustainable, and competitive supply chain systems that are equipped to thrive in a rapidly changing world.

Cross-border data management and artificial intelligence (AI) are at the forefront of the evolving landscape of global technology. As AI systems increasingly permeate various sectors, the international flow of data emerges as both an opportunity for innovation and a challenge to navigate. This multifaceted topic calls for a comprehensive analysis of the mechanisms, regulations, and technologies that facilitate data movement across national boundaries, ensuring that we harness AI's vast potential while upholding stringent privacy and security standards.

The importance of effective cross-border data management is accentuated by the inherently transnational nature of AI development. Advanced AI models, particularly those utilizing machine learning, depend on extensive datasets that are often generated and processed in diverse geographical regions. Take the healthcare sector, for instance. A multinational pharmaceutical company may gather patient data from clinical trials conducted across Europe, analyze this data in research centers situated in the United States, and then apply AI-derived insights to enhance drug development efforts in Asia. This intricate web of data connectivity highlights the urgent need for seamless data transfers while remaining compliant with the ever-evolving legal frameworks of different jurisdictions.

However, the imperative for cross-border data transfer encounters the complexity of varied global data protection regulations. The European Union's General Data Protection Regulation (GDPR) stands out as one of the most stringent legal frameworks, setting a global benchmark for data privacy. GDPR not only governs European entities but also impacts any organization that handles the personal data of EU citizens, imposing rigorous requirements such as the necessity for explicit consent, data minimization practices, and the affirmation of data subject rights. These regulations create substantial challenges for AI systems striving to access diverse datasets essential for training and operational efficiency. Consequently, companies must navigate complex compliance pathways, often relying on tools like standard contractual clauses (SCCs) for cross-border data transfers.

In contrast, the United States adopts a more sector-specific approach to data regulation, relying on laws such as the

Health Insurance Portability and Accountability Act (HIPAA) to safeguard healthcare data. This regulatory landscape of fragmentation necessitates clear and effective strategies for compliance teams within multinational organizations to adeptly maneuver through intricate legal frameworks. One practical approach to managing these complexities is the establishment of regional data hubs, which allow localized data processing and help reduce unnecessary data transfers, ultimately mitigating the risks associated with cross-border data flows. These hubs function as vital nodes that enhance regional data localization strategies while promoting global collaboration in AI initiatives.

AI itself offers transformative potential in optimizing cross-border data management. Advanced data classification systems powered by AI can automatically categorize and label data in accordance with jurisdiction-specific privacy requirements. Additionally, natural language processing (NLP) tools can intelligently analyze and redact sensitive information prior to international sharing, striking a balance between compliance and the integrity of data for analytical use. Employing AI-driven encryption protocols further fortifies data during transmission, providing an extra layer of security against unauthorized access.

Beyond the realms of compliance and security, harnessing AI for cross-border data management paves the way for harmonizing data formats—a common barrier in international data exchange. In global supply chains, for instance, discrepancies in data formats among partners from various countries can hamper effective collaboration and timely decision-making. AI solutions designed to standardize and translate these formats ensure that data remains interoperable and actionable, leading to enhanced efficiency across international operations.

Nevertheless, the integration of AI into cross-border data management is not without obstacles. The complexity of implementing AI systems demands transparency and explainability in decision-making processes. All stakeholders —from corporate leaders to regulatory entities—must have confidence in the ability of AI technologies to manage data ethically and lawfully across jurisdictions. Moreover, understanding the potential economic and societal consequences of AI-facilitated data flows calls for an ongoing dialogue among governments, businesses, and civil society to ensure that all voices are heard and that solutions are equitable and just.

To effectively tackle these challenges, it is essential to develop innovative governance frameworks that keep pace with technological advancements. Collaborative efforts, such as establishing global data governance bodies or forming multilateral agreements on data sharing, represent promising pathways toward achieving standardized and interoperable solutions on a broader scale. Investing in cross-border data infrastructure, advocating for transparent AI models, and fostering robust public-private partnerships will be crucial at the intersection of technology, regulation, and ethical frameworks.

The rise of AI in cross-border data management tells a compelling story about the convergence of global data sharing practices and regional data protection mandates, propelling informed decision-making across a myriad of industries. As AI technologies continue to evolve and proliferate, the capability to manage data effectively across borders will be instrumental not only in driving technological advancements but also in ensuring that these developments respect and embody the diverse values and legal standards of our interconnected global community.

Navigating the Landscape of Global AI Governance

The realm of global governance in artificial intelligence (AI) development is marked by intricate challenges as nations, corporations, and international organizations grapple with the balance between technological advancement and regulatory oversight. As AI continues to transform economies, societies, and cultures, the imperative for cohesive governance frameworks that promote responsible and equitable progress is more urgent than ever. This segment explores the complexity of these governance issues, illuminating the dynamic interplay between national initiatives and international collaborations aimed at regulating and guiding AI evolution.

A fundamental challenge in global AI governance lies in the absence of standardized regulatory frameworks. For instance, while the European Union has taken the lead with comprehensive policies such as the General Data Protection Regulation (GDPR) and is now advancing proposals specifically addressing AI, other regions have embraced a more fragmented, sometimes laissez-faire, approach. This divergence creates a multifaceted development landscape where varying standards can obstruct global interoperability and complicate cross-border collaboration. An illustrative scenario is an AI system crafted under the stringent privacy regulations of the EU, which may not align with the more lenient data practices of other jurisdictions, thus complicating its worldwide deployment and integration efforts.

To bridge these regulatory gaps, prominent international organizations—such as the United Nations and the Organisation for Economic Co-operation and Development (OECD)—have embarked on initiatives to create dialogue aimed at harmonizing AI regulations globally. The OECD's guiding principles for AI focus on nurturing innovation while safeguarding human rights and democratic values. These established principles offer a reference point for countries striving to align their policies. This emerging consensus highlights a recognition that, despite diverse cultural and economic contexts, the fundamental aspects of AI governance must be universally relevant, emphasizing transparency, accountability, and inclusivity.

A crucial dimension of global governance involves addressing the ethical ramifications of AI technologies. The potential for AI systems to reinforce existing biases and inequalities necessitates the development of robust ethical standards that cross national boundaries. For example, facial recognition technologies may demonstrate significantly variable accuracy across different demographic groups, raising profound concerns about fairness and discrimination. Tackling these challenges demands concerted global collaboration to establish guidelines that champion ethical AI practices.

The intersection of security and responsibility in AI deployment adds layers of complexity to the governance landscape. With AI increasingly integrated into critical national security and economic frameworks, there is an urgent need to safeguard these technologies from malicious misuse and unintended repercussions. The autonomous nature of certain AI applications—particularly in cybersecurity and military environments—calls for rigorous oversight to prevent potential exploitation. The debate surrounding the deployment of autonomous drones in military settings exemplifies the pressing need for adherence to international humanitarian laws. Addressing this issue may require multilateral agreements akin to arms control treaties to establish clear boundaries and governance structures.

Moreover, global governance must grapple with the varying capacities for AI development and access among nations. Emerging economies may find themselves lagging in keeping up with rapid technological strides, which could exacerbate the digital divide. Therefore, international collaboration is vital for fostering knowledge transfer and capacity building. Initiatives like the Global Partnership on Artificial Intelligence (GPAI) exemplify efforts to bridge these gaps by promoting research cooperation and sharing best practices among member countries. These initiatives aspire to democratize access to AI technologies and resources, fostering a more equitable environment where all nations can harness AI's transformative capabilities.

The role of non-state actors, including multinational corporations and civil society organizations, also adds significant complexity to the governance landscape. Tech giants like Google and Microsoft, possessing substantial influence over AI advancements, often advance well beyond existing regulatory measures, creating a pressing need for governance models that integrate public-private partnerships. In this scenario, industry leaders must collaborate with governments to formulate ethical and sustainable AI strategies. Civil society plays a crucial role in advocating for transparency and accountability, ensuring that a diverse range of voices contribute to governance frameworks, thereby fostering societal trust in AI initiatives.

Despite the challenges in global AI governance, there exist rich opportunities for frameworks to adapt and evolve in response to the rapid evolution of technology. Strengthening these frameworks through multilateral agreements, investing in secure data-sharing ecosystems, and promoting inclusive dialogues will be instrumental in crafting a governance landscape capable of not only effectively regulating AI but also nurturing confidence in its positive societal contributions.

In summary, the intersection of technology and global regulatory efforts in AI development represents a critical juncture for humanity. This endeavor is not merely a regulatory formality; it is a moral imperative, ensuring that as we unlock the vast potential of AI, we do so grounded in integrity and foresight.

Comparing AI Agent Policies: A Deep Dive into East vs. West

The landscape of artificial intelligence (AI) policy is rich with nuances, revealing a fascinating yet complex dichotomy between Eastern and Western approaches. While both regions aspire to leverage AI's transformative potential for economic growth, they reflect significantly different ethical beliefs, regulatory strategies, and overarching priorities. Recognizing these distinctions is essential for stakeholders seeking to navigate the increasingly interconnected global AI terrain effectively.

In Western nations, especially within the European Union (EU) and North America, AI policies are profoundly shaped by a commitment to data privacy and the safeguarding of human rights. This dedication manifests in robust regulatory frameworks, most notably the EU's General Data Protection Regulation (GDPR) and the proposed Artificial Intelligence Act. These regulations emphasize transparency, accountability, and ethical responsibility, with the aim of mitigating risks associated with AI usage. For example, the GDPR enforces stringent data protection standards that directly influence the design and operational functioning of AI systems within Europe. This strong prioritization of individual privacy reflects a broader cultural ethos in the West, where personal rights and freedoms are often placed above the rapid pace of technological advancement.

Conversely, Eastern policy approaches, particularly in China, exhibit a much more pronounced role for the government in steering AI development. The Chinese strategy is predominantly focused on harnessing AI to enhance economic competitiveness and bolster national security. Key initiatives, such as the New Generation Artificial Intelligence Development Plan, aim to position China as a global leader in AI by 2030, prioritizing rapid innovation and substantial investment in AI research, infrastructure, and talent cultivation. Notably, China's data governance model is more permissive than its Western counterpart, facilitating extensive data aggregation, which is crucial for training advanced AI algorithms on a vast scale.

The application of AI technologies in the public sector starkly illustrates these philosophical divides. In many Western countries, there is an ongoing public discourse centered on the ethical implications of AI, with efforts focused on achieving consensus around algorithmic equity and bias mitigation. This is exemplified by public-private partnerships, such as the Partnership on AI, which work collaboratively to establish voluntary ethical guidelines for AI implementation.

In contrast, China adopts a more directive approach, actively deploying AI technologies in areas like public security and smart city initiatives with minimal public consultation. This strategy, while efficient from a governmental viewpoint, raises significant ethical concerns regarding surveillance and privacy. The widespread use of facial recognition technology in urban areas underscores the broader implications of AI applications in China, highlighting a societal norm where technology serves both commercial interests and extensive state surveillance efforts.

Despite these differences, both Eastern and Western countries confront similar challenges in the realm of AI deployment, particularly in preventing ethical breaches and ensuring fairness in algorithmic outcomes. However, their contrasting policy environments shape their responses to these challenges. Western regulators are more inclined to develop directives that enforce transparency and ethical standards. For instance, the EU's proposed AI Regulation seeks to categorize AI applications based on their associated risks, imposing stringent obligations for high-risk usages.

In the East, the focus is on striking a balance between fostering innovation and maintaining control, often guided by Confucian ideals of harmony and hierarchy. China's approach to AI governance generally revolves around top-down mandates that integrate AI technologies across diverse sectors while managing risks to social stability. While this model enables rapid adoption of AI solutions, it tends to overlook potential ethical dilemmas that may surface from such deployment.

As AI globalization continues to advance, the interplay between Eastern and Western policies will become increasingly crucial. Multinational corporations operating in both landscapes must adeptly navigate these contrasting regulatory frameworks, which dictate their strategic decisions regarding investment, development, and implementation of AI technologies.

Ultimately, while the AI policy landscape in the East and West reveals divergent trajectories, it also presents a unique opportunity for cross-pollination of ideas and best practices. Engaging in constructive dialogue allows these regions to benefit from each other's successes while collaboratively addressing shared challenges. This exchange of knowledge can lead to a global AI ecosystem that champions both innovation and responsibility.

The Future of AI Agents on a Global Scale: Opportunities and Challenges Ahead

As we gaze into the future, the role of AI agents on a global scale appears increasingly vibrant and multifaceted. This horizon is not just a reflection of technological advancements; it also embodies the evolution of societal structures and the necessity for global cooperation. The integration of AI agents across various aspects of daily life and diverse industries promises to fundamentally transform economies, cultural landscapes, and international relations in profound and often unexpected ways.

Economic Transformation: The Engine of Growth

At the forefront of AI's potential impact lies its power to ignite economic transformation. Forecasts suggest that AI technologies will make significant contributions to GDP growth worldwide, rewarding countries that adeptly harness this technology. Regions proficient in deploying AI-driven processes can expect enhanced productivity, optimized operations, and the emergence of new markets. For instance, when examining successful AI implementations across the East and West, we see how these innovations can create a domino effect, leading nations toward rapid modernization. This transformation will necessitate strategic investments in AI-related education and infrastructure, ensuring that the workforce is well-prepared with the skills required in this digital era.

Cultural Integration: A New Dimension of Human Experience

Culturally, we are witnessing a remarkable evolution as AI agents transition from mere tools to co-creators and partners in the arts and education. Particularly in sectors such as entertainment and learning, these agents are revolutionizing the way content is created and delivered, offering hyper-personalized experiences that cater to individual tastes like never before. This expansive reach transcends geographical boundaries, facilitating the exchange and fusion of unique cultural narratives through interactive media powered by AI. Imagine an AI that curates music playlists based on your mood, or an educational platform that adapts its teaching methods to suit your learning style; the possibilities are as diverse as the cultures we represent.

Addressing Global Challenges: AI as a Force for Good

AI agents will also play a crucial role in tackling some of the most pressing challenges facing our world today, including climate change, healthcare disparities, and food security. Advanced climate models powered by AI are being developed to predict environmental threats with unprecedented accuracy, thus informing effective policy-making and resource allocation. In healthcare, AI-driven diagnostic tools have the potential to revolutionize patient care by enabling earlier disease detection and creating tailored treatment plans, ultimately improving health outcomes on a global scale.

Redefining International Relations: The
New Landscape of Diplomacy

In the realm of international relations, the rise of AI agents will inevitably lead to an evolution in diplomatic engagement. As nations weave AI technologies into their national security strategies, new efforts will be required to negotiate agreements that promote the ethical and secure use of these technologies. Establishing robust frameworks to manage AI-powered defense systems and cyber capabilities will be paramount. International treaties may emerge to regulate AI applications in warfare, aiming to prevent escalation and promote global stability.

Navigating Challenges: Bridging the Digital Divide

Despite these promising developments, the global expansion of AI agents brings its own set of challenges. One significant concern is the potential widening of the digital divide, particularly in regions with limited access to technology. Addressing these inequalities will demand inclusive policies and international partnerships that ensure equitable access to emerging AI resources. Initiatives focused on education, targeted investments in technological infrastructure, and collaborations between developed and developing nations will be vital in bridging this gap.

Establishing Ethical Guidelines: A Framework for Responsible AI

On the governance front, the establishment of global standards for AI ethics is essential. These standards should ensure that the deployment of AI agents adheres to principles that protect human rights and promote societal well-being. As countries begin to coalesce around these efforts, there lies a unique opportunity to create a universal framework that balances innovation with ethical considerations, fostering transparency, accountability, and fairness in AI systems.

Looking ahead, the trajectory of AI agents will be significantly influenced by the global context in which they operate. The journey forward will require collaborative efforts, bringing together diverse perspectives to ensure that AI agents become instruments of positive change worldwide.

As these agents increasingly shape our future, the emphasis must lie on fostering systems that prioritize inclusivity, sustainability, and innovation—ultimately guiding humanity along a path that harmonizes technological progress with ethical responsibility. The future of AI is not just about what these agents can do; it's about how they can enhance our shared experience and lead us toward a more equitable and sustainable future.

Chapter 11: Risks and Challenges Facing AI Agents

As we stand on the brink of an era defined by artificial intelligence, it's essential to examine not just the immense potential that AI agents hold but also the nuanced technical limitations and challenges that accompany their deployment. Every facet of AI technology, regardless of its sophistication, faces inherent constraints and vulnerabilities that can significantly influence performance and, at times, lead to failure. Acknowledging these limitations is not merely an academic exercise; it is crucial for ensuring that AI systems operate safely and ethically in a rapidly changing landscape.

One of the most pressing limitations of AI agents is their reliance on the quality of data. Machine learning models, which underpin many AI applications, are fundamentally dependent on vast datasets for training. However, these models are only as effective as the data they learn from. Issues such as poor quality, inherent bias, or incompleteness in datasets can result in erroneous predictions and decisions, often with grave consequences. For example, a medical diagnostic AI trained mainly on data from a specific demographic may fail to accurately diagnose conditions in patients from diverse backgrounds, leading to missed or incorrect diagnoses that could impact patient care significantly.

The implications of such data sensitivities extend into real-world applications in profound ways. Take, for instance, an AI system implemented in financial services. If this system is trained on biased historical data, it risks perpetuating existing inequalities in credit approval processes, effectively sidelining deserving candidates based on flawed algorithms. This scenario underscores the urgent need for an elevated focus on data curation, validation, and ethical sourcing, recognizing that combating bias necessitates holistic strategies. Such strategies should go beyond mere adjustments to algorithms and instead foster systemic changes in the methodologies used to collect and process data.

Another significant hurdle in the AI landscape is the challenge of interpretability, often referred to as the "black-box problem." Many advanced algorithms, especially deep learning models, operate in a manner that is not readily understandable to humans. This opacity can lead to critical challenges when AI systems make unexpected or erroneous decisions. The inability to elucidate how a conclusion was reached can erode trust, particularly in high-stakes domains such as healthcare and autonomous transportation. While advancements in explainable AI (XAI) show promise in enhancing the transparency of AI decision-making processes, this area remains a vibrant field for research and innovation, where breakthroughs are still needed.

Furthermore, the computational demands associated with training and deploying AI models cannot be overlooked. Many sophisticated AI systems require vast processing power, often limiting their use to resource-rich organizations. This disparity not only hinders the equitable distribution of AI benefits but also raises environmental concerns due to the significant energy consumption associated with extensive computing operations. Addressing these challenges necessitates a concerted effort to develop more efficient algorithms that can deliver high performance while mitigating training durations and operational costs.

Despite these obstacles, the AI community is actively pursuing innovative solutions to tackle such limitations. One promising strategy is federated learning, which allows AI systems to learn from distributed data sources without the need to share sensitive information. This approach not only preserves privacy but also reduces biases by leveraging a more diverse range of data while alleviating the burdens on centralized data processing structures. The healthcare sector, for example, is exploring federated learning to enable collaboration among hospitals, allowing them to train AI models without compromising patient confidentiality.

In addition to these strategies, implementing redundancy measures is critical in protecting against potential AI system failures. In high-stakes environments like autonomous vehicles, having such redundancies is not just beneficial; it is essential for safety and reliability.

As the field of AI continues to evolve, there is a dynamic landscape of collaboration between academic institutions, industry leaders, and government entities. These partnerships are invaluable in fostering shared resources, initiating joint research endeavors, and establishing regulatory frameworks to guide ethical AI use and development.

Navigating the intricate interplay of potential and limitation requires a balanced approach characterized by both caution and ambition. In doing so, we ensure that the advancements in technology serve to uplift humanity rather than inadvertently cause harm.

As artificial intelligence agents increasingly permeate our everyday lives, the imperative to address security vulnerabilities and cybersecurity threats becomes ever more critical. This revolutionary technology, while offering transformative benefits, also presents unique challenges that experts and organizations must confront head-on. Cybersecurity in the realm of AI is not a mere side issue; it is a fundamental concern that requires meticulous attention to safeguard sensitive data, maintain user trust, and uphold operational integrity.

AI agents are inherently designed to process and interpret vast quantities of data, enabling them to learn and make decisions. This data-driven approach, however, renders them highly attractive targets for cyber threats. Unlike traditional software systems, AI agents exhibit distinct vulnerabilities linked to their reliance on data for training. One glaring example is adversarial attacks, where malicious actors manipulate input data to mislead AI systems. In image recognition, for instance, an assailant might subtly alter an image in ways that are imperceptible to human perception but drastically affect the AI's interpretation. This manipulation could lead to serious, and potentially harmful, decisions that impact lives and safety.

The complexity deepens when we consider the interconnectedness of AI agents with other systems, which amplifies the points of vulnerability. Particularly in ecosystems where AI interacts with the Internet of Things (IoT), the potential for multi-vector attacks grows exponentially. The healthcare sector exemplifies this risk: AI-driven diagnostic tools interfacing with hospital networks and medical devices become multi-layered targets for cyber intrusions. Safeguarding these expansive networks demands a holistic defense strategy, one that secures not only individual nodes but also facilitates continual oversight of data flows and behavioral patterns.

Machine learning models are not just susceptible to adversarial inputs; they are also vulnerable to model inversion attacks. In these scenarios, adversaries can glean access to sensitive training data by exploiting the AI system. This threat is particularly acute in industries dealing with personal or confidential information, such as financial services or digital assistants. To combat these risks, organizations must deploy advanced security measures like encryption, differential privacy techniques, and stringent access controls to thwart unauthorized access and data leakage.

The rise of AI also raises significant privacy concerns and questions regarding the unauthorized use of data. Many AI systems, particularly those utilizing deep learning architectures, require extensive datasets that often include personally identifiable information. This necessitates compliance with stringent privacy regulations, such as the General Data Protection Regulation (GDPR) in Europe and the California Consumer Privacy Act (CCPA) in the United States. Organizations leveraging AI technologies must implement robust data protection strategies, including encryption, anonymization, and transparent practices surrounding data collection and utilization.

Moreover, preserving the integrity of AI systems in the face of potential sabotage or corruption is paramount. Cyber threat actors may attempt to inject malicious code into AI algorithms, skewing outputs in dangerous ways. For example, if an AI agent is responsible for managing critical infrastructure or financial markets, any form of disruption could lead to catastrophic outcomes. Employing techniques such as code signing, version control, and routine system audits can play a vital role in maintaining the integrity and reliability of these systems.

Ethical considerations in AI development also warrant

attention to prevent misuse of these powerful tools. As governments and organizations become more aware of AI's potential for surveillance and manipulation, the ethical implications of AI deployment gain prominence. Misuse of AI can infringe on individual freedoms or distort public sentiment, as seen in numerous high-profile cases of AI-driven misinformation. To mitigate these concerns, establishing ethical development frameworks paired with rigorous testing environments is essential. This ensures that AI agents are developed and utilized responsibly, without becoming instruments of harm.

International collaboration and knowledge sharing are crucial in bolstering AI security. Cyber threats are inherently borderless, requiring countries and corporations to unite in sharing threat intelligence and best practices to strengthen defenses against global adversaries. Successful models of this collaborative approach can already be observed in various sector-specific cybersecurity information-sharing consortia.

In conclusion, tackling the security vulnerabilities and cyber threats inherent in AI technology requires a multifaceted strategy that encompasses technological innovation, organizational vigilance, and regulatory adherence. This not only protects vital information and upholds public trust but also lays the groundwork for a resilient digital ecosystem where AI-driven innovation can flourish, all while preserving the integrity and safety that society demands.

In the dynamic landscape of artificial intelligence (AI), the integration of intelligent agents into our daily routines prompts complex ethical considerations that demand thoughtful attention and deliberate action. As AI technologies continue to advance, the challenges we face grow increasingly intricate, highlighting the delicate balance between technological potential and moral duty.

One of the foremost ethical dilemmas centers around the

transparency of AI decision-making processes. Many AI systems, particularly those utilizing sophisticated algorithms such as deep learning, operate as "black boxes." This lack of clarity makes it difficult for users to understand the rationale behind AI-generated decisions, leading to mistrust and skepticism. For instance, consider an AI-driven financial advisor that recommends specific stock trades without disclosing how those recommendations were determined. Such obscurity can leave investors questioning their strategies, potentially eroding confidence in the technology. In response to this challenge, the field of explainable AI (XAI) is emerging, aiming to shed light on these processes.

Another pressing ethical concern is the issue of bias embedded within AI decision-making. These systems learn from historical data, which may inadvertently propagate biases that influence their outcomes. The repercussions can be particularly severe in areas like criminal justice, where AI tools are deployed to assist judges in sentencing and parole evaluations. If the historical datasets reflect systemic prejudices, the resulting AI decisions could reinforce or even magnify existing disparities, leading to unjust treatment of marginalized groups. To counteract this problem, organizations can employ comprehensive data auditing, introduce fairness-enhancing algorithms, and consistently monitor AI performance across varied scenarios. These strategies are essential for ensuring equitable and fair outcomes in AI applications.

As autonomous systems gain prominence, ethical questions surrounding accountability in decision-making come to the forefront. Take, for example, autonomous vehicles that must make rapid decisions in potentially life-threatening situations. The dilemma of how to assign responsibility when an AI makes a consequential choice – be it in an accident scenario or a critical maneuver – is inherently complex. Should accountability rest with the developer, the manufacturer, or the user? To tackle these challenges, there is a pressing need for well-defined ethical frameworks and participatory governance models that involve diverse stakeholder input, ensuring that the responsibilities of these technologies are clear and just.

Moreover, the potential misuse of AI technology raises significant concerns, particularly regarding privacy and surveillance. As AI capabilities in data collection and pattern recognition evolve, there is a real risk of these tools being exploited for invasive surveillance practices. Such developments could infringe on individual privacy rights and cultivate a society characterized by pervasive monitoring. For instance, while AI-powered facial recognition technologies may enhance public safety efforts, they can also facilitate the tracking of individuals without their permission. Thus, it becomes vital to find a balanced approach that maximizes the advantages of AI while staunchly defending individual freedoms, necessitating robust regulations and transparent guidelines regarding consent and usage.

In many instances, real-world applications of AI reveal an ethical tension between the pursuit of efficiency and the preservation of human dignity. In the healthcare arena, for example, AI systems may produce recommendations based solely on statistical outcomes, potentially neglecting individual patient preferences and quality-of-life considerations. Healthcare providers must navigate the delicate balance between adhering to AI guidance and respecting the diverse values and choices of those they serve. This underscores the importance of incorporating ethicists and human rights advocates into the design and decision-making processes of AI systems, ensuring that human dignity and autonomy remain at the forefront.

Across these multifaceted challenges, the establishment of clear ethical guidelines and the implementation of educational programs focused on AI ethics are of paramount importance.

Such initiatives can elevate awareness and empower professionals with the necessary tools to address ethical dilemmas effectively. The creation of AI Ethics Boards or Committees that encompass a wide range of perspectives can facilitate ongoing evaluations of AI applications, promoting societal values within technological advancements.

In addressing these ethical dilemmas, a collaborative approach is essential. Organizations must engage actively with regulators, ethicists, and the broader community to craft policies and frameworks that resonate with societal values and expectations.

Ultimately, navigating the ethical landscape of AI extends beyond mere technical solutions; it requires a deep-seated commitment to empathy, inclusivity, and foresight. Our objective is not simply to innovate for innovation's sake but to do so with a conscientious and ethical mindset, paving the way for a future where AI serves as a force for good, empowering humanity while respecting our ethical boundaries.

In an era where artificial intelligence is rapidly permeating various sectors, the integration of AI agents brings significant potential—and with that potential, the critical necessity for reliability and robustness. These two foundational attributes not only ensure seamless operation but also cultivate public trust and acceptance in AI technologies, directly influencing their real-world application and impact.

Understanding Reliability in AI

Reliability in AI refers to the system's ability to produce consistent and accurate results over time. To classify an AI system as reliable, it must perform correctly under specified conditions, yielding predictable outcomes when processing the same data or facing similar scenarios. This consistency is crucial across a plethora of applications. For example, in AI-driven customer service, agents must deliver uniform responses across similar inquiries to maintain customer satisfaction. Similarly, autonomous vehicles rely on a reliable AI system to accurately interpret road signs and detect pedestrians, regardless of changing environmental conditions.

To bolster reliability, robust testing protocols are essential. This involves not only hypothetical scenarios but also extensive simulations and real-world trials that challenge the AI systems in a myriad of situations. For instance, when developing an AI tool for healthcare diagnostics, engineers might expose the system to diverse datasets representing various patient profiles. This exposure allows the algorithms to learn and accurately recognize patterns in medical conditions, ensuring reliable diagnoses despite variability in the data.

The Significance of Robustness

Robustness, conversely, is the ability of an AI system to handle anomalies and unexpected conditions gracefully, without faltering. This resilience is particularly vital in unpredictable environments. Take predictive maintenance systems in manufacturing: these AI tools must not only function effectively across a spectrum of machinery but also adjust to sudden breakdowns or data anomalies caused by sensor malfunctions. This flexibility ensures efficiency, preventing costly downtime.

Achieving robustness poses a unique challenge, demanding sophisticated mechanisms for dynamic adaptation and error rectification. One innovative strategy involves embedding self-correcting protocols within the AI architecture. For example, consider an AI monitoring system in a smart city that utilizes real-time analytics and feedback loops; it can autonomously adjust to fluctuations in traffic patterns caused by unexpected weather changes or public events, ensuring continuous and efficient traffic flow.

Moreover, the aspect of robustness extends to resilience

against cyber threats. With the rising incidence of cyber-attacks targeting AI systems, safeguarding against these vulnerabilities is more critical than ever. Implementing advanced encryption methodologies, utilizing anomaly detection algorithms, and conducting regular security audits are essential practices for fortifying AI systems against exploitation.

Building Trust Through Transparency

The credibility of AI technologies hinges significantly on how effectively stakeholders address concerns around reliability and robustness. This proactive stance is crucial to prevent potential liabilities arising from AI errors—such as inaccurate medical recommendations from a healthcare application or misguided navigation instructions from an autonomous vehicle.

Fostering trust also requires transparency in AI development.

The pursuit of reliability and robustness is not a one-off project but rather a continuous journey. As AI technology evolves, so too must the methods for addressing emerging vulnerabilities and enhancing existing strengths. Engaging multidisciplinary teams—including engineers, ethicists, and domain experts—in this process enriches the development of AI agents, positioning them to be both reliable and robust.

In sum, mastering reliability and robustness is paramount to the successful deployment of AI agents across diverse sectors.

The emergence of artificial intelligence (AI) agents has ushered in a transformative era, sparking a blend of excitement and caution among the public. The relationship people hold with these advanced technologies is inherently complex, characterized by a wide spectrum of emotions—from profound trust in AI capabilities to significant skepticism regarding their broader implications. Effectively navigating this intricate balance is essential for nurturing public acceptance and ensuring that AI can be sustainably woven into our daily lives.

Understanding Public Perception and Its Drivers

At the core of fostering public trust is a nuanced understanding of the factors that fuel skepticism. Much of this concern stems from a fear of the unknown, often exacerbated by sensational media coverage and notable instances where AI systems have failed or exhibited erratic behavior. Take, for instance, the unanticipated malfunctions of autonomous vehicles or the flawed decision-making processes seen in AI-fueled recruitment tools. Such incidents have amplified public wariness, further complicated by a general lack of transparency from tech companies. This reality underscores the urgency for stakeholders to confront these fears head-on through open communication and demonstrable accountability.

Strategies for Building Trust

To effectively address these concerns, companies and developers can implement several key strategies aimed at cultivating trust:

1. Transparent Communication: Transparency is foundational in establishing trust. Clearly articulating the intentions, limitations, and capabilities of AI systems is paramount. Providing detailed insights into data sources, development methodologies, and ethical considerations is vital. A prime example of effective transparency is the open-source AI platform TensorFlow, which empowers users to examine its underlying code and applications, fostering trust and active community engagement.

2. User Involvement and Feedback Loops: Actively involving users through interactive feedback mechanisms can significantly bolster trust. AI

systems should be designed to welcome user feedback as a means of continuous improvement. For instance, virtual assistants like Google Assistant exemplify this principle by learning from user interactions to enhance their responses, thereby demonstrating responsiveness to user needs.

3. Ethical Design and Social Responsibility: Incorporating ethical considerations into the design and development process is crucial. Developers must carefully assess the societal implications of AI systems, ensuring alignment with community values and standards. Microsoft's AI principles, which prioritize fairness, accountability, and transparency, serve as a stellar model, reinforcing public trust in their technologies.

Addressing Ethical Concerns and Cases of Misuse

Despite positive initiatives, concerns regarding ethical misuse and job displacement remain prevalent. These anxieties must be directly addressed through proactive policies and educational initiatives. A demonstrated commitment to ethical AI deployment not only protects against potential abuse but also enhances public perception.

Consider the implementation of AI in predictive policing, where algorithms are employed to forecast potential crime hotspots. Such applications demand meticulous oversight to prevent the reinforcement of societal biases. To nurture trust, it is essential to ensure responsible usage of these systems, coupled with robust monitoring to assess deployment and outcomes.

Public Education and Awareness

Education is instrumental in dispelling myths and misconceptions surrounding AI. Initiatives aimed at increasing AI literacy can empower the public to engage critically with these technologies, shifting the perspective from suspicion to informed understanding. Workshops, seminars, and collaborations with educational institutions can provide individuals with essential knowledge to navigate AI's potential and risks more effectively.

For instance, campaigns led by the Mozilla Foundation illustrate how public education can diminish skepticism.

Building a Collaborative Future with AI

Finally, fostering an environment of collaboration among the public, developers, and policymakers is paramount. Creating platforms for dialogue and feedback ensures that AI evolves in ways that align with societal needs and aspirations. Public consultations, as demonstrated in the European Union's establishment of an AI regulatory framework, highlight how cooperative approaches can lead to policies that resonate with collective values and enhance trust.

In conclusion, managing public trust and skepticism in AI is a multifaceted challenge requiring strategic transparency, ethical responsibility, and active community engagement. As the landscape of AI continues to evolve, maintaining this delicate balance will be crucial for ensuring its beneficial integration into the fabric of our everyday lives.

The Regulatory Landscape: Navigating the Governance of AI

The governance of AI technologies is predominantly complex, demanding a delicate balance between fostering innovation and safeguarding individual rights and societal values. The swift pace at which AI is developing often overtakes existing legal structures, posing challenges for lawmakers striving to create effective and visionary regulations. The diverse applications of AI—from self-driving cars to healthcare diagnostics—necessitate customized legal approaches that account for their specific impacts and associated risks.

Innovative Regulatory Initiatives Worldwide

Globally, various initiatives are emblematic of the diverse methods regulators are employing to tackle the challenges posed by AI:

1. The European Union's General Data Protection Regulation (GDPR): While not exclusively focused on AI, GDPR sets forth critical guidelines regarding data management, which is foundational to AI operations. Principles such as data subject rights, transparency, and accountability are directly applicable to AI, compelling organizations to securely process data and ensure that AI usage respects personal rights.

2. The United States' Algorithmic Accountability Act: Proposed legislation in the United States, including the Algorithmic Accountability Act, seeks to mandate that organizations assess their automated decision-making systems for bias and potential impacts, thereby reinforcing accountability in AI applications. Though still awaiting enactment, this proposal highlights a significant push towards scrutinizing the ramifications of AI-driven decisions.

3. China's Artificial Intelligence Development Plan: In China, a strategic initiative aligns regulatory commitments with national AI objectives, focusing on the establishment of strict standards for ethical and safe AI deployment. This approach illustrates how regional priorities can shape AI governance and affect global discussions around regulatory best practices.

Challenges of Legal and Regulatory Oversight

Navigating the international landscape of AI regulation poses significant challenges for policymakers, including:

1. Standardization Across Jurisdictions: The disparity

in technological capabilities and economic goals among countries makes it difficult to achieve a uniform set of standards. Differences in legal interpretations and ethical frameworks further complicate the development of a cohesive regulatory approach to AI.

2. The Evolving Nature of AI Technologies: AI systems are designed to autonomously evolve and learn, which creates hurdles in maintaining oversight and governance over ever-changing technologies. This necessitates adaptive legislative processes that can promptly respond to new advancements in AI capabilities.

3. Liability and Accountability Issues: Determining liability in incidents involving AI—such as accidents with autonomous vehicles—remains an ambiguous legal frontier. Existing liability frameworks often fall short when addressing situations where decision-making is dispersed across human operators and AI systems.

Illustrating Legal Challenges through Case Studies

Examining real-world scenarios can illuminate the practical legal challenges associated with AI:

- Autonomous Vehicles: Consider a situation where a self-driving car strikes a pedestrian; the ensuing legal disputes may revolve around liability—should it rest with the vehicle manufacturer, the software developer, or the supervising human? Addressing these complexities requires evolving legal standards that acknowledge the collaborative nature of AI decision-making.

- AI in Healthcare Diagnostics: The use of AI in medical diagnostics brings forth questions surrounding liability for misdiagnoses. Legal frameworks must adapt to the distinct dynamics of AI in clinical contexts, balancing innovation against patient safety and accountability.

Strategies for Effective Regulation

Despite the obstacles, several strategies can pave the way for efficient regulation of AI technologies:

1. Collaborative Policymaking: Fostering collaborations across industries and consulting a diverse range of stakeholders can lead to comprehensive legal frameworks that reflect a variety of perspectives and expertise. Engaging technologists, ethicists, and legal professionals ensures that AI regulations are not only sound but also socially responsible.

2. Regular Review and Adaptation of Laws: Legislative bodies should prioritize the periodic reassessment of AI-related laws, incorporating insights from ongoing technological advancements and societal changes. This dynamic approach guarantees that legal protections remain pertinent and responsive to an ever-evolving landscape.

3. Encouraging Global Dialogue and Cooperation: Promoting international collaboration in developing AI regulations can strengthen consistency and facilitate a shared understanding of ethical standards worldwide. Platforms such as international AI forums can provide valuable opportunities for shared learning and the harmonization of policies.

In conclusion, the legal and regulatory challenges surrounding AI agents are intricate and multifaceted, necessitating thoughtful consideration to strike a balance between fostering innovation and ensuring ethical accountability. As AI technologies become increasingly embedded in critical sectors, it is vital for regulatory frameworks to evolve in response to these complexities.

Energy Consumption and Carbon Footprint

AI technologies, especially those leveraging deep learning and neural networks, are notoriously resource-intensive. Training large-scale models necessitates immense computational power, leading to significant energy demands. Remarkably, the carbon emissions produced during the training of a single sophisticated AI model can be equivalent to the lifetime emissions of several vehicles.

- Example: Deep Learning Models Consider the training of state-of-the-art natural language processing models, which typically requires data centers that consume thousands of kilowatt-hours. Research indicated that one such model can use as much energy as a typical household in a developed country over several months. This staggering consumption arises from the extensive calculations needed to refine and optimize model performance, highlighting the urgent need for energy-efficient practices.

AI Hardware and E-Waste

In addition to energy demands, the AI industry significantly contributes to the growing crisis of electronic waste (e-waste). The increasing integration of AI algorithms into various devices drives a surging demand for GPUs, processors, and other specialized hardware components. As AI technology evolves at a breakneck pace, the rapid turnover of these components leads to greater disposal and waste challenges.

- Lifecycle and Recycling Challenges The environmental risks associated with discarded AI hardware are significant. Many electronic components contain harmful substances, such as heavy metals and toxic chemicals, which pose a danger when they are not disposed of properly. Alarmingly, recycling rates for these materials remain low, further exacerbating the e-waste issue. In response, there is a concerted global effort to design AI hardware that utilizes recyclable materials, alongside initiatives aimed at prolonging the lifespan of essential components to lessen environmental strain.

Mitigating Environmental Impact: Sustainable Solutions

Recognizing these challenges, various strategies and innovative approaches are emerging to reduce the ecological impact of AI technologies:

1. Efficient Algorithm Design Researchers are exploring energy-efficient algorithms that deliver comparable results with reduced computational resources. Techniques such as model compression —pruning, quantization, and knowledge distillation —can significantly lower the energy demands for both training and inference without sacrificing performance.

2. Renewable Energy Sources for Data Centers An increasing number of technology firms are committing to renewable energy sources to power their data centers. Some have successfully transitioned to operations entirely reliant on renewable energy, dramatically shrinking the carbon footprint associated with AI processes. This commitment can play a pivotal role in steering the industry toward more sustainable business practices as renewable energy becomes more prevalent.

3. Cloud-Based Optimization Utilizing cloud infrastructure for AI operations offers scalable and effective resource allocation solutions. Cloud

providers are adopting various strategies to enhance energy efficiency, such as dynamic resource allocation and server virtualization, which optimize both energy use and performance of AI applications.

4. Lifecycle Assessment and E-Waste Management Programs To minimize environmental damage from production to disposal, comprehensive lifecycle assessments of AI equipment are becoming standard practice. Organizations are investing in e-waste management programs that promote the recycling and refurbishment of components, thus curbing the volume of harmful waste generated.

5. Policy and Regulation As awareness of the environmental ramifications of AI increases, governmental and international bodies are crafting policies to regulate energy consumption and e-waste management. Incentives designed to promote the creation of sustainable AI technologies will be crucial in guiding the industry towards greener methodologies and practices.

The environmental consequences of AI technologies present a formidable challenge amid our pursuit of innovation. It is imperative that stakeholders across the landscape of this industry actively acknowledge and address these environmental concerns. Achieving sustainability mandates a collaborative effort focused on developing energy-efficient algorithms, enhancing investments in renewable energy, and implementing rigorous e-waste management strategies, all supported by effective regulatory frameworks. As AI continues to evolve and assumes a central role in society, it is vital to manage its environmental footprint, ensuring that we reap the benefits of AI while protecting the ecological stability of our planet for future generations.

As artificial intelligence (AI) technologies increasingly merge into every corner of our lives—transforming how we work, communicate, and access information—the challenge of misinformation generated by these systems presents a formidable obstacle. While AI excels at processing vast amounts of data to make informed decisions, it can also inadvertently (or, at times, even deliberately) spread false or misleading information. This unintended consequence is not just trivial; it threatens trust, public safety, and the very fabric of social cohesion. To effectively tackle this issue, we must gain a deeper understanding of how misinformation arises and implement strategic measures to counteract its impact.

Understanding the Origins of AI-Generated Misinformation

AI systems, especially those leveraging machine learning and natural language processing, depend on vast datasets to operate effectively. The accuracy of AI outputs rests on the quality and integrity of the input information. Misinformation can arise when:

1. Biased or Incomplete Datasets AI models trained on skewed or unrepresentative datasets can inadvertently perpetuate existing inaccuracies. For instance, a chatbot designed to engage in human-like conversation might reflect biases inherent in its training data, resulting in outputs that are both erroneous and potentially harmful. This reaffirms the necessity for diverse and comprehensive data sources.

2. Mimicking Human Language Advanced AI models often generate text that can easily be mistaken for human writing. This capability enables AI to churn out vast volumes of seemingly credible yet misleading information. Consequently, individuals may struggle to distinguish credible sources from cleverly crafted fabrications, as misleading outputs frequently lack clear indicators of their inaccuracy.

3. Misinterpretation and Ambiguity AI systems may misinterpret nuanced language or complex contexts, leading to erroneous conclusions. Without appropriate oversight, these applications can produce misleading information that diverges significantly from the original message or intent, highlighting the challenges inherent in language processing.

Illustrating the Risks of AI Misinformation

One of the most alarming manifestations of AI-generated misinformation is the rise of "deepfakes." These sophisticated audio or video manipulations, created using generative adversarial networks (GANs), can convincingly mimic the likeness and speech patterns of real individuals, blurring the lines between authenticity and deception.

- Case Study: Deepfake Videos The rapid spread of deepfake videos featuring public figures in fabricated situations exemplifies the pivotal threat posed by this technology. Such fake clips can circulate widely on digital platforms, potentially undermining trust in legitimate media sources and inciting political or social unrest. The ability of deepfakes to deceive raises urgent questions about the need for effective detection and prevention strategies.

Strategies for Mitigating AI-Driven Misinformation

Confronting the dangers associated with AI-generated misinformation demands a comprehensive and multi-layered approach involving technological advancements, policy reform, and enhanced public awareness.

1. Developing Robust Detection Tools Advancing detection technologies is fundamental. Algorithms capable of identifying inconsistencies or anomalies in AI-generated content—such as deepfakes—will be crucial. These tools can analyze photorealistic details

and audio cues that may elude human perception, providing an essential layer of verification.

2. Ensuring Data Transparency and Integrity Upholding transparency and high standards of data integrity within AI systems is key to preventing misinformation at its inception. Initiatives aimed at cleansing datasets of biases, coupled with rigorous auditing processes, can profoundly reduce the risk associated with training models on flawed information.

3. Emphasizing Ethical AI Design Principles The integration of ethical considerations in AI design is vital. Developers must establish protocols that prioritize accuracy, reliability, and accountability to minimize the potential for misuse or cascading errors that could lead to misinformation.

4. Implementing Regulatory Measures Governments and regulatory agencies must create policies that promote responsible AI development and deployment.

5. Fostering Public Education and Digital Literacy Empowering the public with knowledge about the intricacies of AI technology and the nature of misinformation serves as a critical defense mechanism. Increasing digital literacy enables individuals to critically evaluate information sources, arming them against the onslaught of deceptive content.

The challenge of managing AI-generated misinformation is an ongoing, complex struggle that calls for a concerted effort from technologists, policymakers, educators, and society at large. This integrated approach is vital to preserving trust in AI systems as they become ever more woven into the social fabric, ultimately fostering a more informed and resilient society.

The growth of artificial intelligence brings incredible opportunities for innovation, efficiency, and problem-solving. However, with these advancements come critical challenges, particularly the risk of misuse that could lead to ethical, moral, and societal dilemmas. For stakeholders involved in the development and deployment of AI technologies, understanding these risks is essential to ensure that AI contributes positively to society and does not lead to unintended consequences.

The Dual-Use Dilemma

At the heart of AI misuse lies the dual-use dilemma: the phenomenon whereby technologies intended for good can be manipulated for malevolent purposes. For example, AI systems designed for natural language processing can be diverted to create large-scale disinformation campaigns or propaganda, eroding trust in truthful communication. This delicate balance between encouraging innovation and implementing safeguards necessitates a proactive approach to mitigate the potential for harm.

Cybersecurity Vulnerabilities

AI is increasingly viewed as a robust tool for bolstering cybersecurity defenses; yet, it also opens doors for exploitation by malicious entities. AI algorithms can facilitate sophisticated cyber-attacks, such as automated phishing schemes that learn from and adapt to target responses. This ominous scenario illustrates how AI can outpace traditional security measures, rendering them ineffective against evolving threats.

- Example: Adaptive Phishing Tactics Imagine a scenario where AI-enhanced phishing campaigns craft emails that resonate deeply with the recipient's online persona, using data harvested from social media. These algorithms could create highly personalized messages that mislead individuals into sharing sensitive information. As this type of adaptive threat evolves, it becomes imperative for security experts to develop preemptive countermeasures, ensuring the integrity of digital spaces.

The Challenge of Autonomous Weapons

The military applications of AI, particularly in the realm of autonomous weapons systems, exemplify a profound ethical conundrum. Although AI can significantly reduce human casualties by undertaking perilous reconnaissance tasks, the deployment of weapons that can make life-and-death decisions autonomously raises alarming questions about accountability and the principles of combat. The delegation of such critical decisions to machines undeniably challenges long-standing legal and ethical norms in warfare.

Privacy Concerns and Surveillance Issues

AI technologies promise enhanced monitoring and capacity for data collection; however, they simultaneously present significant risks regarding mass surveillance and privacy infringement. Consider facial recognition technology: while it can assist law enforcement in preventing and responding to crime, it also raises serious concerns about its potential for invasive tracking and profiling of individuals without their consent.

- Case Study: Facial Recognition in Public Spaces The use of facial recognition in public areas may expedite crime detection, but absent rigorous legal frameworks, it can lead to unwarranted surveillance of everyday individuals. This chilling effect on civil liberties encapsulates the precarious balancing act between security needs and the preservation of personal rights.

Economic Manipulation Risks

AI's potential to revolutionize the financial sector is undeniable, enhancing market forecasting and automating trading processes. However, these capabilities can also be misappropriated for market manipulation. AI-driven algorithms may execute high-frequency trades that destabilize markets or facilitate insider trading, undermining the integrity of financial systems.

- Example: Flash Crashes Induced by AI The phenomenon of flash crashes—rapid, large-scale market declines—illustrates the unpredictable interactions of automated trading algorithms, which can trigger cascading market volatility from seemingly minor fluctuations. To prevent such occurrences, a commitment to stringent monitoring and transparent algorithmic practices is essential.

Safeguarding Against Misuse

To effectively combat the potential misuse of AI, a comprehensive strategy encompassing technological, policy, and ethical dimensions is imperative:

1. Enhanced Algorithmic Transparency Promoting the open auditability of AI systems provides crucial external checks, allowing stakeholders to ensure ethical practices. Developers should prioritize transparency in algorithms, enabling a fuller understanding of decision-making processes while uncovering biases or vulnerabilities.

2. Regulatory Oversight and Enforcement It is essential for governments and international entities to create regulatory frameworks that guide AI advancements and enforce compliance with ethical standards. Laws targeting data privacy, algorithmic accountability, and the development of autonomous systems can

deter misuse and promote responsible adoption of AI.

3. Development of Ethical Standards By integrating ethical principles into AI research and development, we can proactively address the potential for misuse. Widespread adoption of standards that emphasize safety, accountability, and fairness will align technological growth with societal betterment.

4. Collaborative Intelligence Sharing Encouraging cooperation among governments and organizations to facilitate the exchange of information on AI risks fosters a more robust collective response to potential threats. Joint initiatives and shared intelligence platforms will empower stakeholders to navigate and mitigate the complexities of AI misuse effectively.

While the potential for AI misuse presents significant challenges, it also offers an opportunity to establish ethical frameworks that can guide responsible technological advancement. Focusing on transparency, regulatory accountability, and a commitment to ethical standards is essential for mitigating risks and harnessing AI for the greater good.

Future Challenges in AI Development

Artificial intelligence has made astonishing strides, continually redefining the horizon of what machines can achieve. Yet, as AI technology progresses, several critical challenges remain that could fundamentally influence its future trajectory. A comprehensive understanding of these challenges is essential for stakeholders eager to leverage AI's potential while addressing the responsibilities and implications it carries.

Technological Limitations and Unresolved Complexity

Among the foremost challenges in AI development is

the struggle to surmount technological limitations and navigate the complex journey toward achieving artificial general intelligence (AGI). While we've made considerable advancements in narrow AI—systems adept at specific tasks such as playing chess or translating languages—the quest for AGI, which would enable machines to reason, learn, and seamlessly adapt to new situations like humans, continues to be a distant goal.

- Example: Challenges in Machine Creativity Current AI systems can produce remarkable artistic and literary works through sophisticated neural networks like Generative Adversarial Networks (GANs). However, they still lack self-awareness and the ability to understand and appreciate the deeper nuances behind their creations. This shortcoming illustrates the broader challenge of endowing AI with a form of creativity comparable to human intelligence, which involves richer, more intuitive problem-solving capabilities.

Bias and Ethical Standardization

Bias lurking within datasets, algorithmic designs, and resulting AI outputs poses a significant barrier to fairness and equity in technology. Tackling this issue necessitates establishing robust ethical standards and methodologies that prevent AI systems from unintentionally perpetuating discrimination.

- Case Study: Bias in Hiring Algorithms While AI is increasingly being used to streamline recruitment, instances have shown that these systems can inadvertently reinforce gender or racial biases by learning from datasets that reflect historical prejudices. It's crucial to develop comprehensive strategies aimed at identifying, mitigating, and eradicating bias throughout the data and algorithm refinement processes.

Sustainability and Environmental Impact

The energy demands associated with training complex AI models raise serious questions regarding sustainability and their ecological footprint. Finding a way to balance the advancement of AI with environmental responsibility emerges as a formidable challenge.

- Example: The Carbon Footprint of Training Models The training of large-scale language models can significantly contribute to carbon emissions, given the hefty computational power involved. To mitigate this environmental impact, developers are actively investigating more energy-efficient algorithms and practices, highlighting the urgency for eco-conscious innovations within the AI domain.

Alignment with Human Values

Aligning AI systems with human values and societal norms is pivotal for their acceptance and effective integration. However, embedding the complexities of human ethics —varied as they are across cultures and contexts—into algorithms proves to be a daunting task.

- Scenario: Culturally Sensitive AI Applications Take, for instance, an AI deployed for personal healthcare management. While designed to optimize health outcomes, it must navigate and respect diverse cultural attitudes toward healthcare practices. Balancer algorithms need to effectively address these nuances to avoid culturally insensitive recommendations.

Security and Privacy Concerns

The rapid expansion of AI applications also heightens the risks of breaches and privacy violations. It is essential to engineer AI systems equipped with robust safeguards that protect sensitive data and reinforce security protocols.

- Development of Resilient Security Protocols In response to the escalating frequency and sophistication of cyber-attacks on AI systems, engineers must innovate resilient security protocols that can detect and neutralize intrusion attempts, without compromising operational efficacy. This proactive strategy is key to maintaining user trust.

Future-Proofing Legal and Regulatory Frameworks

The absence of coherent legal and regulatory frameworks presents substantial challenges to AI's sustainable growth. As the pace of AI innovation outstrips existing policies, regulators are faced with the daunting task of crafting adaptable frameworks that can both regulate AI developments and foster market innovation.

- Example: Legal Ambiguity in Autonomous Vehicles The rapid evolution of autonomous vehicles exemplifies a case where regulations struggle to keep pace. Policymakers are challenged to devise standards that address safety, liability, and societal acceptance in advance of widespread deployment —emphasizing the critical need for anticipatory legislation.

Addressing the forthcoming challenges in AI development requires a multidisciplinary approach that harmonizes technological innovation with ethical, legal, and societal considerations. Confronting these challenges not only shapes the future of AI but also impacts its global perception and integration.

Chapter 12: Vision for the Future

The next decade holds immense promise for transformative advancements in artificial intelligence, particularly in the realm of AI agents. As we approach this era of rapid technological evolution, understanding the development of these agents is crucial—not simply an exercise in speculation but a vital component of strategic preparation. To effectively navigate the anticipated changes, we must examine the key elements poised to influence their evolution.

At the forefront of this evolution is the remarkable capacity for AI agents to self-evolve. While current agents primarily depend on predetermined algorithms and curated datasets, the next generation will usher in a paradigm of autonomous capability enhancement. Through advancements in unsupervised learning, these agents will extract insights from vast amounts of unlabelled data. A striking example of this innovation can be seen in OpenAI's use of reinforcement learning within simulated environments. Here, agents learn iteratively, honing their abilities through a cycle of successes and failures, much like humans refine their skills through practice. As algorithms advance, we can anticipate AI agents evolving into dynamic learners, capable of adapting to new environments seamlessly and without the need for direct human oversight.

In tandem with this evolution, the way AI agents interact with us will undergo significant transformation. Emerging technologies, such as participatory natural language processing (PNLP), will equip these agents to better understand and respond to human emotions and the nuanced details of conversation. Picture an AI therapist who not only recognizes speech patterns but also discerns the emotional undertones, providing feedback and support infused with genuine empathy. Achieving this level of sophistication demands intricate tuning of AI systems and advanced neural network modeling, reminiscent of how convolutional networks learn to perceive complex patterns in images.

Another critical trend to monitor is the embedding of AI agents within ubiquitous computing environments. As the proliferation of smart devices continues, AI agents will become integral to virtually every aspect of our daily lives. The Internet of Things (IoT) serves as a fertile ground for these agents, enabling the management of interconnected devices to optimize efficiency in homes, cities, and workplaces. For example, the concept of smart cities illustrates a future where AI agents could orchestrate operations ranging from traffic management to energy distribution, providing real-time responsiveness through the power of edge computing, which ensures minimal latency.

The intersection of AI and quantum computing opens an exciting frontier replete with unforeseen possibilities. Quantum processors, leveraging their extraordinary parallel processing abilities, could fundamentally reshape the capabilities of AI agents. Envision the implications for drug discovery, where quantum-enhanced AI could simulate intricate molecular interactions at unprecedented speeds, potentially leading to groundbreaking treatments that were previously thought to be unattainable.

However, as we embrace these remarkable technological advancements, we must confront complex ethical implications. The adaptability and extensive reach of future AI agents demand robust governance frameworks to mitigate biases and ensure responsible deployment. For instance, while predictive policing algorithms hold the promise of crime prevention, their design must be scrutinized carefully to avoid perpetuating systemic biases. Consequently, incorporating ethical auditing into AI agents' frameworks—similar to real-time error checking in software development—will become increasingly paramount.

Moreover, the societal landscape will inevitably shift as these agents redefine various sectors, from healthcare to environmental stewardship. In the healthcare arena, AI agents will serve as decision-support systems, swiftly analyzing complex datasets and providing diagnostic assistance with unprecedented accuracy. Meanwhile, in environmental management, AI agents will monitor ecosystems, generating actionable insights that inform conservation efforts through the analysis of real-time data sourced from satellites and ground-level sensors—efforts that are already in motion in several biodiversity projects.

As we look towards the next decade, envisioning the future of AI agents entails constructing an integrative model that harmonizes technological advancements with ethical responsibility and societal benefit. Our journey in shaping this pathway must consistently orient towards an enduring goal: leveraging AI agents to combat inequality, democratize technology, and pioneer solutions that once resided solely in the realm of science fiction. We stand on the brink of a future where these agents transcend their roles as mere tools, emerging instead as invaluable partners in our progress. The horizon is glowing with the promise of this collaboration.

As we stand on the brink of extraordinary advancements in artificial intelligence over the next few years, we are witnessing the dawn of transformative technologies that have the potential to reshape our societal structures. These innovations promise not only to enhance our current capabilities but to establish entirely new paradigms in our interactions with technology.

One of the most exciting developments on the horizon is the evolution of explainable AI (XAI). While existing AI systems have demonstrated remarkable decision-making prowess, their inner workings often remain mysterious. Upcoming advancements in XAI aim to peel back the layers of these so-called "black boxes," providing users with clear, comprehensible insights into how decisions are made. For instance, in the financial realm, AI algorithms used for credit scoring or fraud detection will soon offer transparent explanations for their conclusions.

Alongside this, we can expect significant strides in AI-driven natural language understanding (NLU). Future systems are anticipated to evolve beyond simple interpretation of language to incorporate emotional intelligence, enabling them to detect subtle nuances in tone and sentiment with unprecedented accuracy. Imagine customer service bots that do more than respond to queries—they will understand a customer's frustration or distress, adjusting their interactions in a way that fosters empathy. Such advancements stand to revolutionize customer experience and loyalty by making digital interactions more human-like and supportive.

The realm of autonomous systems, particularly in robotics, is also on the verge of remarkable evolution. Enhanced robotic dexterity and perception will allow AI-driven robots to perform complicated tasks that have traditionally required human skill. While robots have already made significant inroads into manufacturing and logistics, future innovations could enable them to handle more delicate tasks, such as assembling intricate electronics or conducting minimally invasive surgeries. Breakthroughs in tactile sensor technology will give robots a nearly human-like sense of touch, which will allow them to identify and manipulate objects with a precision that current technology struggles to achieve.

In addition to these developments, the integration of AI with augmented reality (AR) presents a treasure trove of possibilities, blending the physical and digital worlds in ways previously confined to the imaginative realms of science fiction. Future AR systems, powered by AI, could serve as dynamic educational platforms, offering immersive experiences that adjust in real time to each learner's pace and comprehension. Picture a history lesson where students not only read about the Renaissance but also navigate a virtual 3D model of Florence, interacting with historical figures and events as if they were truly there—AI would drive this engagement, tailoring context and interaction dynamically.

On the medical front, the promise of precision medicine will be significantly enhanced by AI's ability to swiftly and accurately analyze vast genomic data. We anticipate innovations that will quickly identify unique patient profiles, allowing for the customization of treatment plans that can markedly improve health outcomes. AI systems will be capable of predicting adverse drug reactions by recognizing genetic predispositions, personalizing therapeutic approaches to an extent that is currently unattainable, and taking predictive analytics in proactive healthcare to new heights.

Moreover, the intersection of quantum computing and AI is set to propel us into a new era of computational capabilities beyond the constraints of Moore's Law. Quantum-enhanced algorithms will enable the rapid processing and analysis of extensive datasets—something our most powerful supercomputers struggle with. This leap forward will pave the way for applications ranging from comprehensive climate models to large-scale drug testing simulations, turning challenges that once seemed insurmountable into tangible realities.

As we anticipate these remarkable advancements, it is crucial to approach each innovation thoughtfully, addressing the ethical implications that accompany them. Particularly for autonomous systems, ethical considerations must guide design and implementation, ensuring that we avert unintended consequences such as algorithmic bias or erosion of human accountability. This careful consideration will be essential in ensuring that the benefits of AI technologies are equitably distributed across society.

In summary, the next decade foresees not merely technological advancement but a profound redefinition of human-AI interaction. This future is characterized by systems that not only amplify human potential but do so with an essential foundation of accountability and transparency.

Transitioning AI from a collection of sophisticated tools to an integral facet of everyday life requires not just breakthroughs in technical capabilities, but also innovations in responsibility and trust. The noble progression of technology hinges on its ethical development, fostering a partnership between humanity and artificial intelligence that transcends the boundaries of innovation.

The evolution of human-AI relationships is a captivating journey marked by increasing complexity, depth, and interdependence. As artificial intelligence continues to advance, it is reshaping our interactions with technology, particularly in personal and professional realms. This evolution is characterized by collaboration, trust, and a host of ethical considerations that guide our engagement with these intelligent systems.

In its nascent phase, AI functioned primarily as a tool —background machinery that processed data and executed tasks without any semblance of interaction. Fast forward to today, and we find ourselves in the midst of a revolutionary shift. AI has emerged as an interactive participant in our lives, significantly enhancing our daily experiences. This transformation is particularly notable in personal assistants like Amazon's Alexa, Apple's Siri, and Google Assistant, which have moved beyond mere functionality to build a more personalized rapport with users. These systems learn from our preferences and behaviors, creating intricate feedback loops that amplify their utility. For example, a virtual assistant can now suggest alternate routes based on an individual's commuting habits or recommend meal options tailored to past dining choices, thus deepening the connection between technology and user needs.

The professional landscape is witnessing an equally profound transformation. In collaborative workspaces, AI serves as a catalyst for productivity and creativity, acting as a co-creator or co-researcher in various fields. From creative design to scientific inquiry, AI helps us navigate complex data sets, generate innovative concepts, and simulate scientific models, expediting processes that would have traditionally taken years for human intellect to accomplish. Take, for instance, AI-driven platforms such as Adobe's Sensei, which anticipates creative suggestions, or IBM's Watson, which aids oncologists in identifying treatment strategies by analyzing vast medical databases.

Yet, as we nurture this budding relationship, we must also address the hurdles that accompany it. Trust emerges as a critical element in this evolving dynamic. Concerns regarding privacy, security, and the accuracy of AI systems loom large, prompting companies to invest heavily in developing AI solutions that prioritize transparency in data usage and decision-making. IBM's principles for trustworthy AI, which emphasize explainability, fairness, and robustness, serve as foundational benchmarks for creating technologies that are not only effective but also accountable.

Emotionally intelligent AI represents yet another important milestone in our relationships with these systems. As AI becomes better equipped to understand and respond to human emotions, it can offer companionship and support in increasingly empathetic ways. For instance, chatbots like Woebot, designed for mental health support, utilize natural language processing and sentiment analysis to deliver personalized emotional guidance. While these bots cannot replace human interaction, they serve as valuable supplements during challenging times, offering companionship and support where needed most.

The workplace, too, is undergoing a transformation as AI augments human capabilities rather than merely displacing them. As companies integrate AI-driven analytics into their decision-making processes, employees learn to harness these insights for more strategic business outcomes. This shift not only enhances productivity but also fosters a workplace culture that views AI as a partner in innovation rather than a competitor for jobs. Initiatives like Microsoft's AI Business School play a vital role in guiding leaders to adopt a strategic mindset toward AI, promoting an ethos that embraces technology as a vital component of organizational success.

On a broader societal scale, attitudes toward AI are gradually shifting from apprehension to acceptance, and even advocacy. Programs aimed at enhancing AI literacy—such as community hackathons, coding workshops for students, and media narratives showcasing AI's role in societal advancement—contribute significantly to this transformation.

As we cultivate this evolving relationship, stakeholders must remain vigilant regarding the implications of integrating AI into social norms. Key issues surrounding consent, privacy, and the potential for bias in AI outputs must be scrutinized and addressed. As the capabilities of AI continue to expand, establishing an ethical framework that champions human rights, dignity, and diversity will be crucial for fostering sustainable and fair progress.

In conclusion, the future of human-AI relationships rests on our ability to integrate these systems thoughtfully and responsibly. It is imperative that we ensure these technologies enhance the human experience while respecting individual autonomy. This evolution is not solely about coexisting with technology but nurturing a symbiotic relationship that amplifies our collective human potential. As we move forward, we aspire to create a future where AI stands not just as a powerful ally, but also as a responsible agent of change, enriching lives and shaping a better world for all.

Navigating Pathways to Sustainable AI Development

The journey toward sustainable AI development demands an intentional balance between technological advancement and environmental stewardship. As AI systems grow in complexity and ubiquity, so do their energy consumption and resource requirements. This escalating demand underscores the urgent necessity for integrating sustainability into AI practices. To responsibly address these challenges, the field of AI must embrace strategies that minimize environmental impacts while fostering innovation.

Optimizing Algorithms for Energy Efficiency

One pivotal avenue for promoting sustainability in AI involves enhancing algorithms for energy efficiency. The computational load involved in training large AI models, especially those utilizing deep learning, can be staggering. Take, for example, models like GPT-3 and BERT; their training requires significant amounts of processing power and electricity. As a response, researchers are actively exploring more efficient algorithms. Techniques such as model pruning, quantization, and knowledge distillation show promise in reducing model size and streamlining inference processes, leading to lower energy consumption.

Model pruning selectively eliminates parts of an algorithm that exert minimal influence on its output, thereby conserving resources without compromising performance. This approach allows for the creation of leaner models that perform effectively while requiring less computational power, setting a precedent for future developments.

Harnessing Renewable Energy for AI Infrastructure

Another critical strategy for sustainable AI involves leveraging renewable energy sources to power AI infrastructure. Leading tech companies like Google and Microsoft have spearheaded initiatives to establish data centers that run on wind and solar energy, underpinning their commitment to carbon-neutral operations. Google's Offset Energy program, for instance, ensures that the carbon footprint of its data activities is neutralized through renewable energy credits, presenting a viable model for other AI enterprises.

The Promise of Edge AI for Sustainability

The emergence of edge AI presents exciting opportunities for reducing environmental impact. Edge AI allows data processing to occur locally on devices rather than relying heavily on centralized cloud systems. This shift not only conserves bandwidth and energy but also enhances the real-time responsiveness of AI applications. Consider mobile applications that leverage edge AI for tasks like facial recognition or language translation; these innovations demonstrate how localized computing can drive functionality and sustainability in tandem.

AI's Role in Environmental Monitoring and Conservation

AI technologies also play an invaluable role in monitoring and conserving the environment. With their adeptness at analyzing extensive datasets, AI algorithms can identify patterns and make predictions relevant to environmental science. For instance, AI-powered satellite imagery is instrumental in tracking deforestation and monitoring wildlife populations, providing critical insights that inform conservation efforts. Furthermore, AI systems are being employed to optimize water resource management in agriculture, ensuring responsible land and water use practices.

Fostering Collaboration and Education for Sustainable AI

Advancing sustainable AI will necessitate collaboration among industry stakeholders, government entities, and academia. Partnerships dedicated to establishing industry-wide standards and benchmarks for sustainability can catalyze widespread change. Global frameworks aimed at assessing the environmental impact of AI technologies are essential in guiding practices across various sectors. Initiatives like the Partnership on AI to Benefit People and Society exemplify the potential of collaborative efforts in tackling sustainability challenges.

Education and training are also vital components of cultivating a sustainable AI ecosystem. Academic curricula integrating ethical AI practices with technical skillsets will inspire a new wave of innovation that is both advanced and environmentally responsible. Institutions leading this charge are shaping an industry that cherishes sustainability alongside technological excellence.

Engaging Public Discourse and Adapting Policy for Sustainability

Engaging the public in conversations about AI's environmental implications and promoting transparency can bolster consumer trust and encourage responsible behavior.

Moreover, policy and regulatory frameworks must evolve to address the novel sustainability challenges posed by AI. Governments can incentivize the development of sustainable AI through mechanisms such as grants and tax benefits for enterprises investing in green technologies.

A Harmonious Future: Merging Technology and Sustainability

Integrating these pathways into AI development paves the way for a future where technology and environmental sustainability coexist harmoniously. It sets the stage for a collective effort across disciplines and sectors to ensure that rapid advancements in AI do not come at the cost of our planet. Through strategic innovation and responsible management, the industry can strike a balance, nurturing technologies that fulfill human aspirations while honoring ecological needs.

As we pursue sustainable AI practices, the potential to enhance global quality of life while safeguarding the environment becomes not just a hope but an achievable reality. Together, we can forge a future that embraces the transformative power of AI within a framework of sustainability and stewardship.

As the impact of artificial intelligence (AI) continues to escalate across diverse sectors, its potential to tackle some of the world's most urgent challenges is becoming increasingly clear. When thoughtfully designed and strategically implemented, AI systems can deliver innovative solutions to pressing issues such as climate change, healthcare crises, economic inequality, and the global scarcity of resources.

Combatting Climate Change with AI Agents

In the fight against climate change, AI agents are emerging as key players in both enhancing our understanding of environmental challenges and in developing mitigation strategies. For instance, advanced AI algorithms analyze comprehensive climate data, empowering researchers and policymakers to predict complex weather patterns with greater accuracy. Machine learning models can simulate different climate scenarios, enabling informed decision-making for potential environmental events.

A prime example of this is IBM's Green Horizon Project, which leverages AI to provide air quality forecasts and suggest strategies to reduce pollution levels.

AI also plays a pivotal role in optimizing renewable energy systems, thereby enhancing sustainability. Smart grid technologies driven by AI expertly balance electricity supply and demand, reducing our dependence on fossil fuels. Startups such as DeepMind are pushing the envelope further by using AI for improved renewable energy forecasting, which enables a more effective management of the energy grid and significantly reduces carbon emissions. Moreover, autonomous vehicles utilizing AI technology can enhance traffic flow and improve public transportation networks, leading to lower overall emissions.

Revolutionizing Healthcare Solutions

In healthcare, AI agents hold the promise to completely transform how we address medical challenges on a global scale. Through sophisticated image recognition algorithms, AI systems can markedly improve the accuracy of disease diagnoses and refine treatment plans. For example, AI platforms can predict patient deterioration within hospital settings, allowing healthcare professionals to take proactive measures before conditions become critical. Tools like Google's ARDA support pathologists in diagnosing diseases with unparalleled speed and accuracy.

Furthermore, AI enhances the efficiency of healthcare logistics by optimizing supply chain management for medical resources. During the COVID-19 pandemic, AI-driven systems were instrumental in vaccine distribution, accurately forecasting demand and optimizing delivery routes to ensure equitable global access.

Tackling Socioeconomic Inequality

AI agents are also vital in addressing socioeconomic disparities. One crucial avenue is through education, as AI-powered platforms create personalized learning experiences in underserved regions, effectively bridging educational gaps. Using advanced algorithms, these platforms assess individual learning styles and deliver tailored resources that cater to each student's unique needs.

In the financial sector, AI agents democratize access to financial services, particularly for unbanked populations. Innovations such as AI-facilitated microloans and enhanced credit risk assessments empower individuals with financial inclusivity where traditional banking options are lacking. For instance, companies like Tala are deploying AI-driven solutions that allow users in developing countries to secure credit through their smartphones, fostering entrepreneurship and driving economic growth.

Ensuring Food and Water Security

AI agents tackle the critical issues of food and water security through precision agriculture and resource management. This data-driven approach not only optimizes agricultural practices but also enhances yield while minimizing waste.

In the domain of water management, AI systems play an

essential role in monitoring water usage and predicting supply and demand. Organizations utilize these technologies to detect leaks and implement efficiency measures within infrastructure, thus conserving this precious resource in areas vulnerable to scarcity. AI algorithms can also monitor aquifer levels and project drought conditions, enabling proactive strategies to safeguard water availability.

Leveraging AI for Global Health Crises

AI agents are crucial in responding to global health emergencies by tracking disease outbreaks and predicting infection patterns. During pandemics, AI-driven models can analyze large datasets to identify trends and recommend containment strategies, facilitating the rapid development and deployment of vaccines and treatments. The role of AI in COVID-19 drug discovery and trial optimization exemplifies how these technologies can accelerate scientific breakthroughs in critical situations.

Harnessing Collaborations and Partnerships

Collaborative efforts stand as a cornerstone in leveraging AI to confront global challenges. Partnerships among governments, tech companies, and non-profit organizations amalgamate resources, knowledge, and technology, enhancing our collective ability to address multifaceted issues. Initiatives like the AI for Good Global Summit unite leaders from various sectors, fostering an exchange of ideas and strategies that are vital for impactful advancements in sustainable development.

A Cohesive Future Through AI Integration

As we pave the way for a future enriched by AI, its integration into global problem-solving mechanisms presents a unique opportunity to confront challenges with creativity and precision. The positive influence of AI on global conditions hinges on our commitment to ethical development and ensuring equitable access. To harness AI effectively for the world's most pressing challenges, we must emphasize not only technological advancements but also collaborative efforts across society. Through conscious and concerted actions, we can unlock the transformative power of AI for the greater good, steering us towards a brighter future.

The vision of smart cities, powered by artificial intelligence (AI), paints an inspiring picture of our urban future—one that champions efficiency, sustainability, and an elevated quality of life through advanced technological integration. As more people flock to urban centers, we face a pressing need for innovative solutions to navigate the complexities of modern city living. At the heart of this transformation lies AI, equipped with the potential to create vibrant urban ecosystems that are responsive and adaptable to the needs of their residents.

Transforming Infrastructure and Transportation

One of the most exciting dimensions of AI in smart cities is its capacity to revolutionize infrastructure and transportation. Traffic congestion is a common challenge in urban environments; however, AI-driven traffic management systems possess the capability to alleviate this issue significantly. For example, Hangzhou, China, has implemented the City Brain project, utilizing AI to manage its road networks effectively, resulting in a remarkable 15% reduction in congestion.

Autonomous vehicles are another groundbreaking component of smart city transportation. With sophisticated machine learning algorithms, these vehicles navigate complex urban landscapes, minimizing accident rates while ensuring smoother journeys for all. Additionally, employing AI for vehicle-to-infrastructure communication can create a seamless interaction landscape, where cars receive real-time updates on road conditions and available transit options, facilitating a more organized transportation system.

Pioneering Sustainable Energy Solutions

The influence of AI extends far beyond transportation; it also plays a crucial role in energy management within smart cities. AI algorithms predict consumption patterns, enabling more effective electricity distribution and significantly reducing waste. For instance, during peak production times, AI systems can redirect surplus energy generated by solar panels to storage solutions, ensuring optimal use of renewable resources.

The integration of AI into smart meters and grid systems provides utilities with valuable insights into consumption patterns, fostering dynamic pricing models that promote energy conservation among residents. Industry leaders like Siemens are at the forefront of this innovation, developing smart grids that connect decentralized energy sources and empower consumers to make informed energy-related decisions.

Promoting Environmental Health and Efficient Waste Management

AI-driven monitoring systems have the potential to substantially enhance environmental quality within urban areas. Air and water quality sensors, strategically distributed throughout the city, continuously gather data that AI analyzes to identify pollution trends and alert authorities to emerging hazards. The deployment of such technologies not only safeguards public health but also ensures compliance with environmental regulations.

In the realm of waste management, AI applications are equally transformative. This approach not only reduces operational costs but also promotes sustainability. For example, Copenhagen has effectively utilized AI for dynamic waste collection management, optimizing resources by adjusting schedules and routes based on real-time data.

Elevating Public Safety and Security

AI technologies are also pivotal in reinforcing public safety and security within smart cities. Advanced surveillance systems powered by computer vision and deep learning can intelligently analyze video footage in real time, enabling the detection of suspicious activities or potential threats, and facilitating swift interventions by authorities. Moreover, these systems can integrate with emergency response networks, streamlining crisis management and resource allocation.

When implemented responsibly, biometric technologies such as facial recognition provide an additional layer of security by verifying identities in sensitive locations. However, it is crucial to balance such advancements with ethical considerations and data privacy concerns to maintain public trust.

Delivering Personalized Citizen Services

Smart cities embrace the idea of leveraging AI to offer personalized services that enhance citizens' everyday experiences. Virtual personal assistants and chatbots can disseminate real-time information regarding city services, public transportation schedules, and local events, tailored to individual preferences. These personalized interactions not only foster civic engagement but also reinforce the city's commitment to responsiveness.

AI also plays a transformative role in urban planning by analyzing multifaceted datasets to refine zoning, development, and infrastructure investments. Tools that simulate various growth scenarios empower planners to make well-informed decisions aligned with long-term sustainability goals, ultimately bolstering urban resilience and livability.

Harmonizing Diverse Data Streams for Comprehensive Management

A pivotal aspect of AI-powered smart cities is the integration of diverse data streams, which creates a cohesive framework for managing urban environments. This requires seamless coordination among IoT devices, urban databases, and AI systems to guarantee data accuracy and reliability. Centralized data management platforms enable city planners to adopt a holistic perspective on urban dynamics, fostering informed policies and efficient resource allocation.

Fostering Equitable and Inclusive Smart Cities

The successful implementation of AI in urban environments hinges on ensuring equitable access to technology and resources. Smart city initiatives must prioritize inclusivity and address disparities in service provision and digital literacy. Encouraging public dialogue and community involvement in the development process guarantees that these initiatives reflect the diverse needs and aspirations of all residents.

Charting a Path Toward Resilient Urban Spaces

Imagining AI-powered smart cities invites us to consider a future where urban living transcends mere efficiency, evolving to become responsive and enriching for all inhabitants. Through thoughtful AI integrations, the cities of tomorrow promise not only to mitigate environmental impacts but also to enhance public safety and civic life. Realizing this vision demands a steadfast commitment to collaborative innovation, robust ethical standards, and an unwavering focus on inclusivity—principles that will guide successful urban centers in the age of intelligent systems.

Long-term ethical frameworks for AI agents are essential for navigating the intricate balance between rapid technological advancements and their societal implications. As AI agents become more autonomous and interwoven into the fabric of our daily lives, the establishment of robust ethical guidelines becomes vital. These guidelines ensure that these technologies resonate with human values and uphold individual rights, ultimately paving the way for a future where innovation flourishes without compromising ethical standards.

A key principle in the development of these long-term ethical frameworks is fostering transparency in AI decision-making processes. It is imperative that AI systems are interpretable and their actions are comprehensible to human stakeholders, as this fosters trust. When users understand how decisions are made, including the criteria and data that inform these choices, it mitigates skepticism. For instance, the emergence of explainable AI models is a significant stride toward this goal. In healthcare diagnostics, these models can provide insights into complex decision-making processes, empowering clinicians to interpret AI-generated predictions effectively. This transparency not only bolsters trust but also cultivates a collaborative dynamic between human experts and AI systems.

Accountability serves as another cornerstone of ethical AI frameworks, ensuring that responsibility for AI actions is clearly defined. It is crucial to articulate liability structures, especially in scenarios where AI agents operate independently. This encompasses outlining whether developers, operators, or users bear responsibility for the outcomes of AI-driven processes. Take, for example, the evolving legal landscape surrounding autonomous vehicles; legal frameworks are currently being shaped to determine liability in the event of accidents or malfunctions, effectively balancing the dynamic of technological innovation with public safety imperatives.

Additionally, it is vital that long-term ethical frameworks actively address the issue of bias within AI systems. Bias can manifest from skewed datasets or flawed algorithmic designs, leading to unjust or discriminatory outcomes. As AI agents increasingly influence significant decisions in areas such as hiring, law enforcement, and financial lending, rectifying these biases is of paramount importance. Implementing techniques such as continuous bias monitoring, deploying anti-discriminatory algorithms, and conducting iterative testing throughout the development process are integral practices. Companies like IBM are at the forefront of this effort, embedding fairness checks into their AI development lifecycles to identify and address potential biases before their systems are deployed.

Another critical element of ethical AI usage is the protection of user privacy. AI systems must prioritize data confidentiality and be vigilant against overreaching surveillance practices. This necessitates the implementation of stringent data protection measures and the acquisition of informed consent for any data usage. In this context, privacy-first architectures are gaining prominence, especially as Internet of Things (IoT) devices expand across smart cities. For instance, Apple exemplifies industry leadership in this regard by employing differential privacy methods, allowing it to safeguard user data while still delivering quality services.

Moreover, fostering inclusivity and equitable access to AI technologies should be at the forefront of ethical frameworks. It is essential that these innovations benefit a diverse array of populations and do not perpetuate existing disparities. Engaging a broad spectrum of stakeholders in the AI design process is vital to capturing varied perspectives and requirements. Initiatives like Google's AI for Social Good demonstrate a commitment to applying AI to global challenges, focusing on inclusive strategies that reflect the needs of marginalized communities.

Lastly, the journey toward ethical AI development calls for the establishment of continuous learning and adaptive mechanisms within organizations. This can be achieved by forming ethics boards or committees tasked with regularly reviewing AI implementations and evolving frameworks in response to emerging ethical concerns and advancements in technology. Microsoft's AETHER (AI and Ethics in Engineering and Research) committee is a notable example of an organization actively steering ethical AI research and deployment to uphold rigorous ethical standards.

In conclusion, the process of crafting long-term ethical frameworks for AI agents demands a multifaceted approach that emphasizes transparency, accountability, bias mitigation, privacy protections, inclusivity, and ongoing evaluation. These frameworks offer guiding principles that not only shield users and society from potential adverse effects but also bolster the legitimacy and acceptance of AI technologies.

In an age where technology is woven into the very fabric of society, the role of education in shaping future AI professionals is more crucial than ever. As artificial intelligence continues to evolve and integrate into various aspects of our lives, the demand for a workforce that is both technically skilled and ethically informed has surged. Education transcends mere knowledge transfer; it is a vital platform that cultivates the ethical, creative, and collaborative competencies essential for thriving in AI-centric environments.

At the core of effective AI education is a curriculum that harmoniously merges theoretical foundations with practical applications. Students need not only a solid grasp of fundamental concepts such as machine learning algorithms, data analytics, and computational theories, but also hands-on experience through engaging projects, internships, and laboratory work. Renowned institutions, such as the Massachusetts Institute of Technology (MIT) and Stanford University, exemplify this dual approach, offering courses that seamlessly blend academic learning with real-world applications in cutting-edge AI research environments. This immersion in authentic projects allows students to bridge the gap between theory and practice—a vital skill set for aspiring AI professionals.

The relevance of interdisciplinary studies within AI education programs is increasingly recognized. The implications of AI extend beyond technical frameworks, intersecting with ethics, law, psychology, and management. For instance, Carnegie Mellon University's AI program stands out by integrating technology courses with ethical considerations and policy studies. This comprehensive approach enables future AI professionals to navigate the intricate societal dimensions of their work, ensuring that their innovations are not only groundbreaking but also socially accountable and ethically sound.

Moreover, collaboration between educational institutions and industry is paramount in addressing the rapidly shifting landscape of AI technologies. Initiatives like the AI4K12 Guidelines in the United States aim to introduce AI concepts into K-12 curricula, providing young learners with foundational insights into the field. This early exposure ignites interest and fosters inclusivity, creating pathways for diverse talent to enter the world of AI. Partnerships among schools, universities, and technology companies can help make AI education more accessible, attracting a wide array of perspectives and experiences.

Fostering creativity and innovation should also be a central focus in developing AI competencies. Today's AI professionals must possess strong problem-solving abilities and critical thinking skills that extend far beyond coding and algorithm design. Encouraging students to engage in hackathons, innovation labs, and creative workshops can significantly enhance these vital skills. For example, the AI+World Challenge invites students from around the globe to develop AI solutions addressing pressing global issues. Such initiatives not only promote technical proficiency but also inspire inventive thinking, driving students to explore the extensive possibilities of AI as they tackle real-world challenges.

Mentorship plays a crucial role in preparing the next generation of AI professionals. Seasoned mentors offer invaluable insights into industry trends, career pathways, and ethical dilemmas. Programs like Women in Machine Learning (WiML) actively connect female students and early-career professionals with experienced mentors, fostering diversity and inclusion in the AI field. These mentorship opportunities empower students with clarity and confidence as they navigate their professional journeys, enriching the landscape of future AI leaders with a multitude of perspectives.

As the influence of AI continues to reshape our world, it is essential for educational methodologies to evolve in tandem with technological advancements. Institutions must stay agile, incorporating cutting-edge technologies and novel methodologies into their curricula. The introduction of simulation-based learning and virtual reality environments can significantly enhance students' understanding of complex AI models while providing immersive training experiences. Schools and universities that embrace these innovations will not only elevate the quality of AI education but also prepare students to adapt swiftly and effectively to future technological shifts.

In summary, the challenge of shaping future AI professionals extends beyond traditional teaching paradigms. It calls for an adaptable, inclusive, and holistic approach that embraces interdisciplinary knowledge, practical skills, creativity, and ethical awareness. This strategic educational framework not only facilitates personal and professional growth but also serves as a catalyst for transformative advancements that resonate positively with the global community.

Community engagement in the development of artificial intelligence (AI) is not just a visionary idea; it is a crucial foundation for building ethical and effective AI systems. As we see AI becoming an integral part of our daily lives, the need for active participation from all corners of society becomes ever more pressing. Engaging diverse communities ensures that AI technologies are responsive to the unique needs and values of different groups, enhancing the relevance and effectiveness of these innovations. Moreover, such participation serves as a safeguard against the pitfalls of biased or exclusionary practices in technology development.

A pivotal step in fostering community involvement is

creating collaborative platforms that promote open dialogue between AI developers and the public. These initiatives can take various forms—community forums, workshops, and hackathons that enable individuals to share their insights and propose solutions. For example, the OpenAI community forum exemplifies this concept by bringing together developers, researchers, and AI enthusiasts to discuss advancements, ethical challenges, and user experiences. This collaborative atmosphere cultivates transparency and inclusivity, enriching the research and deployment of AI technologies.

Integrating community feedback into AI projects is essential for ensuring that these solutions are grounded in real-world experiences. Take, for instance, urban development initiatives that employ AI to create smart cities. It is critical that these projects reflect the voices of local residents who will be directly impacted. Implementing town hall meetings and conducting surveys can help developers glean valuable insights about community priorities, privacy concerns, and accessibility challenges. A notable success story in this realm is Barcelona's smart city initiative, where citizen feedback significantly influenced data collection methods, thereby enhancing privacy and enabling informed local decision-making.

To truly embrace a holistic approach, developers and organizations must strive for cultural competency by actively involving participants from a wide range of ethnic and socioeconomic backgrounds in the design and testing phases of AI products. This inclusivity is vital for mitigating bias and ensuring that AI systems are universally applicable. For example, in the development of speech recognition software, incorporating voices from diverse dialects and accents into training datasets allows AI to cater accurately to users from various linguistic backgrounds, enhancing the technology's overall effectiveness.

Engagement should also extend to academic institutions and civil society organizations, which can provide valuable oversight and direction. Collaborating with universities and think tanks can lead to in-depth research into the societal implications of AI and help establish ethical frameworks for measuring these effects. Partnerships with non-profits committed to technology ethics, such as the Partnership on AI, exemplify this collaborative spirit, offering guidelines and best practices for responsible AI development that upholds human rights and fosters societal well-being.

Moreover, educational outreach plays a pivotal role in empowering communities to participate effectively in AI development. Programs aimed at enhancing AI literacy can demystify complex technologies, paving the way for informed discussions and decision-making. Libraries, community centers, and schools can serve as hubs for this education, as illustrated by initiatives like the AI Experience Lab, which deploys mobile labs to underserved regions, empowering residents with knowledge about AI concepts and inspiring grassroots innovation.

Furthermore, open-source AI projects can act as catalysts for widespread community engagement, promoting inclusivity in the development process. This democratization of AI promotes a broader base of contributions and critiques, driving the creation of higher-quality and more equitable AI systems.

In essence, fostering community engagement in AI development is about establishing a dynamic feedback loop that benefits both technology and society. This approach cultivates accountability in AI production, equipping individuals with the knowledge and influence necessary to shape technologies that significantly impact their lives. Ultimately, this model creates AI systems that are not only robust in their technical design but also attuned to social needs, fostering greater trust and acceptance among users around the globe.

As we conclude our exploration of AI agents, we stand at a crucial crossroads where reflection meets action. This journey has revealed the intricate dimensions of AI agents—from their technological underpinnings to their real-world applications, alongside the ethical and socio-economic dilemmas they bring to the forefront. The landscape we traverse is one of profound change, ripe with extraordinary opportunities for innovation and growth. Our current challenge is to harness this potential with a sense of responsibility, ensuring that AI emerges as a beacon of positive change within society.

Our first imperative is to become staunch advocates for ethical AI development. Whether you are a seasoned professional, a passionate tech enthusiast, or a concerned citizen, we collectively hold the power to influence the evolution of AI technologies. This responsibility goes beyond mere technical comprehension; it encompasses engaging with the ethical and philosophical questions that arise. Let's foster dialogues in our communities, workplaces, and online spaces—championing the ideals of transparency and accountability in AI practices. We must insist that AI-driven decisions uphold privacy, fairness, and equity, mirroring the rich tapestry of values and needs within our society.

Next, embrace the ethos of lifelong learning in this rapidly evolving field. With AI advancing at breakneck speed, continuous education is no longer optional; it's essential. I encourage you to explore courses that blend technical skills with ethical considerations, such as those offered on platforms like Coursera or edX. These programs deliver a comprehensive curriculum that encompasses both the mechanics of AI and its broader societal implications.

Recognizing AI's potential as a catalyst for social good, we must also support or engage in initiatives that harness AI to address global challenges. From combating climate change to enhancing healthcare and improving education, AI offers transformative tools capable of driving substantial progress. Consider collaborating with organizations like AI for Good or Data Science for Social Good, which are dedicated to using AI for humanitarian and environmental advancements. Your involvement in these initiatives can make a significant impact, illustrating how technology can improve lives and foster sustainable development for communities around the globe.

Collaboration across disciplines presents yet another powerful avenue for action. The complex challenges posed by AI demand a holistic approach that incorporates diverse fields such as computer science, ethics, law, and social sciences. Engage in cross-disciplinary projects and think tanks that strive to craft solutions that are both technically sound and ethically grounded.

Moreover, let's adopt a mindset of local engagement with a global perspective. Tackle AI challenges that are unique to your community or region by partnering with local governments, businesses, or educational institutions to implement tailor-made AI solutions. Whether it involves addressing traffic management, optimizing resource allocation, or enhancing educational accessibility, localized initiatives can set significant precedents for broader applications, demonstrating responsible and effective technological use on a global scale.

Finally, we must cultivate a sense of stewardship for future generations. As pioneers in the AI frontier, the foundations we lay today will shape the world our children and grandchildren inherit. We should remain vigilant about the long-term consequences of our AI solutions, advocating for sustainable practices and ethical frameworks that protect the interests of future societies. Let's inspire young minds to engage with AI not only with curiosity but also with a deep sense of responsibility and foresight, guiding them to become thoughtful innovators and leaders.

In conclusion, the future of AI development hinges on our intentional actions and unwavering commitments. Your engagement is a vital catalyst for the responsible evolution of AI, and together, we can forge a future where technological advancements enhance human welfare and enrich our society as a whole.

APPENDIX A:
TUTORIALS

Project Title: Exploring the Technological Landscape of AI Agents

Objective: The purpose of this project is to provide students with a comprehensive understanding of the technological landscape that drives AI agents. Students will explore various AI technologies, including Natural Language Processing (NLP), machine learning frameworks, robotics, IoT, cloud computing, and cybersecurity.

Materials Needed: - Computer with internet access - Access to online AI tools and platforms (e.g., Google Colab, TensorFlow, etc.) - Research resources (e.g., academic journals, articles, books) - Presentation software (e.g., PowerPoint, Google Slides)

Project Timeline: This project is designed to be completed over a four-week period.

Week 1: Introduction and Research

Step 1: Introduction to AI Technologies - Read Chapter 2: The Technological Landscape. - Take notes on key concepts, technologies, and terms mentioned in the chapter.

Step 2: Topic Assignment - Divide the class into small groups. - Assign each group one of the following topics: 1. Overview of AI technologies driving agent capabilities 2. Natural Language Processing (NLP) advancements 3. Machine learning frameworks and tools 4. Robotics and physical AI agents 5. The Internet of Things (IoT) and AI agents 6. Cloud computing and AI scalability 7. Data management and real-time processing 8. Cybersecurity challenges and solutions 9. Open-source vs proprietary AI agent platforms 10. Future technology predictions

Step 3: Research - Each group will conduct in-depth research on their assigned topic. - Utilize online databases, academic journals, articles, and other reliable sources. - Focus on understanding how the technology works, its applications, and its significance in the context of AI agents.

Week 2: Deep Dive and Analysis

Step 4: Detailed Analysis - Each group will create a detailed report on their assigned topic. - The report should include: - An introduction to the technology - How it works (technical explanation) - Current applications and examples - Benefits and challenges - How it contributes to the capabilities of AI agents - Future trends and predictions

Step 5: Case Study Selection - Each group will select a case study that exemplifies the use of their assigned technology. - Analyze the case study and integrate it into the report.

Week 3: Presentation Preparation

Step 6: Presentation Creation - Groups will create a presentation based on their report. - The presentation should include: - Key points from the report - Visual aids (diagrams, charts, images) - Real-world examples and case studies - A summary of future trends

Step 7: Presentation Rehearsal - Groups will rehearse their presentation. - Focus on clarity, engagement, and time management. - Prepare to answer questions from classmates and the instructor.

Week 4: Presentation and Discussion

Step 8: Group Presentations - Each group will present their findings to the class. - All group members should participate in the presentation.

Step 9: Q&A Session - After each presentation, there will be a Q&A session. - Encourage students to ask questions and engage in discussions.

Step 10: Reflective Essay - Each student will write a reflective essay on what they learned from the project. - The essay should include: - Insights gained from their research - How their understanding of AI technologies has evolved - The significance of their assigned technology in the bigger picture of AI agents - Any remaining questions or areas of interest they wish to explore further

Assessment Criteria: - Quality and depth of research - Clarity and organization of the report - Effectiveness and creativity of the presentation - Participation and collaboration within the group - Engagement during the Q&A session - Insightfulness and reflection in the essay

Submission: - Submit the group report and presentation slides at the end of Week 3. - Submit the individual reflective essay at the end of Week 4. This project aims to foster research skills, teamwork, critical thinking, and effective communication.

Project Title: Exploring the Technological Landscape of AI Agents

Objective: The purpose of this project is to provide students with a comprehensive understanding of the technological landscape that drives AI agents. Students will explore various AI technologies, including Natural Language Processing (NLP), machine learning frameworks, robotics, IoT, cloud computing, and cybersecurity.

Materials Needed: - Computer with internet access - Access to online AI tools and platforms (e.g., Google Colab, TensorFlow, etc.) - Research resources (e.g., academic journals, articles, books) - Presentation software (e.g., PowerPoint, Google Slides)

Project Timeline: This project is designed to be completed over a four-week period.

Week 1: Introduction and Research

Step 1: Introduction to AI Technologies - Read Chapter 2: The Technological Landscape. - Take notes on key concepts, technologies, and terms mentioned in the chapter.

Step 2: Topic Assignment - Divide the class into small groups. - Assign each group one of the following topics: 1. Overview of AI technologies driving agent capabilities 2. Natural Language Processing (NLP) advancements 3. Machine learning frameworks and tools 4. Robotics and physical AI agents 5. The Internet of Things (IoT) and AI agents 6. Cloud computing and AI scalability 7. Data management and real-time processing 8. Cybersecurity challenges and solutions 9. Open-source vs proprietary AI agent platforms 10. Future technology predictions

Step 3: Research - Each group will conduct in-depth research on their assigned topic. - Utilize online databases, academic journals, articles, and other reliable sources. - Focus on understanding how the technology works, its applications, and its significance in the context of AI agents.

Week 2: Deep Dive and Analysis

Step 4: Detailed Analysis - Each group will create a detailed report on their assigned topic. - The report should include: - An introduction to the technology - How it works (technical explanation) - Current applications and examples - Benefits and challenges - How it contributes to the capabilities of AI agents - Future trends and predictions

Step 5: Case Study Selection - Each group will select a case study that exemplifies the use of their assigned technology. - Analyze the case study and integrate it into the report.

Week 3: Presentation Preparation

Step 6: Presentation Creation - Groups will create a presentation based on their report. - The presentation should include: - Key points from the report - Visual aids (diagrams, charts, images) - Real-world examples and case studies - A summary of future trends

Step 7: Presentation Rehearsal - Groups will rehearse their presentation. - Focus on clarity, engagement, and time management. - Prepare to answer questions from classmates and the instructor.

Week 4: Presentation and Discussion

Step 8: Group Presentations - Each group will present their findings to the class. - All group members should participate in the presentation.

Step 9: Q&A Session - After each presentation, there will be a Q&A session. - Encourage students to ask questions and engage in discussions.

Step 10: Reflective Essay - Each student will write a reflective essay on what they learned from the project. - The essay should include: - Insights gained from their research - How their understanding of AI technologies has evolved - The significance of their assigned technology in the bigger picture of AI agents - Any remaining questions or areas of interest they wish to explore further

Assessment Criteria: - Quality and depth of research - Clarity and organization of the report - Effectiveness and creativity of the presentation - Participation and collaboration within the group - Engagement during the Q&A session - Insightfulness and reflection in the essay

Submission: - Submit the group report and presentation slides at the end of Week 3. - Submit the individual reflective essay at the end of Week 4. This project aims to foster research skills, teamwork, critical thinking, and effective communication.

Comprehensive Project Based on Chapter 4: The Role of Data in AI Agents

Project Title: Mastering Data Utilization in AI Agents

Objective: The goal of this project is to provide students with a thorough understanding of the role of data in AI agents. Students will explore the importance of big data, data sources, collection methodologies, privacy, security concerns, data ethics, and the impact of data quality on AI performance.

Materials Needed: - Computer with internet access - Data analysis software (e.g., Python, R, etc.) - Access to datasets (e.g., Kaggle, UCI Machine Learning Repository) - Research resources (e.g., academic journals, articles, books) - Presentation software (e.g., PowerPoint, Google Slides)

Project Timeline: This project is designed to be completed over a five-week period.

Week 1: Introduction and Research

Step 1: Introduction to Data in AI - Read Chapter 4: The Role of Data in AI Agents. - Take notes on key concepts, technologies, and terms mentioned in the chapter.

Step 2: Topic Assignment - Divide the class into small groups. - Assign each group one of the following subtopics: 1. Importance of big data for AI agents 2. Data sources: structured vs unstructured 3. Data collection methodologies 4. Data privacy and security concerns 5. Data ethics and responsible AI use 6. The impact of poor data quality on AI performance 7. Techniques for data augmentation and manipulation 8. Real-time data processing and responsiveness 9. The role of user feedback in improving AI agents 10. Future trends in data utilization for AI

Step 3: Research - Each group will conduct in-depth research on their assigned subtopic. - Utilize online databases, academic journals, articles, and other reliable sources. - Focus on understanding the role of data in AI, its challenges, and best practices.

Week 2: Data Collection and Analysis

Step 4: Data Gathering - Each group will identify and gather relevant datasets related to their subtopic. - Use platforms like Kaggle, UCI Machine Learning Repository, or other data sources.

Step 5: Data Analysis - Perform data analysis using Python, R, or any other data analysis tool. - Analyze the data to extract meaningful insights related to their subtopic.

Step 6: Detailed Analysis Report - Each group will create a detailed report on their findings. - The report should include: - An introduction to the subtopic - Data collection methods and sources - Analysis techniques used - Insights derived from the data - Challenges faced during data analysis - How data impacts the performance and functionality of AI agents

Week 3: Practical Application

Step 7: Practical AI Implementation - Each group will implement a simple AI model using the data they analyzed. - Use machine learning frameworks like TensorFlow, Scikit-learn, or PyTorch. - Document the process, including data preprocessing, model training, and evaluation.

Step 8: Case Study Selection - Each group will select a case study that exemplifies the use of data in AI agents. - Analyze the case study and integrate it into their report.

Week 4: Presentation Preparation

Step 9: Presentation Creation - Groups will create a presentation based on their report and practical implementation. - The presentation should include: - Key points from the report - Visual aids (data visualizations, charts, images) - Real-world examples and case studies - Summary of practical implementation and results - Future trends and predictions

Step 10: Presentation Rehearsal - Groups will rehearse their presentation. - Focus on clarity, engagement, and time management. - Prepare to answer questions from classmates and the instructor.

Week 5: Presentation and Discussion

Step 11: Group Presentations - Each group will present their findings to the class. - All group members should participate in the presentation.

Step 12: Q&A Session - After each presentation, there will be a Q&A session. - Encourage students to ask questions and engage in discussions.

Step 13: Reflective Essay - Each student will write a reflective essay on what they learned from the project. - The essay should include: - Insights gained from their research - How their understanding of data in AI has evolved - The significance of their assigned subtopic in the bigger picture of AI agents - Any remaining questions or areas of interest they wish to explore further

Assessment Criteria: - Quality and depth of research - Clarity and organization of the report - Effectiveness and creativity of the presentation - Participation and collaboration within the group - Engagement during the Q&A session - Insightfulness and reflection in the essay

Submission: - Submit the group report and presentation slides at the end of Week 4. - Submit the individual reflective essay at the end of Week 5. This project aims to foster research skills, teamwork, technical proficiency, critical thinking, and effective communication.

Comprehensive Project Based on Chapter 5: Designing and Developing AI Agents

Project Title: Designing and Developing Effective AI Agents

Objective: The goal of this project is to provide students with hands-on experience in designing and developing AI agents. Students will explore best practices in AI agent design, user-centric design principles, development frameworks, stakeholder feedback integration, prototyping, testing, and performance evaluation.

Materials Needed: - Computer with internet access - AI development tools (e.g., Python, TensorFlow, Keras, PyTorch) - Integrated Development Environment (IDE) (e.g., PyCharm, Jupyter Notebook) - Research resources (e.g., academic journals, articles, books) - Presentation software (e.g., PowerPoint, Google Slides)

Project Timeline: This project is designed to be completed over a six-week period.

Week 1: Research and Planning

Step 1: Introduction to AI Agent Design - Read Chapter 5: Designing and Developing AI Agents. - Take notes on key concepts, design principles, and methodologies mentioned in the chapter.

Step 2: Topic Assignment - Divide the class into small groups. - Assign each group one of the following subtopics: 1. Best practices in AI agent design 2. User-centric design principles 3. Development frameworks and methodologies 4. Integrating stakeholder feedback 5. Prototyping and iterative development 6. Testing and performance evaluation 7. Cross-disciplinary collaboration in AI projects 8. Managing project timelines and resources 9. Case studies of successful AI agent development 10. The role of design thinking in AI innovation

Step 3: Research - Each group will conduct in-depth research on their assigned subtopic. - Utilize online databases, academic journals, articles, and other reliable sources. - Focus on understanding the best practices, challenges, and methodologies involved in AI agent design and development.

Week 2: Design and Conceptualization

Step 4: Ideation and Concept Development - Each group will brainstorm and come up with a concept for an AI agent. - Clearly define the purpose and functionality of the AI agent. - Identify the target users and their needs.

Step 5: User-Centric Design - Apply user-centric design principles to create initial design sketches and wireframes. - Consider user experience (UX) and user interface (UI) design elements.

Step 6: Stakeholder Feedback - Identify potential stakeholders (e.g., target users, industry experts). - Create a survey or conduct interviews to gather feedback on the initial design concept. - Document the feedback and plan how to integrate it into the design.

Week 3: Development Frameworks and Prototyping

Step 7: Selection of Development Frameworks - Choose appropriate development frameworks and tools for building the AI agent. - Justify the choice based on the agent's functionality and requirements.

Step 8: Prototyping - Develop a low-fidelity prototype of the AI agent. - Focus on core functionalities and user interactions. - Use rapid prototyping techniques to iterate and improve the design.

Week 4: Implementation and Testing

Step 9: Implementation - Begin the implementation of the AI agent using the chosen development frameworks. - Follow best practices in coding and software development. - Document the development process, including challenges and solutions.

Step 10: Testing and Performance Evaluation - Develop test cases to evaluate the performance of the AI agent. - Conduct functional testing, usability testing, and performance testing. - Collect and analyze test results to identify areas for improvement.

Week 5: Refinement and Finalization

Step 11: Iterative Development - Based on the test results, refine and improve the AI agent. - Implement necessary changes and enhancements. - Conduct additional rounds of testing as needed.

Step 12: Final Documentation - Create comprehensive documentation for the AI agent, including: - Design principles and methodologies used - Development process and frameworks - Stakeholder feedback and integration - Testing and performance evaluation - Final implementation details

Week 6: Presentation and Reflection

Step 13: Presentation Preparation - Groups will create a presentation based on their project. - The presentation should include: - An overview of the AI agent concept and design - User-centric design principles applied - Development frameworks and methodologies - Stakeholder feedback and integration - Prototyping and iterative development - Testing and performance evaluation results - Challenges faced and solutions implemented

Step 14: Presentation Rehearsal - Groups will rehearse their presentation. - Focus on clarity, engagement, and time management. - Prepare to answer questions from classmates and the instructor.

Step 15: Group Presentations - Each group will present their project to the class. - All group members should participate in the presentation.

Step 16: Q&A Session - After each presentation, there will be a Q&A session. - Encourage students to ask questions and engage in discussions.

Step 17: Reflective Essay - Each student will write a reflective essay on what they learned from the project. - The essay should include: - Insights gained from their research and development process - How their understanding of AI agent design and development has evolved - The significance of their assigned subtopic in the bigger picture of AI agents - Any remaining questions or areas of interest they wish to explore further

Assessment Criteria: - Quality and depth of research - Clarity and organization of the report and presentation - Effectiveness and functionality of the AI agent prototype - Participation and collaboration within the group - Engagement during the Q&A session - Insightfulness and reflection in the essay

Submission: - Submit the group report, prototype code, and presentation slides at the end of Week 5. - Submit the individual reflective essay at the end of Week 6. The project aims to foster technical proficiency, teamwork, creativity, problem-solving skills, and effective communication.

Comprehensive Project Based on Chapter 6: Ethical and Social Implications

Project Title: Evaluating the Ethical and Social Implications of AI Agents

Objective: The goal of this project is to provide students with a deep understanding of the ethical and social implications associated with AI agents. Students will explore AI ethics frameworks, identify sources of bias, evaluate job displacement concerns, and propose solutions for trust, transparency, and regulatory compliance.

Materials Needed: - Computer with internet access - Research resources (e.g., academic journals, articles, books) - Presentation software (e.g., PowerPoint, Google Slides) - Survey or interview tools (e.g., Google Forms, SurveyMonkey) - Video conferencing tools (e.g., Zoom, Microsoft Teams) for remote collaboration and interviews

Project Timeline: This project is designed to be completed over a six-week period.

Week 1: Introduction and Research

Step 1: Introduction to Ethical and Social Implications - Read Chapter 6: Ethical and Social Implications. - Take notes on key concepts such as AI ethics frameworks, bias, job displacement, trust, transparency, and regulatory landscape.

Step 2: Topic Assignment - Divide the class into small groups. - Assign each group one of the following subtopics: 1. Understanding AI ethics frameworks 2. Bias in AI agents: sources and solutions 3. Job displacement concerns and reskilling 4. Trust and transparency in AI decisions 5. Regulatory landscape for AI agents 6. Social impact assessments of AI technology 7. The importance of accountability in AI actions 8. Public perception of AI agents 9. Global disparities in AI access and development 10. Long-term implications of AI agent integration into society

Step 3: Research - Each group will conduct in-depth research on their assigned subtopic. - Utilize online databases, academic journals, articles, and other reliable sources. - Focus on understanding the best practices, challenges, and methodologies involved in addressing ethical and social implications of AI agents.

Week 2: Analysis and Conceptualization

Step 4: Problem Identification - Each group will identify specific problems or ethical dilemmas related to their subtopic. - Clearly define the scope and impact of these problems.

Step 5: Data Collection - Design surveys or interview questions to gather insights from various stakeholders (e.g., AI users, developers, ethicists). - Conduct surveys or interviews to collect data on perceptions, challenges, and potential solutions.

Step 6: Data Analysis - Analyze the collected data to identify common themes, concerns, and recommendations. - Document findings and prepare for further exploration.

Week 3: Solution Development

Step 7: Ideation and Proposal Development - Brainstorm potential solutions or strategies to address the identified problems. - Develop comprehensive proposals that include ethical guidelines, policy recommendations, or technological solutions.

Step 8: Stakeholder Feedback - Present the proposals to relevant stakeholders (e.g., classmates, industry experts) for feedback. - Document the feedback and plan how to integrate it into the final proposal.

Week 4: Implementation and Testing

Step 9: Proposal Refinement - Refine the proposals based on stakeholder feedback. - Ensure that the proposals are practical, feasible, and address the identified problems effectively.

Step 10: Simulation or Case Study - Develop a simulation or case study to test the effectiveness of the proposals. - Use real-world scenarios to evaluate the potential impact of the proposed solutions.

Week 5: Documentation and Finalization

Step 11: Report Writing - Create a comprehensive report that includes: - Introduction to the subtopic and identified problems - Research findings and data analysis - Detailed proposals and solutions - Stakeholder feedback and integration - Simulation or case study results - Conclusion and recommendations

Step 12: Presentation Preparation - Groups will create a presentation based on their project. - The presentation should include: - Overview of the subtopic and identified problems - Research methodology and findings - Proposed solutions and stakeholder feedback - Simulation or case study results - Conclusion and recommendations

Week 6: Presentation and Reflection

Step 13: Presentation Rehearsal - Groups will rehearse their presentation. - Focus on clarity, engagement, and time management. - Prepare to answer questions from classmates and the instructor.

Step 14: Group Presentations - Each group will present their project to the class. - All group members should participate in the presentation.

Step 15: Q&A Session - After each presentation, there will be a Q&A session. - Encourage students to ask questions and engage in discussions.

Step 16: Reflective Essay - Each student will write a reflective essay on what they learned from the project. - The essay should include: - Insights gained from their research and development process - How their understanding of AI ethics and social implications has evolved - The significance of their assigned subtopic in the broader context of AI - Any remaining questions or areas of interest they wish to explore further

Assessment Criteria: - Quality and depth of research - Clarity and organization of the report and presentation - Practicality and feasibility of proposed solutions - Participation and collaboration within the group - Engagement during the Q&A session - Insightfulness and reflection in the essay

Submission: - Submit the group report, stakeholder feedback documentation, and presentation slides at the end of Week 5. - Submit the individual reflective essay at the end of Week 6. The project aims to foster critical thinking, ethical reasoning, teamwork, and effective communication skills.

Comprehensive Project Based on Chapter 7: The Future of Work with AI Agents

Project Title: Exploring the Future of Work with AI Agents

Objective: The objective of this project is to provide students with an in-depth understanding of how AI agents are reshaping the future of work. Students will explore human-AI collaboration models, the automation vs augmentation debate, future skill sets, and the impact of AI on remote work and job roles.

Materials Needed: - Computer with internet access - Research resources (e.g., academic journals, articles, books) - Presentation software (e.g., PowerPoint, Google Slides) - Survey or interview tools (e.g., Google Forms, SurveyMonkey) - Video conferencing tools (e.g., Zoom, Microsoft Teams) for remote collaboration and interviews

Project Timeline: This project is designed to be completed over a six-week period.

Week 1: Introduction and Research

Step 1: Introduction to the Future of Work with AI - Read Chapter 7: The Future of Work with AI Agents. - Take notes on key concepts such as human-AI collaboration, automation vs augmentation, future skill sets, remote work, and new job roles.

Step 2: Topic Assignment - Divide the class into small groups. - Assign each group one of the following subtopics: 1. Human-AI collaboration models 2. Automation vs augmentation debate 3. Skill sets for the future workforce 4. AI agents and remote work trends 5. New job roles created by AI agents 6. Employee sentiment and AI integration 7. Continuous learning and adaptation 8. Leadership strategies for AI-enhanced teams 9. Workplace safety and ethical AI use 10. Predicting the future job market landscape

Step 3: Research - Each group will conduct in-depth research on their assigned subtopic. - Utilize online databases, academic journals, articles, and other reliable sources. - Focus on understanding the best practices, challenges, and methodologies involved in the future of work with AI agents.

Week 2: Analysis and Conceptualization

Step 4: Problem Identification - Each group will identify specific problems or challenges related to their subtopic. - Clearly define the scope and impact of these problems.

Step 5: Data Collection - Design surveys or interview questions to gather insights from various stakeholders (e.g., industry experts, employees, HR professionals). - Conduct surveys or interviews to collect data on perceptions, challenges, and potential solutions.

Step 6: Data Analysis - Analyze the collected data to identify common themes, concerns, and recommendations. - Document findings and prepare for further exploration.

Week 3: Solution Development

Step 7: Ideation and Proposal Development - Brainstorm potential solutions or strategies to address the identified problems. - Develop comprehensive proposals that include models, guidelines, policy recommendations, or technological solutions.

Step 8: Stakeholder Feedback - Present the proposals to relevant stakeholders (e.g., classmates, industry experts) for feedback. - Document the feedback and plan how to integrate it into the final proposal.

Week 4: Implementation and Testing

Step 9: Proposal Refinement - Refine the proposals based on stakeholder feedback. - Ensure that the proposals are practical, feasible, and address the identified problems effectively.

Step 10: Simulation or Case Study - Develop a simulation or case study to test the effectiveness of the proposals. - Use real-world scenarios to evaluate the potential impact of the proposed solutions.

Week 5: Documentation and Finalization

Step 11: Report Writing - Create a comprehensive report that includes: - Introduction to the subtopic and identified problems - Research findings and data analysis - Detailed proposals and solutions - Stakeholder feedback and integration - Simulation or case study results - Conclusion and recommendations

Step 12: Presentation Preparation - Groups will create a presentation based on their project. - The presentation should include: - Overview of the subtopic and identified problems - Research methodology and findings - Proposed solutions and stakeholder feedback - Simulation or case study results - Conclusion and recommendations

Week 6: Presentation and Reflection

Step 13: Presentation Rehearsal - Groups will rehearse their presentation. - Focus on clarity, engagement, and time management. - Prepare to answer questions from classmates and the instructor.

Step 14: Group Presentations - Each group will present their project to the class. - All group members should participate in the presentation.

Step 15: Q&A Session - After each presentation, there will be a Q&A session. - Encourage students to ask questions and engage in discussions.

Step 16: Reflective Essay - Each student will write a reflective essay on what they learned from the project. - The essay should include: - Insights gained from their research and development process - How their understanding of the future of work with AI agents has evolved - The significance of their assigned subtopic in the broader context of AI - Any remaining questions or areas of interest they wish to explore further

Assessment Criteria: - Quality and depth of research - Clarity and organization of the report and presentation - Practicality and feasibility of proposed solutions - Participation and collaboration within the group - Engagement during the Q&A session - Insightfulness and reflection in the essay

Submission: - Submit the group report, stakeholder feedback documentation, and presentation slides at the end of Week 5. - Submit the individual reflective essay at the end of Week 6. The project aims to foster critical thinking, problem-solving, teamwork, and effective communication skills.

Comprehensive Project Based on Chapter 8: Innovations Driving AI Agent Evolution

Project Title: Exploring Innovations Driving AI Agent Evolution

Objective: The objective of this project is to provide students with a comprehensive understanding of the latest innovations driving the evolution of AI agents. Students will delve into various technological advancements, including breakthroughs in algorithms, computer vision, speech recognition, quantum computing, and more.

Materials Needed: - Computer with internet access - Research resources (e.g., academic journals, articles, books) - Presentation software (e.g., PowerPoint, Google Slides) - Survey or interview tools (e.g., Google Forms, SurveyMonkey) - Video conferencing tools (e.g., Zoom, Microsoft Teams) for remote collaboration and interviews

Project Timeline: This project is designed to be completed over a six-week period.

Week 1: Introduction and Research

Step 1: Introduction to Innovations in AI - Read Chapter 8: Innovations Driving AI Agent Evolution. - Take notes on key concepts such as breakthroughs in algorithms, advancements in computer vision, speech recognition, quantum computing, and other emerging technologies.

Step 2: Topic Assignment - Divide the class into small groups. - Assign each group one of the following subtopics: 1. Breakthroughs in algorithm development 2. Advancements in computer vision 3. Enhancements in speech recognition 4. Quantum computing and its potential impact 5. Advances in AI ethics technology 6. Innovative human-computer interfaces 7. Exploratory AI: creativity and problem-solving 8. Swarm intelligence and collective behavior in AI 9. Integration of AI with blockchain technology 10. Future technologies to watch for AI agents

Step 3: Research - Each group will conduct in-depth research on their assigned subtopic. - Utilize online databases, academic journals, articles, and other reliable sources. - Focus on understanding the latest developments, challenges, and potential future impacts of the innovation.

Week 2: Analysis and Conceptualization

Step 4: Problem Identification - Each group will identify specific problems or challenges related to their subtopic. - Clearly define the scope and impact of these problems.

Step 5: Data Collection - Design surveys or interview questions to gather insights from various stakeholders (e.g., industry experts, researchers). - Conduct surveys or interviews to collect data on perceptions, challenges, and potential solutions.

Step 6: Data Analysis - Analyze the collected data to identify common themes, concerns, and recommendations. - Document findings and prepare for further exploration.

Week 3: Solution Development

Step 7: Ideation and Proposal Development - Brainstorm potential solutions or advancements to address the identified problems. - Develop comprehensive proposals that include models, guidelines, policy recommendations, or technological solutions.

Step 8: Stakeholder Feedback - Present the proposals to relevant stakeholders (e.g., classmates, industry experts) for feedback. - Document the feedback and plan how to integrate it into the final proposal.

Week 4: Implementation and Testing

Step 9: Proposal Refinement - Refine the proposals based on stakeholder feedback. - Ensure that the proposals are practical, feasible, and address the identified problems effectively.

Step 10: Simulation or Case Study - Develop a simulation or case study to test the effectiveness of the proposals. - Use real-world scenarios to evaluate the potential impact of the proposed solutions.

Week 5: Documentation and Finalization

Step 11: Report Writing - Create a comprehensive report that includes: - Introduction to the subtopic and identified problems - Research findings and data analysis - Detailed proposals and solutions - Stakeholder feedback and integration - Simulation or case study results - Conclusion and recommendations

Step 12: Presentation Preparation - Groups will create a presentation based on their project. - The presentation should include: - Overview of the subtopic and identified problems - Research methodology and findings - Proposed solutions and stakeholder feedback - Simulation or case study results - Conclusion and recommendations

Week 6: Presentation and Reflection

Step 13: Presentation Rehearsal - Groups will rehearse their presentation. - Focus on clarity, engagement, and time management. - Prepare to answer questions from classmates and the instructor.

Step 14: Group Presentations - Each group will present their project to the class. - All group members should participate in the presentation.

Step 15: Q&A Session - After each presentation, there will be a Q&A session. - Encourage students to ask questions and engage in discussions.

Step 16: Reflective Essay - Each student will write a reflective essay on what they learned from the project. - The essay should include: - Insights gained from their research and development process - How their understanding of AI innovations has evolved - The significance of their assigned subtopic in the broader context of AI - Any remaining questions or areas of interest they wish to explore further

Assessment Criteria: - Quality and depth of research - Clarity and organization of the report and presentation - Practicality and feasibility of proposed solutions - Participation and collaboration within the group - Engagement during the Q&A session - Insightfulness and reflection in the essay

Submission: - Submit the group report, stakeholder feedback documentation, and presentation slides at the end of Week 5. - Submit the individual reflective essay at the end of Week 6. The project aims to foster critical thinking, problem-solving, teamwork, and effective communication skills.

Comprehensive Project Based on Chapter 9: Integrating AI Agents into Existing Systems

Project Title: Seamlessly Integrating AI Agents into Legacy Systems

Objective: The goal of this project is to give students a deep understanding of the challenges and best practices for integrating AI agents into existing systems.

Materials Needed: - Computer with internet access - Research resources (e.g., academic journals, articles, books) - Programming environment (e.g., Python, Java) - API development tools (e.g., Postman) - Presentation software (e.g., PowerPoint, Google Slides) - Survey or interview tools (e.g., Google Forms, SurveyMonkey) - Video conferencing tools (e.g., Zoom, Microsoft Teams) for remote collaboration and interviews

Project Timeline: This project is designed to be completed over a six-week period.

Week 1: Introduction and Research

Step 1: Introduction to AI Integration - Read Chapter 9:

Integrating AI Agents into Existing Systems. - Take notes on key concepts such as challenges of legacy system integration, API development, cloud vs on-premises deployment, and data synchronization.

Step 2: Topic Assignment - Divide the class into small groups. - Assign each group one of the following subtopics: 1. Challenges of integration with legacy systems 2. API development and interoperability 3. Cloud vs on-premises deployment considerations 4. Ensuring seamless user experiences 5. Change management strategies 6. Data synchronization and integrity 7. Performance metrics for integrated systems 8. Case studies of successful integrations 9. Training and support for end-users 10. Future trends in system integration

Step 3: Research - Each group will conduct in-depth research on their assigned subtopic. - Utilize online databases, academic journals, articles, and other reliable sources. - Focus on understanding the latest developments, challenges, and potential solutions related to their subtopic.

Week 2: Analysis and Conceptualization

Step 4: Problem Identification - Each group will identify specific problems or challenges related to their subtopic. - Clearly define the scope and impact of these problems.

Step 5: Data Collection - Design surveys or interview questions to gather insights from various stakeholders (e.g., industry experts, IT professionals). - Conduct surveys or interviews to collect data on perceptions, challenges, and potential solutions.

Step 6: Data Analysis - Analyze the collected data to identify common themes, concerns, and recommendations. - Document findings and prepare for further exploration.

Week 3: Solution Development

Step 7: Ideation and Proposal Development - Brainstorm

potential solutions or advancements to address the identified problems. - Develop comprehensive proposals that include integration models, guidelines, policy recommendations, or technological solutions.

Step 8: Stakeholder Feedback - Present the proposals to relevant stakeholders (e.g., classmates, industry experts) for feedback. - Document the feedback and plan how to integrate it into the final proposal.

Week 4: Implementation and Testing

Step 9: Proposal Refinement - Refine the proposals based on stakeholder feedback. - Ensure that the proposals are practical, feasible, and address the identified problems effectively.

Step 10: Mock API Development - Develop a mock API to demonstrate how an AI agent could be integrated into an existing system. - Use API development tools like Postman to create and test the mock API. - Provide documentation for the API, including endpoints, methods, and data formats.

Week 5: Documentation and Finalization

Step 11: Report Writing - Create a comprehensive report that includes: - Introduction to the subtopic and identified problems - Research findings and data analysis - Detailed proposals and solutions - Stakeholder feedback and integration - Mock API documentation - Conclusion and recommendations

Step 12: Presentation Preparation - Groups will create a presentation based on their project. - The presentation should include: - Overview of the subtopic and identified problems - Research methodology and findings - Proposed solutions and stakeholder feedback - Mock API demonstration - Conclusion and recommendations

Week 6: Presentation and Reflection

Step 13: Presentation Rehearsal - Groups will rehearse their presentation. - Focus on clarity, engagement, and time management. - Prepare to answer questions from classmates and the instructor.

Step 14: Group Presentations - Each group will present their project to the class. - All group members should participate in the presentation.

Step 15: Q&A Session - After each presentation, there will be a Q&A session. - Encourage students to ask questions and engage in discussions.

Step 16: Reflective Essay - Each student will write a reflective essay on what they learned from the project. - The essay should include: - Insights gained from their research and development process - How their understanding of AI integration has evolved - The significance of their assigned subtopic in the broader context of AI - Any remaining questions or areas of interest they wish to explore further

Assessment Criteria: - Quality and depth of research - Clarity and organization of the report and presentation - Practicality and feasibility of proposed solutions - Participation and collaboration within the group - Engagement during the Q&A session - Insightfulness and reflection in the essay

Submission: - Submit the group report, stakeholder feedback documentation, mock API documentation, and presentation slides at the end of Week 5. - Submit the individual reflective essay at the end of Week 6. The project aims to foster critical thinking, problem-solving, teamwork, and effective communication skills.

Comprehensive Project Based on Chapter 10: Global Perspectives on AI Agents

Project Title: Comparative Analysis of AI Agent Adoption Across Global Regions

Objective: The goal of this project is to help students understand the varying approaches to AI agent adoption and integration across different regions of the world. Students will analyze regional variations, government roles, international collaborations, cultural impacts, and the future of AI on a global scale.

Materials Needed: - Computer with internet access - Research resources (e.g., academic journals, articles, books) - Data analysis tools (e.g., Excel, Google Sheets) - Presentation software (e.g., PowerPoint, Google Slides) - Survey or interview tools (e.g., Google Forms, SurveyMonkey) - Video conferencing tools (e.g., Zoom, Microsoft Teams) for remote collaboration and interviews

Project Timeline: This project is designed to be completed over a six-week period.

Week 1: Introduction and Research

Step 1: Introduction to Global Perspectives - Read Chapter 10: Global Perspectives on AI Agents. - Take notes on key concepts such as regional variations in AI adoption, AI initiatives in emerging markets, the role of government, international collaborations, and cultural impacts.

Step 2: Topic Assignment - Divide the class into small groups. - Assign each group one of the following subtopics: 1. Regional variations in AI adoption 2. AI initiatives in emerging markets 3. The role of government in AI development 4. International collaborations and partnerships 5. Cultural impacts on AI application 6. AI agent impacts on global supply chains 7. Cross-border data management and AI 8. Global governance issues in AI development 9. Comparing AI agent policies: East vs West 10. Future of AI agents on a global scale

Step 3: Research - Each group will conduct in-depth research on their assigned subtopic. - Utilize online databases, academic journals, articles, and other reliable sources. - Focus on understanding the latest developments, challenges, and potential solutions related to their subtopic.

Week 2: Analysis and Conceptualization

Step 4: Problem Identification - Each group will identify specific problems or challenges related to their subtopic. - Clearly define the scope and impact of these problems.

Step 5: Data Collection - Design surveys or interview questions to gather insights from various stakeholders (e.g., industry experts, government officials, cultural analysts). - Conduct surveys or interviews to collect data on perceptions, challenges, and potential solutions.

Step 6: Data Analysis - Analyze the collected data to identify common themes, concerns, and recommendations. - Document findings and prepare for further exploration.

Week 3: Solution Development

Step 7: Ideation and Proposal Development - Brainstorm potential solutions or advancements to address the identified problems. - Develop comprehensive proposals that include integration models, guidelines, policy recommendations, or technological solutions.

Step 8: Stakeholder Feedback - Present the proposals to relevant stakeholders (e.g., classmates, industry experts) for feedback. - Document the feedback and plan how to integrate it into the final proposal.

Week 4: Implementation and Testing

Step 9: Proposal Refinement - Refine the proposals based on stakeholder feedback. - Ensure that the proposals are practical, feasible, and address the identified problems effectively.

Step 10: Comparative Analysis - Conduct a comparative analysis between different regions based on the research and proposals. - Highlight key differences, similarities, and unique approaches to AI integration.

Week 5: Documentation and Finalization

Step 11: Report Writing - Create a comprehensive report that includes: - Introduction to the subtopic and identified problems - Research findings and data analysis - Detailed proposals and solutions - Stakeholder feedback and integration - Comparative analysis - Conclusion and recommendations

Step 12: Presentation Preparation - Groups will create a presentation based on their project. - The presentation should include: - Overview of the subtopic and identified problems - Research methodology and findings - Proposed solutions and stakeholder feedback - Comparative analysis - Conclusion and recommendations

Week 6: Presentation and Reflection

Step 13: Presentation Rehearsal - Groups will rehearse their presentation. - Focus on clarity, engagement, and time management. - Prepare to answer questions from classmates and the instructor.

Step 14: Group Presentations - Each group will present their project to the class. - All group members should participate in the presentation.

Step 15: Q&A Session - After each presentation, there will be a Q&A session. - Encourage students to ask questions and engage in discussions.

Step 16: Reflective Essay - Each student will write a reflective essay on what they learned from the project. - The essay should include: - Insights gained from their research and development process - How their understanding of global AI integration has evolved - The significance of their assigned subtopic in the broader context of AI - Any remaining questions or areas of interest they wish to explore further

Assessment Criteria: - Quality and depth of research - Clarity and organization of the report and presentation - Practicality and feasibility of proposed solutions - Participation and collaboration within the group - Engagement during the Q&A session - Insightfulness and reflection in the essay

Submission: - Submit the group report, stakeholder feedback documentation, comparative analysis, and presentation slides at the end of Week 5. - Submit the individual reflective essay at the end of Week 6. The project aims to foster critical thinking, problem-solving, teamwork, and effective communication skills.

Comprehensive Project Based on Chapter 11: Risks and Challenges Facing AI Agents

Project Title: Identifying and Mitigating Risks and Challenges in AI Agent Development

Objective: The goal of this project is to help students explore and understand the various risks and challenges associated with AI agents. Students will analyze technical limitations, security vulnerabilities, ethical dilemmas, public trust issues, environmental impacts, and more.

Materials Needed: - Computer with internet access - Research resources (e.g., academic journals, articles, books) - Data analysis tools (e.g., Excel, Google Sheets) - Presentation software (e.g., PowerPoint, Google Slides) - Survey or interview tools (e.g., Google Forms, SurveyMonkey) - Video conferencing tools (e.g., Zoom, Microsoft Teams) for remote collaboration and interviews

Project Timeline: This project is designed to be completed over a six-week period.

Week 1: Introduction and Research

Step 1: Introduction to AI Risks and Challenges - Read Chapter 11: Risks and Challenges Facing AI Agents. - Take notes on key concepts such as technical limitations, security vulnerabilities, ethical dilemmas, public trust, legal challenges, and environmental impacts.

Step 2: Topic Assignment - Divide the class into small groups. - Assign each group one of the following subtopics: 1.

Technical limitations and failures 2. Security vulnerabilities and cyber threats 3. Ethical dilemmas in decision-making 4. Reliability and robustness concerns 5. Managing public trust and skepticism 6. Legal and regulatory challenges 7. Environmental impact of AI technologies 8. Handling misinformation generated by AI 9. Potential misuse and harmful applications 10. Future challenges in AI development

Step 3: Research - Each group will conduct in-depth research on their assigned subtopic. - Utilize online databases, academic journals, articles, and other reliable sources. - Focus on understanding the latest developments, challenges, and potential solutions related to their subtopic.

Week 2: Analysis and Conceptualization

Step 4: Problem Identification - Each group will identify specific problems or challenges related to their subtopic. - Clearly define the scope and impact of these problems.

Step 5: Data Collection - Design surveys or interview questions to gather insights from various stakeholders (e.g., industry experts, government officials, ethical analysts). - Conduct surveys or interviews to collect data on perceptions, challenges, and potential solutions.

Step 6: Data Analysis - Analyze the collected data to identify common themes, concerns, and recommendations. - Document findings and prepare for further exploration.

Week 3: Solution Development

Step 7: Ideation and Proposal Development - Brainstorm potential solutions or advancements to address the identified problems. - Develop comprehensive proposals that include technical solutions, policy recommendations, ethical guidelines, or educational initiatives.

Step 8: Stakeholder Feedback - Present the proposals to relevant stakeholders (e.g., classmates, industry experts) for feedback. - Document the feedback and plan how to integrate it into the final proposal.

Week 4: Implementation and Testing

Step 9: Proposal Refinement - Refine the proposals based on stakeholder feedback. - Ensure that the proposals are practical, feasible, and address the identified problems effectively.

Step 10: Comparative Analysis - Conduct a comparative analysis between different risks and challenges based on the research and proposals. - Highlight key differences, similarities, and unique approaches to risk mitigation.

Week 5: Documentation and Finalization

Step 11: Report Writing - Create a comprehensive report that includes: - Introduction to the subtopic and identified problems - Research findings and data analysis - Detailed proposals and solutions - Stakeholder feedback and integration - Comparative analysis - Conclusion and recommendations

Step 12: Presentation Preparation - Groups will create a presentation based on their project. - The presentation should include: - Overview of the subtopic and identified problems - Research methodology and findings - Proposed solutions and stakeholder feedback - Comparative analysis - Conclusion and recommendations

Week 6: Presentation and Reflection

Step 13: Presentation Rehearsal - Groups will rehearse their presentation. - Focus on clarity, engagement, and time management. - Prepare to answer questions from classmates and the instructor.

Step 14: Group Presentations - Each group will present their project to the class. - All group members should participate in the presentation.

Step 15: Q&A Session - After each presentation, there will be a Q&A session. - Encourage students to ask questions and engage in discussions.

Step 16: Reflective Essay - Each student will write a reflective essay on what they learned from the project. - The essay should include: - Insights gained from their research and development process - How their understanding of AI risks and challenges has evolved - The significance of their assigned subtopic in the broader context of AI - Any remaining questions or areas of interest they wish to explore further

Assessment Criteria: - Quality and depth of research - Clarity and organization of the report and presentation - Practicality and feasibility of proposed solutions - Participation and collaboration within the group - Engagement during the Q&A session - Insightfulness and reflection in the essay

Submission: - Submit the group report, stakeholder feedback documentation, comparative analysis, and presentation slides at the end of Week 5. - Submit the individual reflective essay at the end of Week 6. The project aims to foster critical thinking, problem-solving, teamwork, and effective communication skills.

Comprehensive Project Based on Chapter 12: Vision for the Future

Project Title: Envisioning the Future of AI Agents

Objective: The purpose of this project is for students to explore and predict the future landscape of AI agents. They will analyze potential breakthroughs, ethical frameworks, and socio-economic impacts, ultimately crafting a vision that balances technological advancement with ethical considerations.

Materials Needed: - Computer with internet access - Research resources (e.g., academic journals, articles, books) - Data analysis tools (e.g., Excel, Google Sheets) - Presentation software (e.g., PowerPoint, Google Slides) - Survey or interview tools (e.g., Google Forms, SurveyMonkey) - Video conferencing tools (e.g., Zoom, Microsoft Teams) for remote collaboration and interviews

Project Timeline: This project is designed to be completed over a six-week period.

Week 1: Introduction and Research

Step 1: Introduction to Future Trends in AI - Read Chapter 12: Vision for the Future. - Take notes on key concepts such as predicted breakthroughs, ethical frameworks, human-AI relationships, sustainable AI development, and global challenges.

Step 2: Topic Assignment - Divide the class into small groups. - Assign each group one of the following subtopics: 1. Predicting the next decade of AI agents 2. Expected breakthroughs and innovations 3. The evolution of human-AI relationships 4. Pathways to sustainable AI development 5. The impact of AI agents on global challenges 6. Envisioning smart cities powered by AI 7. Long-term ethical frameworks for AI agents 8. The role of education in shaping future AI professionals 9. Community engagement in AI development 10. Final thoughts and calls to action for readers

Step 3: Research - Each group will conduct in-depth research on their assigned subtopic. - Utilize online databases, academic journals, articles, and other reliable sources. - Focus on understanding the latest developments, challenges, and potential solutions related to their subtopic.

Week 2: Analysis and Conceptualization

Step 4: Vision Crafting - Each group will identify specific trends, predictions, and challenges related to their subtopic. - Clearly define the scope and impact of these elements.

Step 5: Data Collection - Design surveys or interview questions to gather insights from various stakeholders (e.g., industry experts, government officials, ethical analysts). - Conduct surveys or interviews to collect data on perceptions, future trends, and potential solutions.

Step 6: Data Analysis - Analyze the collected data to identify common themes, concerns, and recommendations. - Document findings and prepare for further exploration.

Week 3: Vision Development

Step 7: Ideation and Proposal Development - Brainstorm potential future scenarios and advancements to address the identified trends and challenges. - Develop comprehensive visions that include technical solutions, policy recommendations, ethical guidelines, or educational initiatives.

Step 8: Stakeholder Feedback - Present the visions to relevant stakeholders (e.g., classmates, industry experts) for feedback. - Document the feedback and plan how to integrate it into the final vision.

Week 4: Implementation and Testing

Step 9: Vision Refinement - Refine the visions based on stakeholder feedback. - Ensure that the visions are practical, feasible, and address the identified trends and challenges effectively.

Step 10: Comparative Analysis - Conduct a comparative analysis between different trends and predictions based on the research and visions. - Highlight key differences, similarities, and unique approaches to future scenarios.

Week 5: Documentation and Finalization

Step 11: Report Writing - Create a comprehensive report that includes: - Introduction to the subtopic and identified trends - Research findings and data analysis - Detailed visions and solutions - Stakeholder feedback and integration - Comparative analysis - Conclusion and recommendations

Step 12: Presentation Preparation - Groups will create a presentation based on their project. - The presentation should include: - Overview of the subtopic and identified trends - Research methodology and findings - Proposed visions and stakeholder feedback - Comparative analysis - Conclusion and recommendations

Week 6: Presentation and Reflection

Step 13: Presentation Rehearsal - Groups will rehearse their presentation. - Focus on clarity, engagement, and time management. - Prepare to answer questions from classmates and the instructor.

Step 14: Group Presentations - Each group will present their project to the class. - All group members should participate in the presentation.

Step 15: Q&A Session - After each presentation, there will be a Q&A session. - Encourage students to ask questions and engage in discussions.

Step 16: Reflective Essay - Each student will write a reflective essay on what they learned from the project. - The essay should include: - Insights gained from their research and development process - How their understanding of the future of AI agents has evolved - The significance of their assigned subtopic in the broader context of AI - Any remaining questions or areas of interest they wish to explore further

Assessment Criteria: - Quality and depth of research - Clarity and organization of the report and presentation - Practicality and feasibility of proposed visions - Participation and collaboration within the group - Engagement during the Q&A session - Insightfulness and reflection in the essay

Submission: - Submit the group report, stakeholder feedback documentation, comparative analysis, and presentation slides at the end of Week 5. - Submit the individual reflective essay at the end of Week 6. The project aims to foster critical thinking, problem-solving, teamwork, and effective communication skills.

APPENDIX B: GLOSSARY OF TERMS

A

AI Agents: Artificial Intelligence entities capable of perceiving their environment, reasoning to take actions, and learning to improve over time. Types include reactive, deliberative, and hybrid agents.

Algorithm: A set of rules or calculations designed to solve problems or perform tasks in AI development.

B

Big Data: Large and complex data sets that traditional data-processing software cannot handle. Crucial for training AI agents to enhance performance and accuracy.

Blockchain Technology: A decentralized digital ledger that records transactions across many computers securely and transparently. Potentially useful for securing and verifying AI agent operations.

C

Cloud Computing: Delivery of computing services (e.g., servers, storage, databases, networking) over the internet (the cloud). Enables AI scalability and accessibility.

Computer Vision: A field of AI that enables computers to interpret and process visual data similarly to human vision.

D

Data Augmentation: Techniques used to increase the diversity of data available for training AI models without actually collecting new data.

Data Ethics: Principles and standards that guide how data is collected, managed, and utilized, ensuring fair, transparent, and respectful usage.

Data Management: The practice of collecting, keeping, and using data securely, efficiently, and cost-effectively.

Deliberative AI Agents: AI agents that use decision-making processes to determine actions based on a reasoning process rather than reacting to stimuli.

E

Ethical AI: The practice of designing and deploying AI systems in a manner that is fair, transparent, accountable, and respects individual rights and privacy.

Exploratory AI: AI systems designed to discover new solutions, processes, or approaches through creative and innovative methods.

F

Framework: A foundational structure supporting the development and deployment of AI systems, often including software libraries, tools, and best practices.

H

Hybrid AI Agents: AI agents that combine elements of both reactive and deliberative systems to leverage the benefits of both approaches.

I

Internet of Things (IoT): A network of interconnected devices that communicate and exchange data. AI agents often utilize IoT data for enhanced functionality.

Interoperability: The ability of AI systems and components to work together across various platforms and environments seamlessly.

L

Legacy Systems: Older computer systems or applications that are still in operation, often posing integration challenges for new AI technologies.

M

Machine Learning: A subset of AI that entails training algorithms to improve their performance over time using data.

Milestones: Significant achievements or events in the development and evolution of AI agents.

N

Natural Language Processing (NLP): A branch of AI focused on the interaction between computers and humans through natural language.

Neural Networks: Computing systems inspired by the biological neural networks of animal brains crucial for tasks like pattern recognition and decision-making in AI.

O

Open-source AI: AI systems and tools that have their source code made available to the public for use, modification, and distribution.

P

Prototyping: The process of creating early models of AI systems to test and refine concepts and functionalities.

Q

Quantum Computing: Advanced computing technologies based on quantum mechanics, promising to significantly enhance AI capabilities.

R

Reactive AI Agents: Basic AI agents that respond to specific stimuli or changes in the environment without internal state-based decision-making processes.

S

Smart Cities: Urban areas that integrate various information and communication technologies to enhance the quality of services, reduce costs and resource consumption, and engage more effectively and actively with their citizens via AI.

Swarm Intelligence: The collective behavior of decentralized, self-organized systems, which can be applied to AI to solve complex problems.

T

Transparency: Ensuring that AI operations and decision-making processes are understandable and accessible to users and stakeholders, fostering trust and accountability.

U

User-centric Design: Design principles focusing on creating AI systems that prioritize and meet the needs and preferences of end-users.

V

Vision for the Future: Envisions the future impact and trajectory of AI agents, addressing technological advancements, ethical frameworks, and societal integration.

W

Workforce Automation: The use of AI to automate tasks that were previously performed by human workers, affecting job dynamics and skill requirements.

Y

Yield Enhancement: The use of AI agents in agriculture and food production to improve crop yields, efficiency, and sustainability.

This glossary serves as a comprehensive guide to understanding the key terms and concepts discussed in "The Future of AI Agents: Emerging Trends and Opportunities."

APPENDIX C: ADDITIONAL RESOURCES

Books

1. "Artificial Intelligence: A Modern Approach" by Stuart Russell and Peter Norvig
2. A comprehensive guide to the fundamental concepts and various aspects of artificial intelligence, including agent-based systems and machine learning.
3. "Superintelligence: Paths, Dangers, Strategies" by Nick Bostrom
4. Explores the potential future impacts of superintelligent AI systems, including ethical and safety considerations.
5. "Life 3.0: Being Human in the Age of Artificial Intelligence" by Max Tegmark
6. An accessible discussion on how AI might affect society, economics, and the future of work, with a vision of coexistence between humans and AI agents.
7. "Deep Learning" by Ian Goodfellow, Yoshua Bengio, and Aaron Courville
8. Focuses on the machine learning technologies underpinning modern AI agents, especially deep

learning models.

9. "Human + Machine: Reimagining Work in the Age of AI" by Paul Daugherty and H. James Wilson

10. Examines how human-AI collaboration can enhance productivity and create new job roles.

Academic Papers

1. "The Ethics of Artificial Intelligence" by Nick Bostrom and Eliezer Yudkowsky

2. A seminal paper discussing the ethical dimensions of AI development and deployment.

3. "Building Machines That Learn and Think Like People" by Joshua B. Tenenbaum, et al.

4. Explores advancements in cognitive AI aiming to replicate human learning and thinking processes.

5. "A Survey on Transfer Learning" by Sinno Jialin Pan and Qiang Yang

6. An extensive review of transfer learning methodologies, crucial for the adaptation and scalability of AI agents.

Online Courses and Tutorials

1. Coursera: Machine Learning by Andrew Ng

2. A highly popular and comprehensive course on the basics of machine learning, essential for understanding the core technologies behind AI agents.

3. edX: Artificial Intelligence: Principles and Techniques by Stanford University

4. An advanced course covering the principles and applications of AI, including agent-based systems and decision making.

5. Udacity: AI for Robotics by Sebastian Thrun

6. Focuses on the application of AI techniques in robotics, covering practical aspects of deploying physical AI agents.

Websites and Blogs

1. Towards Data Science (https://towardsdatascience.com/)
2. A platform with articles and tutorials on AI, machine learning, and data science, written by practitioners and researchers.
3. OpenAI Blog (https://openai.com/blog/)
4. Offers insights into cutting-edge AI research, developments, and practical applications from one of the leading AI research organizations.
5. AI Alignment Forum (https://alignmentforum.org/)
6. A community blog focused on discussing AI safety, ethics, and alignment challenges.

Conferences and Workshops

1. NeurIPS (Conference on Neural Information Processing Systems)
2. One of the premier conferences on AI and machine learning, showcasing the latest research and breakthroughs.
3. AAAI Conference on Artificial Intelligence
4. Organized by the Association for the Advancement of Artificial Intelligence, focusing on all aspects of AI.
5. ICML (International Conference on Machine Learning)
6. Covers a wide range of topics in machine learning, providing insights into new techniques and applications relevant to AI agents.

Government and Industry Reports

1. "The National Artificial Intelligence Research and Development Strategic Plan" by the U.S. National Science and Technology Council
2. Offers a comprehensive strategy for AI research and development, highlighting government efforts to advance AI technology.
3. "Artificial Intelligence and Life in 2030" by the Stanford University One Hundred Year Study on Artificial Intelligence (AI100)
4. Provides an in-depth look at the anticipated impact of AI in various sectors by 2030.
5. "The Age of AI: And Our Human Future" by the AI Council for the World Economic Forum
6. Explores the global landscape of AI adoption, addressing economic, social, and ethical implications.

Open-Source Projects and Tools

1. TensorFlow (https://www.tensorflow.org/)
2. An open-source machine learning framework developed by Google, widely used for developing AI agents.
3. PyTorch (https://pytorch.org/)
4. An open-source deep learning platform that provides flexibility and ease of use, particularly popular in academic and research settings.
5. OpenAI Gym (https://gym.openai.com/)
6. A toolkit for developing and comparing reinforcement learning algorithms, often used in training AI agents.

Ethical Guidelines and Frameworks

1. "Ethics Guidelines for Trustworthy AI" by The European Commission's High-Level Expert Group on

AI

2. Provides principles and guidance to ensure AI is developed and used in a trustworthy manner.

3. "The IEEE Global Initiative on Ethics of Autonomous and Intelligent Systems" by IEEE

4. Addresses the ethical implications of autonomous and intelligent systems, offering standards and recommendations.

Professional Organizations

1. Association for the Advancement of Artificial Intelligence (AAAI)

2. Promotes research and responsible utilization of AI technologies for the benefit of society.

3. Partnership on AI

4. An organization bringing together a diverse coalition of companies, academics, and non-profits to collaborate on AI issues and best practices.

These resources provide deeper insights and a broad understanding of the complex and evolving field of AI agents, complementing the topics discussed within "The Future of AI Agents: Emerging Trends and Opportunities."

Epilogue: Navigating the Future with AI Agents

As we stand on the brink of a new era defined by digital transformation, the emergence of AI agents heralds opportunities and challenges we never thought possible. Through the exploration of the expansive realm presented in this book, "The Future of AI Agents: Emerging Trends and Opportunities," we have delved into the various dimensions that define AI agents today and envisioned what lies ahead.

A Recap of Our Journey

From the foundational principles in Chapter 1 to the forward-looking predictions of Chapter 12, we have journeyed through the intricacies and potential of AI agents. We began with a comprehensive introduction, gaining clarity on definitions, categorizations, and the distinct evolution of AI agents. We examined key technologies — from Natural Language Processing to the advent of quantum computing — that are pushing the frontiers of AI capabilities.

We explored sector-specific implementations, witnessing how AI agents transform industries such as healthcare, finance, retail, and beyond. The critical role of data, as both a fuel and a challenge for AI agents, underscored the importance of quality, security, and ethical stewardship. As we immersed in the design and development process, we encountered best practices, frameworks, and real-world case studies that illustrated the meticulous effort behind every AI application.

In addressing ethical and social implications, we confronted the biases, regulatory landscapes, and societal impacts necessitating careful navigation. Our focus extended to the evolving workplace, the redefinition of job roles, and the synergy between human capabilities and AI enhancements. We celebrated breakthroughs driving AI evolution and recognized the importance of seamless integration with existing systems.

Unveiling the Future: Opportunities and Cautions

Recognizing the global perspective, we explored how different regions adopt and adapt AI, the role of governance, and international collaborations shaping a unified yet diversified AI landscape. However, amidst these promising developments, we acknowledged the significant risks and challenges: technical, ethical, and societal.

In our vision for the future, we anticipated groundbreaking innovations, the evolution of human-AI relationships, and pathways to sustaining AI development ethically and responsibly. We centered on education's pivotal role in preparing future professionals and called for community engagement in shaping AI's trajectory.

A Call to Collective Responsibility

As AI agents become more integrated into the fabric of our lives, our collective responsibility is paramount. We must foster a culture of ethical considerations, ensuring transparency, accountability, and inclusivity in AI advancements. Stakeholders across industries, governments, and communities must collaborate to navigate the complexities and harness the full potential of AI agents for the greater good.

Embracing Innovation for a Better Tomorrow

While AI agents promise to revolutionize various aspects of society, the journey toward their optimal use is ongoing. The wisdom in our approach, the ethics in our deployment, and the inclusivity in our innovation will determine the legacy we leave for future generations. With curiosity, caution, and collaborative spirit, we can pave a path that leverages AI agents for unprecedented opportunities, while mitigating risks and championing the ethical evolution of technology.

Final Thoughts

The narrative woven through these chapters is one of potential — brimming with the promise of what AI agents can achieve when aligned with human values and societal goals. It is a call to action for policymakers, technologists, educators, and users to envision a future where AI agents enhance our capabilities, augment our tasks, and contribute positively to the tapestry of human progress.

So, as we close this book, let us remain committed to questioning, learning, and innovating with a steadfast aim: to shape a future molded by the harmonious collaboration between human intelligence and artificial agents, ensuring a brighter, more sustainable world for all.

Let this be our guiding vision as we embark on the exciting

journey ahead.